D1526964

The Frontier Newspapers and the Coverage of the Plains Indian Wars

The Frontier Newspapers and the Coverage of the Plains Indian Wars

Hugh J. Reilly

NATIVE AMERICA: YESTERDAY AND TODAY
Bruce E. Johansen, Series Editor

PRAEGER

AN IMPRINT OF ABC-CLIO, LLC
Santa Barbara, California • Denver, Colorado • Oxford, England

Copyright 2010 by Hugh J. Reilly

Library of Congress Cataloging-in-Publication Data
Reilly, Hugh J.
   The frontier newspapers and the coverage of the Plains Indian Wars / Hugh J. Reilly.
      p. cm. — (Native America: yesterday and today)
   Includes bibliographical references and index.
   ISBN 978-0-313-35440-3 (alk. paper) — ISBN 978-0-313-35441-0 (ebook)
   1. Indians of North America—Wars—1866–1895—Press coverage.   2. Indians of
North America—Wars—Great Plains—Press coverage.   3. Newspapers—Great Plains—
History—19th century.   4. Great Plains—History—19th century.   I. Title.
   E83.866.R377   2010
   978.004'97—dc22   2009051215

14   13   12   11   10   1   2   3   4   5

This book is also available on the World Wide Web as an eBook.
Visit www.abc-clio.com for details.

Praeger
An Imprint of ABC-CLIO, LLC

ABC-CLIO, LLC
130 Cremona Drive, P.O. Box 1911
Santa Barbara, California 93116-1911

This book is printed on acid-free paper ∞

Manufactured in the United States of America

For My Father,
Robert T. Reilly

Contents

Foreword

THE FRONTIER PRESS AND THE COVERAGE
OF THE PLAINS INDIAN WARS 1863–1891

History that has been written from a temporal distance often comes out in monochrome. Too many writers rely on footnote flipping—citing of other works—leading to an exchange of muddy generalities. Writing about the early days of European–American movement into the center of North America, for example, readers often receive a standardized account describing episodic "Indian wars," in which the immigrants invade the homelands of indigenous peoples backed by the army, aided by the spread of disease and alcoholism, justifying their invasion under the legalistic rubric of their own real-estate law ("highest and best use"), popularized as "Manifest Destiny." The federal government negotiates treaties and then violates them. The invading culture breaks down Native social and economic structures as the first peoples defend their shrinking land base in shrinking numbers, as if caught in a flood.

All of this happened, of course, but history without street smarts ignores considerable nuance. Not all of the immigrants thought or acted alike. Nor did all the Native peoples. They engaged in conflict, to be sure, but there also was considerable intermixing, some alliances, and even marriage. We have been a multicultural society from the beginning.

Hugh Reilly's accounts, which follow, have been drawn from the newspapers of the time and carry all the diversity and contradictions of life at street level. The story is full of unexpected twists and turns. An Omaha newspaper, the *World-Herald*, for example, sent a Native American correspondent, a woman, to report on the aftermath of what the army called a "battle" at Wounded Knee in 1890.

She may have been the only newspaper reporter to interview the survivors of what history today nearly universally regards as a massacre. She was Susette La Flesche, an Omaha (actually, U'ma'ha), was married to Thomas Tibbles, one of the newspaper's senior editors. (How's that for multiculturalism?) They had met years before.

During the late 1870s, Standing Bear and a small group of fellow Poncas arrived in Omaha under the escort of soldiers, having marched from Oklahoma in winter, their bare feet bleeding in the snow. They were so hungry they had eaten their moccasins; Standing Bear's party wanted to go home, to the Niobrara, in northernmost Nebraska, rejecting the government's plans to exile them in "Indian Territory," now Oklahoma.

The Poncas' case was so compelling that General George Crook allowed them to sue him in federal court, setting the stage for the first legal ruling in the United States, in 1879, that recognized Native American legal rights under *habeas corpus* (essentially recognizing Standing Bear as a human being with civil rights). La Flesche and Tibbles then set out on a national tour with Standing Bear to win back the Poncas' homeland, an errand that helped turn a well-known poet, Helen Hunt Jackson, into a crusading historian who created a sensation with her expose, entitled *A Century of Dishonor,* of the government's mistreatment of Indians.

The Poncas' history is well known today in Omaha, where a large lake is named for Standing Bear. His visage nearly ended up on the Nebraska state quarter. Standing Bear came in second to the more familiar display of a covered wagon chosen by Republican governor Dave Heineman.

The frontier was a complex place in the last years of the 19th century. As the Tibbles crusaded for justice in Standing Bear's case and La Flesche provided a Native point of view at Wounded Knee, another newspaper, the *Bee,* editorialized ceaselessly that Indians should be hunted down like wild beasts. At the same time, a newspaper editor in Aberdeen, South Dakota, L. Frank Baum (who later wrote the *Oz* books), was celebrating the "battle" at Wounded Knee as a necessary step on the road to obliteration of remaining Native peoples.

Hugh Reilly's history bristles with enlightening and instructive detail. It transports readers to a different time, in all its complexity, providing a new, richly nuanced view of a tumultuous period in our past.

—*Bruce E. Johansen*
Series Editor
Omaha, Nebraska
May 2009

Acknowledgments

A book like this could never have been written without the advice and assistance of many individuals. Reading newspapers from the 1860s to 1890s often requires poring over microfilm and microfiche. It was not unusual for some pages to be nearly impossible to read because they were torn or smudged. The librarians' unfailing courtesy and willingness to go above and beyond never ceased to amaze me. The staffs at the Omaha Public Library, the University of Nebraska at Omaha's Criss Library, the Denver Public Library, and the Minnesota State University Library were all exceptionally helpful. I especially want to single out Wendel Cox of the Denver Public Library and Kellian Clink of the Minnesota State Library, who each introduced me to some invaluable resources.

Professor Warren Francke of the University of Nebraska at Omaha (UNO) provided me with critical advice on journalistic practices. UNO's Professor Michael Tate was invaluable in helping me to keep my manuscript historically accurate as well as giving me many ideas for sources. I also want to thank Tisha Hooks, Senior Editor, Multicultural Studies for Praeger Publishers, for her patience and enthusiastic guidance through the maze of publishing requirements.

Finally, I must single out three individuals: first, my wife, Deanna, who was always supportive and kept the kids out of my office so I could work on the book. Second, Professor Bruce Johansen, who was instrumental at every step in the process from serving as my thesis committee chairman to pushing me to turn the thesis into a book and who never stopped encouraging me despite all the setbacks along the way. Finally, I want to thank my father, Professor Robert T. Reilly, who took me on a memorable journey to Wounded Knee when I was 10 years old and taught me the importance of human dignity and undaunted courage.

—*Hugh J. Reilly*

Introduction: Frontier Newspapers

The frontier press was an information lifeline for early settlers. It kept them informed of the local, national, and international news of the day. Newspapers featured advertisements of local products and gave settlers the latest local market prices for their livestock and grain. The press also offered fiery editorials and opinions.

According to historian David Dary, "Like [James Gordon] Bennett [editor of the *New York Herald*], the best editors in the West were masters of vigorous English. They knew or concocted virile expressions. They applied the barbed epithet when they thought it would do the most good. They understood the value of editorial abuse in attracting readers, to show pride in their papers, or to show indignation about rival editors or people they did not like."[1]

The Plains Indian Wars were covered by large and small newspapers in the Great Plains states. Each newspaper had its own unique history. Some papers lasted only months, while others are still publishing. The *Minnesota Pioneer*, founded by James Goodhue in 1849, has—through mergers and name changes—morphed into the *St. Paul Pioneer Press*. The other Minnesota paper featured in the chapter on the Sioux Uprising of 1862, the *Mankato Semi-Weekly Record*, published its first issue on July 4, 1859. It was sold in 1868 and soon disappeared.

The *Rocky Mountain News* began publishing in April 1859, shortly after gold was discovered in the front range of the Rocky Mountains. It was founded by William Newton Byers, who moved to Colorado from Omaha. He brought the printing press from the defunct *Bellevue Gazette* with him by oxcart and published the first edition of the *News* just 20 minutes ahead of its rival, the *Cherry Creek Pioneer*. The *Rocky Mountain News* closed in February 2009, after 150 years of publishing.

Byers had moved to Omaha in 1854 and been a member of the city's first city council; he had also served as a member of the Nebraska Territorial legislature.

By the time he left Omaha, the area had already seen several newspapers start and then disappear. The subjects they covered, their editorial policies, and their life spans are representative of frontier newspapers as a whole.

Although a small post newspaper was printed at Fort Atkinson (located 18 miles north of present-day Omaha, Nebraska) in the 1820s, the first generally recognized Nebraska newspaper was the *Nebraska Palladium*. It was first published by Daniel Reed and Company on July 15, 1854, and the initial issues were printed in Iowa. It was four months before the first issue was actually printed in Bellevue, Nebraska Territory.[2]

The second Nebraska paper, the *Omaha Arrow*, was also first printed in Iowa, on July 28, 1854. Publisher and editor Joe Ellis Johnson "set up his Omaha office, not under a tree but on the stump of one. His desk was a beaver hat, as he began composing an editorial in praise of this 'highly favored and beautiful territory upon which we have now established a regular weekly paper.' "[3] The *Arrow* was not Johnson's first publishing effort. He had also been the editor of the *Western Bugle* in Kanesville (now Council Bluffs), Iowa, from 1852 to 1856.

Most of those early frontier newspapers were filled more with advertisements than news stories. They were created by land companies hoping to attract settlers to their town sites. A press and an editor were considered essential to the success of any land venture. The *Nebraska Palladium* was published by the Bellevue Town Company and the *Omaha Arrow* by the Council Bluffs and Nebraska Ferry Company, which in addition to publishing the newspaper operated a Missouri River crossing and speculated on land. According to John Myers' *Print In a Wild Land*, "The *Arrow* was singing the praises of the little shack town [Omaha] as if it were a glamorous metropolis. Unlike many of the boomer papers, the *Arrow* was more prophetic as Omaha prospered, while the other town sites failed to live up to their advance promotion."[4]

Johnson himself was involved in what may have been the first editorial war between Nebraska newspapers. He championed Omaha's claim to be the territorial capital of Nebraska, in direct competition with the editor of Bellevue's *Nebraska Palladium*.[5] Despite the fact that Bellevue was the more established town, Omaha was chosen as territorial capital in 1854. Omaha remained the capital until Nebraska became a state in 1867, and the capital was transferred to Lincoln.

Johnson editorialized on many issues, including that frontier favorite, the Indian problem. Near Fort Laramie in August 1854, Brevet Second Lieutenant John L. Grattan and his entire command of 30 men were killed by a band of Brule Sioux. Grattan had gone to the camp of the Brule chief, Conquering Bear, to arrest a visiting Miniconjou warrior, High Forehead. This warrior had killed and skinned a sickly cow belonging to a Mormon immigrant. The Indians offered to pay for the cow but refused to hand over their visitor. The confrontation escalated and a shot rang out. General gunfire erupted and Grattan's two howitzers shelled the Indian camp, mortally wounding Conquering Bear as he cried out for his people to stop shooting. The Indians responded with fury and wiped out Grattan and his men.[6]

Johnson wrote about the skirmish in his paper and used it as a pretext to bring more federal troops into Nebraska Territory. "The massacre at Fort Laramie in the fall of 1854 and the inclination of the 'Shian' [Cheyenne] to be troublesome, gave Johnson ammunition for his propaganda campaign to get more troops into Nebraska Territory. He suggested that unless more soldiers were dispatched to this territory, the pioneers themselves would 'have to shoulder their trusty rifles and, in true frontier style, take to the bush for a free fight.' "[7]

The last issue of the *Arrow* was published in December 1854. Although short-lived, the *Arrow* had made its mark. "The *Arrow* was one of the institutions which brought Nebraska nationwide attention before the Civil War. The flamboyant nature of its editorials, its obvious appeal to people of culture and refinement, and its relentless crusade for democracy, all combined to give the *Arrow* an audience far beyond the confines of Territorial Nebraska."[8] Johnson left Omaha for Wood River, Nebraska Territory, where he published the *Huntsman's Echo* for two years. A Mormon with two wives, Johnson eventually moved to Utah owing to strong feelings in Nebraska against polygamy.[9]

By the 1860s, Omaha had become Nebraska's largest city and the territory's principal news center. The *Arrow* had folded after a few months, but it was soon followed by the *Omaha Daily Telegraph*, which became the town's first daily newspaper in 1860. That journal was followed by the *Omaha Republican Weekly* in 1858, which became a daily in 1864; the *Omaha Daily Herald* in 1865; the *Omaha Bee*, in 1871; the *Omaha Evening News* in 1878; and the *Omaha Daily World* in 1885. Eventually the *Omaha Daily Herald* was bought by Gilbert M. Hitchcock and merged with the *Omaha Daily World* to form the *Omaha World Herald* in October 1889.

The *Republican* was founded in 1858 by E. F. Schneider and Harrison J. Brown to promote the political causes of the Republican Party. The *Republican* flourished for several years. "Typographically it was a gem, and editorially [it] scintillated with wit sarcasm, philosophy, politics, science and art."[10] Unfortunately, the paper's expenses exceeded its income and it began to fail. It was sold in 1883 to S. P. Rounds and Cadet Taylor but lost money every year from then on until it closed in the mid-1890s.[11]

The *Omaha Daily Herald* was founded in October 1865 by George L. Miller and Daniel W. Carpenter. Miller later indicated that he started the *Daily Herald* to counteract the treatment Democrats had received at the hands of the *Republican*. Carpenter came to Omaha after having assisted in the publication of the *Palladium* in Bellevue, Nebraska. Miller was the editor and Carpenter the business manager; he also looked after the newspaper's printing plant.[12]

Miller first came to Nebraska as a physician in 1854. He referred to this period in his career in a speech later given at a banquet for General George Crook, where he declared that, "he was entitled to the distinction of being the pioneer Indian slayer in Nebraska, inasmuch as his first and almost his only patient in the state, was an Omaha papoose, which he succeeded in sending to the happy hunting grounds within a few hours after he had been called to attend it."[13] Fortunately, Miller's editorial skills proved to be better than his medical skills.

The editorial policy of the *Herald* can be illustrated by an item that appeared on November 13, 1878: "The *Omaha Daily Herald* has not been sued for libel in 30 days. We are almost tempted to call the acting Governor of Nebraska sober, and an honest man, just to see whether we will be charged with lying by the Republican press, or sued for libel by the temperance societies and churches."

The *Herald* was also active in promoting Democratic political causes, and Miller was a member of the Democratic National committee for many years, until poor health forced him to resign in 1880.[14] The newspaper also touted the Union Pacific Railroad as the shining light that would attract new citizens to Omaha and help keep the city's economy healthy and growing. James Savage, in an article about Miller in the *Magazine of Western History* wrote, "Of that great and maligned corporation, the Union Pacific, the doctor has always been a firm and consistent friend."[15]

The *Omaha Bee* was initially started by Edward Rosewater simply to promote a bill in the state legislature to create an Omaha board of education. The first issue was only two pages long and was distributed free. After the bill had successfully passed the legislature, Rosewater decided that there was still a need for his editorial voice, and he kept publishing the *Bee* as an evening paper. Rosewater's *Bee* considered itself a champion of the common man and fought for civic improvements such as permanent buildings, paved streets, and concrete sidewalks. It was a financial and a popular success for Rosewater. Along with the *Republican*, the *Bee* represented a faction of the Republican political viewpoint.[16]

The *Bee* was engaged in fierce competition with its rivals, the *Herald* and the *Republican*, from the beginning. In addition to personal attacks upon each other through their editorial columns, the newspapers also competed in their business practices. Victor Rosewater, son of *Omaha Bee* founder Edward Rosewater, recalled rival newspapers paying local newsboys not to sell the *Bee*. As a result, young Rosewater sold the papers himself for five cents a copy.[17]

Gilbert M. Hitchcock, Frank J. Burkley, W. V. Rooker, and Alfred Miller founded the *Omaha Daily World* in August 1885. Hitchcock claimed that he founded the *World* to give Omaha a neutral, objective newspaper, a unique idea in that era of fierce partisanship. He wrote, "The *World* stands fairly and frankly upon a platform alone. It believes there is room for a newspaper of virtue in the state. It has no alliances of any kind."[18] Hitchcock was confident that the community would support such a newspaper to provide balance in local news coverage.

While the *Herald* and the *Republican* cordially welcomed the *World*, Rosewater's *Bee* snubbed the new paper. "The appearance of the *World* was greeted with mingled feelings by its journalistic contemporaries. The *Omaha Bee* described it as "one of those mushrooms which flourish and die in Omaha each succeeding season."[19] Rosewater and Hitchcock soon developed a bitter rivalry that would extend beyond their respective newspaper's editorial page to politics, civic improvements. and personal insults. The feud continued unabated until Rosewater's death in 1906.

In 1889, Hitchcock purchased the *Herald* and merged it with his *World* to create the *Omaha World-Herald*. Although these newspapers covered many issues of the day, to many Nebraskans no issue was more important than "the Indian problem." Rarely would a week pass without some mention of Native Americans in the editorial and news columns.

As an example, an April 13, 1873, editorial in the *Omaha Republican* focused on the sale of the western part of the Omaha Indian Tribe's reservation, "for the benefit of the tribe":

> This is to our mind only the beginning of the end. It seems certain that these Indian reservations are designed to be sold and settled by a white population. The Indian does not take kindly to civilization. He cannot or will not endure constraints. They either pass away or become so mixed by intermarriage with the Whites that their nationality is lost, and they become, to all intents and purposes, citizens. We confess that we have but little faith in the ultimate civilization of these roving savages. More than two and one-half centuries have passed since the savage tribes came into contact with civilization, and yet today they retain very nearly the same characteristics by which they were known when the Pilgrims landed on Plymouth Rock. They die well. They waste rapidly away before the breath of civilization, but they do not civilize. They are the same wild, free, independent roving savages as ever, with all the vices, and few of the virtues, of the dominant race. They are often chiefs and beggars. Some of them are very great in the scale of humanity, but most of them are very small, and to our limited vision, they seem to be of no possible use in this great busy, stirring, world. We are inclined to the opinion that the good of Nebraska and the best interests of the Indians requires their removal wholly from the state.[20]

This editorial, written about an Indian tribe that had traditionally allied itself with the whites, reveals the antipathy many frontier editors felt even toward peaceful tribes. When they wrote about warlike tribes such as the Sioux and Apache, their venom was even more pronounced.

The correspondents who covered the Indian wars for the frontier editors were a rare combination of adventurers and journalists. Many were "volunteer correspondents more gifted in imaginative writing than in accurate reporting, they spread before their readers the kind of highly-colored accounts of Indian raids and 'massacres' that the most sensational yellow journal of a later period might have envied."[21] Examples of the work of these amateur journalists included reports of Sitting Bull's death 20 years before he was killed and detailed reports of the 1867 Fort Buford "massacre"; a massacre that never occurred.

The editors of these frontier newspapers were a slightly different breed. Often highly educated, these men held strong opinions about the events of the day. According to Barbara Cloud in *The Business of Newspapers in the Western Frontier,* "Publishers also knew that sensationalism and controversy sold newspapers. Stories about deaths, violent or otherwise, crime, Indian raids, and allegations of corruption did not get big headlines because nothing got big headlines, but they mingled with items about visitors to town and plans for the new library and provided readers with both information and titillation."[22] Cloud adds that frontier newspapermen were not averse to a little exaggeration if it would help sell newspapers. "So when newspapermen took to the wings of invention, in preference to having nothing to report, they were as true to the spirit of the world in which they moved as by journalists have in general forever been. . . . The prince of Western journalism was not the skilled assembler of facts, but the juggler who could ram fiction down the public throat and have it digested as news."[23]

Cloud adds that "Newspapers employed relatively few staff journalists—smaller papers rarely had more than the local editor—and relied on correspondents, who were paid by the story, to fill the columns."[24] It was also common for the editors to be involved in other businesses. Joe Ellis Johnson, in addition to being the editor of the *Omaha Arrow,* "ran a general store, sold vegetables to wagon trains passing through, operated a mill and furnished accommodations for man and board."[25]

Technological advances changed the nature of newspaper journalism during the early years of the frontier press in Nebraska Territory. According to Cloud, "Before the Morse code made rapid communication between journalists possible, the best they could do to cooperate with each other was an exchange system. . . . The four sources of news might be resident's letters from others, outside magazines, books and competent amateur writers. From these sources, the pioneer journalist drew the main items of his paper."[26]

In September of 1860, telegraph wires were installed across Nebraska, linking the isolated territory with the Pacific and Atlantic coasts and, via the transoceanic cable, with the rest of the world.[27] Johnson, while serving as editor of *The Huntsman's Echo,* described the event in his September, 1860 newspaper: "Whoop! Hurrah! The pole—wire—the telegraph—the lightning! The first are up, the second stretched, the third playing on the line between St. Joe and Omaha: and the people of Omaha are exulting in the enjoyment of direct communication with the balance of the earth and the rest of mankind. . . . Thoughts that breathe and words that burn will glide along the wires with lightning rapidity."[28]

The advent of the telegraph wires meant that information could spread from the remote frontier outposts to the big cities of the East in a matter of days instead of weeks. It also meant that small-town editors now had the ability to get stories off the wire to print in their local papers. They no longer had to rely quite as much on stringers and letter writers for their news. Their stories were more immediate.

News stories reprinted from wire services or from local or regional newspapers offer a contrast to editorial columns. While many stories in frontier newspapers were written with what would now be considered an opinionated style, it was in frontier editorials that true personality and bias could emerge.

The years 1862–1891 are the main focus of the present study of frontier newspapers. This time period covers most of the significant events in the history of what some have called the "winning of the West." From the Sioux uprising of 1862 to what many consider the final battle of the Plains Indian wars at Wounded

Knee in 1890, these years saw the final desperate struggles by Native Americans of the Great Plains to retain their traditional ways of life.

In contrast to other books that usually cite the Indian War coverage of newspapers from New York or Chicago, the focus of this book is on newspapers relatively close to the events described. These include newspapers from Nebraska, Colorado, South Dakota, Montana, Kansas, and Minnesota.

In an attempt to further narrow the scope of study, the focus is on eight watershed events in Native American history from 1862 to 1891. These events were chosen for three reasons: (1) their historical significance, (2) the fact they received extensive coverage in the frontier newspapers of the time, and (3) the fact that events occurred in or near the Great Plains region. Unlike the large eastern newspapers, which were reporting on events remote from their offices, the frontier newspapers were reporting about events taking place in their own backyards.

Beginning with the coverage of the Great Sioux Uprising (February–May 1862), this study also analyzes newspaper coverage of the Sand Creek Massacre (January–April 1864); the 1868 Fort Laramie Treaty (February–May 1868); the 1876 campaign against the Sioux, culminating in the Little Big Horn battle (January–July 1876); the flight of the Nez Perce (March–October 1877); the Cheyenne Outbreak (September 1878–January 1879); the Standing Bear Trial (January–April 1879); and, finally, the Wounded Knee Massacre (August 1890–January 1891).

Also included are a few other news stories concerning Indians that were written at the same time as the coverage of these watershed events. In contrast to wartime coverage, they serve as a comparison and insight into day-to-day newspaper coverage of Native Americans by the frontier press.

News stories and editorials from frontier newspapers allow us to examine the attitudes of the frontier press toward Native Americans. Rhetorical patterns in the press coverage of the seven selected watershed events fall into basic stereotypes. There is a wide spectrum of views regarding the Native Americans—from paternalism to persecution, from "Kill the Indian, Save the man," attributed to General Richard Pratt, founder of the Indian boarding school system, to General Philip Sheridan's infamous "The only good Indian is a dead Indian."

According to historian Robert Berkhofer in *The White Man's Indian,* there were three major stereotypes used by the whites and their press to portray the Native Americans. First, there was the "Noble Savage." Berkhofer writes, "the good Indian appears friendly, courteous and hospitable to the invaders of his land. According to this version, the Indian, in short, lived a life of simplicity and innocence."[29]

In contrast to the "Noble Savage," Berkhofer describes the second major stereotype. "On the other side, a list of almost contradictory traits emerged of the bad Indian in White eyes. Nakedness and lechery, passion and vanity, led to lives of polygamy and sexual promiscuity among themselves and constant warfare and fiendish revenge against their enemies."[30]

Berkhofer also identified a third major stereotype. "If there is a third White image of the Indian, then this degraded, often drunken Indian constitutes the essence of that understanding. Living neither as an assimilated White nor an Indian of the classic image, and therefore neither noble nor wildly savage, but always scorned, the degraded Indian exhibited the vices of both societies in the opinions of White observers."[31]

An attack on this third stereotype can be found in an editorial from the May 7, 1873, edition of the *Omaha Daily Herald*:

> Red Cloud is taunted with being "drunken." There are none so low as to deny he
> is able. But who deals out liquid demolition to this untutored savage? Who introduced the alcoholic demon to the peer of RED JACKET, BLACK HAWK, and
> OSCEOLA! And are not White "chiefs" drunken too? How about U.S. Grant,
> whose intoxicated toe caused the scene in the Kansas City Opera House, no
> longer than two weeks ago? How about DICK YATES, whose bestial boots the
> cowardly libeler of Red Cloud licked all over, when this interesting person was
> chasing his "drunken" hat through the streets of Omaha, a few years ago? How
> about scores of other "drunken" men who have disgraced public stations in the
> State and Nation?[32]

In addition to examining the rhetorical side of the coverage of Native Americans, the present volume also analyzes the newspapers in terms of their historical accuracy. It uses the method recommended by L. John Martin and Harold L. Nelson in the article "The Historical Standard in Analyzing Press Performances," published in *Journalism Quarterly*.

Martin and Nelson write that the "traditional methods of history do not produce a historical standard that is 'objective' in the sense that it can be duplicated by every other historian working independently."[33] They add that "there are many clearly-established 'facts' of history that are stable and stand as constants—date, names, and certain acts of official persons and bodies, for example. Historians do not quarrel over the date of firing on Fort Sumter, although they may be in severe disagreement as to the causes of the Civil War."[34]

Martin and Nelson outlined four basic measures used to judge the historical quality of a newspaper story. First, *accuracy*: is the report factual, unambiguous, up to date, and precise? Second, *prediction*: does it accurately predict the effects of the event on the future of those involved in the event? Third, *selection*: is the news story significant, balanced and comprehensive? Fourth, *judgment*: are the opinions and analyses based on and grow logically from facts and do they show a good grasp of the meaning of events?[35] These measures are used to examine significant issues and differences, not merely minute differences. The yardsticks for measuring historical accuracy are the works of several historians, including Robert Utley, David Lavender, Rex Alan Smith, Loring Benson Priest, Richard Dillon, and Elmo Scott Watson.

Historian Robert Berkhofer points out that the first inhabitants of the Western Hemisphere did not call themselves by a single name or think of themselves as a single people. "The idea and the image of the Indian must be a White conception. Native Americans were and are real, but the *Indian* was a White invention and still remains largely a White image, if not a stereotype."[36]

Berkhofer writes of three persistent misinterpretations that whites created to analyze and judge Indians. First, they equated one Indian tribe's society and culture with all Indian society and culture; second, they thought of Indians in terms of their deficiencies according to white ideals rather than in terms of their own various cultures; and third, they used moral evaluations to describe Indians. He concludes that "Noble Indians could exist before the coming of White society or they could help the White settler and then die forecasting the wonders and virtues of the civilization that was to supersede the simplicity and naturalness of aboriginal life. Savage Indians could scalp helpless Whites or die under torture singing their defiant death songs according to the old ways of native life."[37]

In 1854, Josiah Nott and George Glidden wrote an ethnological treatise that reflected one of the many attitudes of the day toward Native Americans. Nott and Glidden opined that "Furthermore, certain savage types can neither be civilized or domesticated. The barbarous races of America (excluding the Toltecs) although nearly as low in intellect as the Negro races, are essentially untamable. Not merely have all attempts to civilize them failed, but also every endeavor to enslave them. Our Indian tribes submit to extermination, rather than wear the yoke under which our Negro slaves fatten and multiply."[38]

Attitudes and philosophies by some correspondents helped to shape frontier press coverage of Native Americans. However, other factors also helped shape this portrayal, including economics and geography: "western publishers used Eastern newspapers as their models, and their experiences differ mainly in degree from their contemporaries in the East. . . . But there are differences; for example, what Australian historian Geoffrey Blainey described as the 'tyranny of distance.' Western publishers operated, as a rule, in greater isolation and farther from material, labor and news sources than most publishers in other parts of the continent."[39]

There is also something of the aura of the myth about the frontier press. We visualize the crusading editor fighting a lonely battle against the forces of power and corruption in his own small town. Barbara Cloud writes, "In considering the frontier press, one must deal with the legends and mythology that have developed, both about the region and about the press itself. Western literature, both fiction and nonfiction, has created people and place larger than even the wide-open spaces of the West can accommodate with honesty, and journalism history has added its own mystique.[40]

In his book *Following The Indian Wars,* Oliver Knight quotes General William Tecumseh Sherman, who described Indian fighting as the most difficult type of war. Knight writes that this analogy might be extended to the coverage of the Indian wars. "Surrounded by the wilderness, the correspondent was one with the soldier—a White man, one to be slain, not a noncombatant bearing credentials. He had also to meet the soldier's test of rugged endurance—long hours and days in an unaccustomed saddle, sometimes months in the field, marching through dust or scorching heat or freezing snow or sub-zero temperatures. . . . Worse yet, communications facilities were as far removed from the reporter as civilization from wilderness."[41]

Some early correspondents were in fact literate soldiers who took the time to write for their hometown newspaper or other local newspapers. They were hardly unbiased observers. Their stories were colored by their own experience of being outmaneuvered, and frequently outfought, by their Native American adversaries. Lieutenant Colonel George Armstrong Custer was a frequent correspondent for the *New York Herald* and other papers. His reputation as a peerless Indian fighter was not always accurate. His mid-1860s campaigns against the Cheyenne and Kiowa were often frustrating and fruitless. Historian Robert Utley writes of Custer, "Defeated by the Indians, by the land, by the weather, by his own officers and men, by his superiors, and ultimately by himself, Custer may well have been plunged by the setbacks and frustrations of 1867 into what a later generation would call an identity crisis."[42]

The main correspondents were the editors of the small frontier town weeklies. Historian Elmo Scott Watson notes, "These papers naturally reflected local sentiment on the Indian question, including the frontiersman's traditional hostility toward the red man and his determination to possess the Indian's lands, by fair means or foul. So it is obvious that their editors were considerably less than 'objective reporters' of Indian affairs, whether for their own papers or as correspondents for the Eastern journals."[43]

Army records show 1,065 engagements with Indians between 1866 and 1891. About 70 percent of these actions were fought between soldiers and Indians and the remaining 30 percent were fought between civilians and Indians. Of the actions between soldiers and Indians, 63 percent were fought by small bodies of troops of less than 100 men. Only 70, or 7 percent, were fought by groups of more than 200 men.[44] These latter 7 percent were the actions most likely to be covered by correspondents.

The first American war correspondents began to emerge during the Mexican War, as technological advances provided for larger presses and more rapid communication. In addition, there was a new breed of editors and publishers in the newspaper business, including men who would become prominent in later years. These men—James Gordon Bennett, Horace Greeley, and Benjamin Day—realized that news had a commodity value. They changed newspapers from a collection of editorial pieces to a collection of news stories.

The Indian wars added a new twist to the role of war correspondent. Unlike previous wars, during which correspondents reported on the action from behind the lines, there were no distinct lines in Indian warfare. "There was no rear echelon in Indian fighting, and anyone on a near-by point of vantage might never have another haircut. The reporter went all the way or went home."[45] Editors portrayed their correspondents in the Indian wars as combination reporters and combatants. Knight notes that, "Adventure and the hero rated high in reader appeal and war correspondents contributed their bit with accounts of their own adventures as well as the adventures of others."[46]

While it was an arduous job, the reporters themselves often relished the role and were not above stretching the truth for a good story. John F. Finerty, who covered several Indian campaigns, embellished the truth a little when he described the difficulty of covering Indian wars. "Let no easy-going journalists suppose that an Indian campaign is a picnic. If he goes out on such business he must be prepared to ride his forty or fifty miles a day, freeze, and make the acquaintance of such vermin that may flourish in the vicinity of his couch; and finally, be ready to fight Sitting Bull or Satan when the trouble begins, for God and the United States hate non-combatants."[47]

While correspondents certainly accompanied some of the larger campaigns, most of the reporting on the Indian wars was not first-hand. According to Oliver Knight in *Following the Indian Wars*, the American press relied heavily on second-hand sources to report on Indian campaigns. They borrowed clippings from other papers who had staff correspondents on the scene or excerpted letters from soldiers. The frontier press also used stories from the Associated Press wire or gleaned information from governmental sources or military reports and dispatches.[48]

The history of the frontier is replete with examples of alarming news of Indian trouble being sent to the eastern press. Historian Watson notes, "Much of this so-called news was nothing more than propaganda to influence the federal government to send more soldiers to the 'threatened' areas, thus giving local tradesman an opportunity to sell more supplies to the troops."[49]

The winter of 1866–67 brought an early example of the coverage of Indian wars. Captain William Fetterman had boasted that with 80 men he could "ride roughshod over the entire Sioux nation." He was given his opportunity when, with slightly more than 80 men, he went to relieve a wood-gathering detail that had been attacked by Indians near Fort Phil Kearny, in present-day northern Wyoming. He was cautioned by his commanding officer, Colonel Henry B. Carrington, not to pursue the Indians past Lodge Trail Ridge. He rashly chose to ignore his orders and pursued the Indians beyond the ridge, where his command was ambushed and wiped out to the last man.

Harper's Weekly of March 23, 1867, quoted a purported eyewitness who claimed to have watched the entire battle hidden in the woods only 50 yards away. In truth, this witness accompanied a rescue that arrived too late, and what he saw of the battle was what others rescuers saw of the battle—nothing. Similarly, the April 5 edition of the *New York Semi-Weekly Tribune* claimed that Fort Buford, a small fort manned by 80 men on the mouth of the Yellowstone River, was attacked and overwhelmed by 2,000 to 3,000 Indians. According to the newspaper, the soldiers repulsed the first few attacks, killing 300 Indians and wounding 1,000 more. The commander was said to have saved the last two bullets for his wife and himself. The report soon spread to other publications, which added small, previously unknown, details. It was not until a month later that the *New York Semi-Weekly Tribune*, which had first broken the story, admitted that the account had been a complete fabrication. "The future was to see numerous examples of rumors being expanded into 'eyewitness accounts' and 'reliable intelligence' as well as just faking the news of later Indian wars," said historian Watson.[50]

Even when the western correspondent was actually at the scene of the conflict and did an accurate job of covering the event, he was usually hampered by one crucial deficiency: he could not interview the other side in the conflict. He could not interview the Indians. Knight points out in his book, *Following the Indian Wars,* that "The Western war correspondent reported the story in detail, but did not have and could not have had the Indian side of the story. Often, however the reporter did reveal the Indian side when he sought to explain the cause of a conflict, not in terms of Indian interpretations, but in terms of criminal mismanagement of Indian affairs by civilians. In that connection, the reporter generally reflected the feelings, attitudes and thoughts of the military."[51] Even while attempting to portray the Indian side of the story, the western correspondent was forced to rely on the soldier's interpretation of how the Indian might feel. The next chapters examine, in detail, the coverage of eight watershed events in the history of Native Americans from 1862 to 1891, by these correspondents and their editors, just as they appeared in several frontier newspapers.

CHAPTER 1

Great Sioux Uprising:
August–December 1862

Over the earth I come;
Over the earth I come;
A soldier I come;
Over the earth I am a ghost.

It was December 26, 1862. Back east, the Civil War raged and Abraham Lincoln had just celebrated his second Christmas in the White House. In Mankato, Minnesota—where they had hoped to execute more than 300—38 men dangled from the gallows. It was the largest mass hanging in the history of the United States and, but for the intervention of President Lincoln, it would have been much worse.

The roots of the tragedy went back many years to the expulsion of the Sioux, or Dakota, from northern Wisconsin and Minnesota by the Ojibwa. Settling into southern Minnesota, the Dakota achieved an uneasy truce with the white settlers who were moving into the state. The first serious crack in the truce occurred in 1857. The Wahpekute band of the Dakota, led by Inkpaduta, massacred settlers they found near Spirit Lake, Iowa, just over the Minnesota border. It was considered a sacred place by the Indians and the settlers' presence was deemed a desecration.

Soldiers led by Charles Flandrau pursued Inkpaduta's band, but since they were on foot, they had little hope of capturing the mounted warriors.[1] The Dakota under Little Crow were ordered to bring in the outlaws or lose their annuity payments. They were able to kill four of Inkpaduta's men but unable to bring in the chief or the remaining warriors. Despite their failure, the annuities were still distributed to the Dakota. According to historian Kellian Clink, "This lack of resolve on the part of the U.S. is mentioned in almost every account as being a factor in the events of 1862."[2] The whites had threatened, but in the end they had backed down.

Since the whites had arrived, the Dakota's land had been whittled away through a succession of treaties. The year following the Spirit Lake massacre, the Dakota signed a treaty that reduced their reservation to a narrow strip along the Minnesota River. It was 10 miles wide and 150 miles long. They realized all treaties with the whites were transitory and their lands could be taken away on a whim.

The Dakota were expected to cease their nomadic lifestyle and support themselves as farmers. The heads of household were supplied with annuity payments, and this reduced the influence of the tribal chiefs. In addition, most of the annuities were eaten up in debts already owed to traders. Historian William Folwell writes that "Profit on sales to Indians ranged from one hundred to four hundred per cent, it was comfortable for the agent to have a share in the business . . . substantially all the money paid out for annuities went immediately into the pockets of traders in payment."[3]

In the summer of 1862, the war was not going well for the Union forces. The Confederates had claimed a series of victories and the new state of Minnesota was being asked to provide more soldiers for the Union armies. The Dakota watched and waited. Their annuities, both food and money, promised for June had still not been paid by August. It was the practice to deliver both parts of the annuities together. Congress had delayed the payment of money, preferring to shift it to pay for the war effort. So the food, while delivered, was kept locked in storehouses and began to rot. Pleas by the Dakota to release the food were ignored. Little Crow warned the whites that when men are starving, they help themselves.

Negotiations between the Dakota, the United States government, and local traders were launched in early August to try and find a solution to the impasse. The Dakota asked Andrew Myrick, who was representing the traders, to help the Dakota plead their cause to the government. Myrick, mocking the Dakota's plight, taunted, "So far as I am concerned, if they are hungry, let them eat grass."[4]

On August 16, 1862, the annuity payments finally arrived in St. Paul, Minnesota; they were transported to Fort Ridgely the next day. Tragically, it was too late. The same day the goods were delivered to Fort Ridgely, August 17, 1862, four young Dakota warriors—Killing Ghost, Breaking Up, Runs against Something When Crawling, and Brown Wing—attacked a farmhouse near Acton, Minnesota. There was an argument about stealing eggs from a white family and the courage of one man was challenged. To prove they were not cowards, they went to the house and killed the owner, Robinson Jones; his son-in-law Howard Baker; Mr. Webster; Mrs. Jones; and a girl of 14.[5]

Returning to their camp, the four warriors met with Little Crow and a hasty counsel was held. The Dakota feared retribution for the murders these young men had committed. Many believed the Americans would take vengeance on the whole tribe for the killings, especially since women as well as men had been killed. Many felt certain their long awaited annuities would be denied. They argued that the Dakota should strike first rather than wait for the inevitable.[6]

Others saw an opportunity. The army was distracted by the war far to the east, which the Union forces seemed to be losing. Perhaps now was the time to regain their lost lands. Many of the chiefs, including Little Crow, foresaw only disaster, but stung by the taunts of the young warriors, the council decided to go to war. According to Jerome Big Eagle's memoirs, Little Crow stated, "Blood had been shed, the payment would be stopped, and the white would take dreadful vengeance because women had been killed. Kill the whites and kill all these cut hairs [Dakota who had become farmers and cut their hair short] who will not join us."[7]

The Dakota did not wait long to begin their war. The morning after the council, war bands spread out across the state. A group of Dakota attacked the Redwood Agency, populated by government employees and their families, "cut hairs," and some other mixed- and half-blood Indians. Thirteen Americans were killed in the attack, seven more were killed while fleeing and ten were captured.[8] Among the first killed was trader Andrew Myrick, caught while trying to escape through a window. His body was later found with grass stuffed in his mouth.

The *Mankato Semi-Weekly Record* was among the first to report on the uprising:

> We have sufficient information to justify the belief that most all of the white persons at the two agencies, including traders, have been murdered, stores and buildings burned and the goods all carried off or destroyed.
>
> At the Upper Agency, there were about 25 white persons, all of whom are believed to have been killed. This brave little band fought the Indians for two and a half days, when most of the men having been killed, the remainder were forced to surrender. No quarters were shown them, but all were butchered in the most brutal manner.[9]

Contrary to the report in the Mankato paper, 47 people escaped from the Redwood Agency to nearby Fort Ridgely. The fort's commander, John S. Marsh, set out for the agency with 46 men and an interpreter, despite warnings that he would be outnumbered. He was attacked at the Redwood Ferry and he and 24 of his men were killed. The survivors fled back to Fort Ridgely in panic.[10]

In an effort to calm the fears that it, in part, had created, the *Semi-Weekly Record* tried to put the Indian War in perspective:

> All kinds of false and silly rumors have been circulated down the river in regard to the Indian depredations. One to the effect that Mankato was in ashes and St. Peter would be in a few hours; another that the people of this and adjoining counties had all been butchered, and that the whole country was a complete waste.

Of course, nothing could be more absurd. We question whether a Sioux Indian has been within our county since the difficulty commenced, and we are sure if there was an instance of this kind, no white person knew of it. New Ulm, 28 miles distant, is the nearest point that has been threatened, and that would not have occurred if the people there had been supplied with arms.[11]

The Mankato newspaper mocked the fears of its readers when they wrote about a rumor among the area's Indian tribes. "A Sioux Indian predicted to a Winnebago a few days ago, that his tribe would plant corn next year where the towns of Mankato and St. Peter now are. We rather think this prediction will not be fulfilled, but a more likely one is that the Sioux reservation will be converted into a Sioux burying ground."[12]

The *Semi-Weekly Record*'s prediction was eerily accurate.

Emboldened by their early success, the Dakota attacked the settlement of New Ulm. They approached the town from the west and quickly surrounded it. According to the *Record,* "They commenced their attack by firing a number of buildings on the outskirts. Some of the attacking party were on horseback and others on foot. Their approach was characterized with caution and system as they closed in on the town."[13]

The Dakota surrounding New Ulm may have been more than 20 miles away, but the citizens of Mankato felt certain the warriors lurked just outside their town. "Sunday was the gloomiest day in Mankato since the outbreak," the Mankato paper declared. Martial law was proclaimed in the town and families deserted their houses to seek shelter in the fortified buildings. Armed men patrolled the streets. "Reports that the little garrison at New Ulm was surrounded by flames and hundreds of Indians, rumors of a threatened attack by the combined Sioux and Winnebago forces—all combined to excite and terrify the people. In the evening, not less than twenty-five wagon loads of men, women and children deserted the town to seek safety elsewhere."[14]

The night, however, passed without the slightest disturbance and by Monday morning, the excitement in Mankato had died down.

The newspaper shifted its focus to the defense of New Ulm, which was described in heroic terms by the newspaper, relying on "eyewitness" accounts.

From these buildings, and behind fences, wood piles and other places as offered protection to our men, there was a most vigorous fire directed at the savages until evening with considerable loss on both sides. Many incidents occurred which brought the recollection of the scenes of the early pioneers of Ohio and Kentucky. The savage war whoop, their insatiable thirst for murder and barbarity scarcely fins a parallel in American history. In every instance where a hand to hand conflict occurred, our men repulsed the red devils with that cool determination that characterizes brave men. On Sunday morning, after consultation, Judge Flandreau ordered such Buildings as could not be safely held to be destroyed and the whole of the population, consisting of about 2000 men, women and children, were concentrated in about two squares, in order to be more successfully defended. During the burning of these buildings, the Indians renewed the attack with the same determined vigor that characterized the previous day's fight and they were met with a firm, unyielding resistance on the part of our soldiers. After about an hour's fighting, the savages withdrew, driving off such stock as they could conveniently take with them.[15]

Reinforcements were sent to New Ulm and they evacuated the survivors from the ruined town and escorted them to Mankato. According to the *Record,* in the absence of the town's citizens, many of New Ulm's homes were looted by their fellow settlers passing through on their way to safety.[16]

In an article entitled, "The Remedy," the *Record* wrote that it was a "settled fact" that the southwest portion of the state would lose a large percentage of its population due to the "recent massacre."[17] It stated that the state's citizens could not be expected to settle in a place where peace and safety could not be guaranteed. "It will be folly to attempt to restore public confidence so long as there is a hostile Indian within our state limits, and not until they are totally exterminated or driven beyond our boundary and our frontier guarded by a line of forts—a sure barrier to further depredation—will peace and prosperity again smile upon us."[18]

The newspaper feared not only the immediate consequences of depopulation but also that the conflict would hinder immigration to their state. It claimed that most of the settlers who had been killed were recent immigrants from Europe and the news would soon spread to that continent and make the name Minnesota synonymous with Indian massacres. To the *Record,* the die had been cast and there was no going back.

> The cruelties perpetrated by the Sioux nation in the last two weeks demand that our government shall treat them for all time as outlaws who have forfeited all rights to property and life. They must cease to be the wards of government and their whole possessions and annuities converted into a fund to recuperate, so far as money will do so, for the depredations already committed.
>
> Nothing short of this policy will appease our people. We want no more treaties or compromises. Minnesota must be either a Christian land or a savage hunting ground— either the white man must exercise undisputed sway or the Indian—the two races can never live peaceably and prosperously together again.[19]

Jane Grey Swisshelm, editor of Minnesota's *St. Cloud Democrat,* agreed with the sentiments of the *Record* that no quarter should be given to the Dakota. "Let our present Legislature offer a bounty of $10 for every Sioux scalp, outlaw the tribe and so let the matter rest. It will cost five times that much to exterminate them by the regular modes of warfare and they should be got rid of in the cheapest and quickest manner."[20]

Amid the stories of destruction and death, the *Record* also found time to tell stories of heroism and humor. One young boy carried his toddler brother to safety because he had promised his mother he would. "This heroic little fellow travelled 60 miles carrying his little brother in his arms and on his back the entire distance and living on raw corn and such victuals he could find at the deserted home- steads along the way. We question whether history records a parallel instance of such bravery, determination and physical endurance as evinced by this lad, only 12 years old, in his efforts to rescue his infant brother."[21]

The paper also wrote of an Indian dressing himself in "Rev. Mr. Hinman's min- isterial robes, in which he presented quite a ludicrous appearance. While thus strutting around, a white woman trying to escape met him, and with a savage grin he asked, 'if she belonged to his church.' The force of the fellow's wit seemed to have so mollified him that he allowed her to escape to the fort in safety."[22]

Settlers, fleeing the threat of marauding Dakota warriors, continued to stream from their isolated farms to refuge in places like Fort Ridgely and Mankato. Back in Washington, President Lincoln had called a national draft for soldiers to fight the Civil War. Minnesota politicians asked for an extension, "on account of Indian troubles," and Lincoln responded: "Attend to the Indians. If the draft cannot pro- ceed, of course it will not proceed. Necessity knows no law."[23]

On September 2, 1862, the Dakota attacked a detachment of soldiers at Birch Coulee about 16 miles from Fort Ridgely. The soldiers had been sent out to bury the men killed during an earlier attack and to discover just where the hostiles were. According to the *Record,* the fight was between about 125 soldiers and 600 to 700 Indians. "The soldiers were surprised, but the promptness of the men saved the little band from destruction. After a few hours fight, the Indians were driven into the timber, from which they kept up a continuous fire for 86 hours. On the second day of the fight, Colonel Sibley's command arrived and dispersed the Indians. Twenty-two soldiers were killed and about fifty wounded."[24] While the newspaper tried to claim the battle as a victory, it was another major defeat for American forces.

Still the tide of the war was beginning to change. General Pope and Colonel Sibley were in the field with strong forces and closing in on the Dakota. Many of the Dakota who had been reluctant to go to war in the first place now believed their cause was lost. Colonel Sibley sent a messenger to Little Crow demanding the return of the white captives. Little Crow replied that the Dakota had started the war because their children were starving and their agent and the traders would not give them the food they needed to survive. Sibley replied: "Little Crow, you have murdered many of our people without sufficient cause. Return the prisoners under a flag of truce and I will talk with you like a man."[25]

Messengers delivered Little Crow's reply asking General Sibley to meet to ar- range peace terms: "I want to know from you as a friend what way I can make peace for my people—in regard to prisoners; they fare with our children or our self as well as us." Sibley's reply was reprinted in the *Record*: "You have not done as I wished in giving up to me the prisoners taken by your people. It would be better for you to do so. . . . You have allowed your young men to commit some murders since you wrote your first letter. This is not the way for you to make peace."[26]

The war was stumbling to a close but one sharp fight remained. On the morning of September 23, 1862, Sibley's camp "was attacked by about three hundred Indians, who suddenly made their appearance and dashed down toward us, whooping and yelling in their usual style, and firing with great rapidity." Some of the Dakota ran down a nearby ravine in an attempt to outflank the soldiers, but Sibley sent five companies of his reserves to counterattack. "Lieut. Colonel Marshall advanced at a double-quick amidst a shower of balls from the enemy, which fortunately did little damage to his commands: and after a few volleys, he led his men in a charge and cleared the ravine of savages."[27]

The battle raged for about two hours. Sibley brought up his six-pounder cannon and mountain howitzer and shelled the Dakota. Outnumbered, outgunned and suffering heavy losses, the Dakota were forced to flee the battlefield. Sibley reported that four soldiers were killed and between 30 and 40 wounded. "The enemy lost 30 killed and a large number wounded [according to a half-breed who visited their camp]." The Dakota sent a flag of truce asking to gather up their dead and wounded but were not allowed to unless they turned over their captives first.[28]

It was the first clear-cut victory for the military and it signaled the effective end to the war. Now all that was left was to work out the surrender terms and free the white captives. Little Crow and his followers fled north while most of the Dakota waited for Sibley to enter their camp to negotiate the surrender of the white captives. These Dakota were tired of the war and wished to seek peace.

Sibley described the scene: "After speeches in which they seriously condemned the war party, denied any participation in their proceedings, and gave me assurances that they would not have dared to come and take my hand if their own were bloodstained with the blood of captive women and children, they formally delivered up to me to the number of ninety-one pure whites."[29]

The Dakota were splitting up into factions opposed to the war and in favor of the war. There were reports that some Indians said they would give up their captives for $200 each. "Indians are coming in every day—One day 32 tepees arrived, another five with one white child prisoner and about 70 were expected the day after we left. All these Indians are humble and say they are 'good Indians.'"[30]

Colonel Sibley abandoned his pursuit of Little Crow and turned his attention to White Lodge and his band. "Sibley's own opinion is that the number of really good Indians is exceedingly small and this is also the impression of others familiar with the Indian character. John Other Day says there are about six or a dozen 'good Indians' and all others are bad."[31] Sibley told the *Record* that he had about 500 Indian prisoners and he estimated there were around 350 hostiles still at large. These Indians had the remaining white prisoners. In addition to counting prisoners, the settlers began to count their losses. The *Record* reported that: "The military authorities in Brown County buried 343 victims of last August's massacre. In the township of Milford only four out of 44 total citizens survived. Major Brant estimates that the Indians have killed 900 people since the trouble began."[32] A more accurate death total would be nearer to 500 whites killed than 900. According to historical records, in 37 days of fighting, 77 American soldiers, 29 citizen soldiers, and approximately 358 settlers had been killed.[33]

With the war drawing to a close, the people of Minnesota began to look around and try to affix blame for the slaughter. The *Record,* in an editorial titled, "Where the Responsibility Lies," chastised the Dakota, but it also pointed its finger at the government and local traders.

> We do not pretend to apologize in the slightest for the atrocities so lately perpetrated by the Sioux upon our defenseless frontier settlers, but demand in retaliation therefore their total extermination; yet we sincerely believe that when the whole matter has been thoroughly and fairly investigated, the main cause of the outbreak will be the fraudulent conduct of Indian officials. The Indian ideas of justice are such that he does not discriminate between the men committing the wrongs and innocent persons, and in seeking revenge, has made an indiscriminate war on the whole white race.
>
> The Department at Washington is not wholly blameless for the murder of our frontier settlers, for time and again the frauds of Indian officials have been made known there, to all of which a deaf ear was turned.
>
> The amount of annuities furnished by the Government, if properly distributed, are ample for all of their wants, but in the hands of a thieving agent, leagued with equally dishonest traders, not sufficient is meted out to keep them from starvation and they are turned loose to supply the deficiency by stealing from white settlers. The bulk of their goods go to fill the coffers of those in whose care they are entrusted.[34]

It was not shocking that the Indians would be held accountable for the massacres of the last several weeks. However, it was surprising that this frontier newspaper bluntly stated that the actions of greedy traders and corrupt government officials were also greatly to blame. The *Record* followed up its earlier editorial with a companion piece a week later. Some of its vitriol may have been inspired by politics, as elections were coming up and the newspaper saw an opportunity to embarrass and defeat political rivals.

> One thousand lives have been sacrificed by this band of thieves in the accomplishments of their hellish purposes and the blood of our frontier settlers is now being used to corrupt and control our elections and maintain the supremacy of the heartless and guilty wretches. It remains for the people of our State to say whether they will succeed or whether the murder of our fellow citizens shall be

avenged by breaking up the band of conspirators. On Tuesday next, every voter will be called upon to render his verdict and we appeal to each and all, by the thousand lives already sacrificed, by our depopulated and desolated frontier, by the thousands of women and children driven from their homes penniless and dependent on public charity—to consider well the responsibility. The opportunity will never again return and we beseech the voters of our State to lay aside all party feeling and cast their votes for men who will remove every Indian from our borders and dedicate the rich and virgin soil of Minnesota to civilization and Christianity.[35]

Some Indian agents, ministers, and government officials, anxious to protect their wards from what they considered unjust accusations, began to make statements minimizing the actions of the Indians. The *Record* was quick to try and set the matter straight. The Reverend W. S. Williamson claimed that he had made inquiries into alleged Dakota "cruelties," but could find no evidence of anything beyond acts of war. The *Record* countered, criticizing Williamson for his half-hearted efforts. "The Doctor has not been very energetic in prosecuting his inquiries or he might have heard of outrages such as only a Sioux Indian could perpetrate. A number of instances have occurred where females have been brutally ravished after death. We have it upon good authority that two children were found in Brown County with their feet tied together and strung across a fence. Also one instance where a body was found nailed to a wall. In the face of such facts, we fear the doctor will not make much headway in manufacturing sympathy for his Indian Wards."[36]

The *St. Paul Pioneer* echoed the sentiments of the *Record* and welcomed the opportunity to tweak its rival, the *St. Paul Press*. "If the [St. Paul] *Press* correspondent, who was so shocked to see the Sioux scalp in Third street, could have seen the horribly mutilated condition of the corpses of Andrew Austin and others I could name, but do not out of regard to surviving friends and relatives—wives, sisters and children—see how their hearts have been torn out from their bosoms, their heads cut off and stuck in their bowels. It is thought here that his Christian sympathy would take another direction."[37]

Historian Carol Chomsky argues that the accusation of widespread barbarity by the Dakota was inaccurate. "In most cases the Dakota killed the men and took the women and children prisoners. Wild stories of mutilation by the Dakota in these encounters spread among the settlers, but historians have concluded that these reports were probably exaggerations of isolated instances of atrocities."[38]

Many Minnesota citizens accused the Winnebago tribe of at least tacitly assisting the Dakota in their uprising. In an editorial entitled "Are the Winnebagoes Implicated with the Sioux?" the *Record* laid out its case:

It is the general and firm belief of our people that a portion of the Winnebago tribe has been and even now is engaged with the Sioux in murdering and plundering the white settlers. This belief is founded principally upon circumstantial evidence, but is sufficiently strong to justify the most positive conviction on the part of those best acquainted with the Indians.

The above are but a portion of the circumstances that have caused our people to distrust the Winnebago nation, and upon which is based the belief that the tribe is implicated with the Sioux in murdering the whites. The conviction is firmly impressed upon the public mind, and so long as they remain in our midst, they will be recognized and treated as enemies. Our people can never again feel secure so long as the very heart of our agricultural district is owned and occupied by two thousand savages, the mere contemplation of those wily and barbarous mode of warfare—sparing neither helpless women nor innocent children—strikes terror to the stoutest hearts.

The old stereotype story is repeated, and our farmers are told that if the Winnebagoes are removed, we shall lose a market for our agricultural surplus. But thank God, this sordid appeal has lost its charms. Winnebago gold, piled mountain high, cannot offset the atrocities of the past two months, or reconcile the remnant of our population to again confidently place ourselves at the mercy of the savages. They must either leave the country or we will. Our rich and fertile prairies must either be the abode of thrift, industry and wealth, or the hunting ground of a barbarous and worthless race. Which shall it be Mr. President?[39]

While a few individual Winnebago may have fought alongside the Dakota, the evidence is overwhelming that the tribe was peaceful and tried to remain neutral in the fight between the whites and the Dakota. Commissioner William P. Dole believed that only a few Winnebago had joined the Sioux in their war and did not think it was proper to punish the whole tribe. The public sentiment, however, considered the Winnebago equally guilty and called for their expulsion from the state. In the end, both the Winnebago and the Dakota would be removed beyond the borders of Minnesota.

With Little Crow and the few surviving hostiles now on the run, the focus of Minnesota's citizens shifted to a surprising and unprecedented event. There was going to be a public trial for almost 400 Indians captured by the military. General John Pope expected the execution of the prisoners as a matter of course. Only the president could pardon the Indians, and Pope did not expect him to interfere. In an earlier letter to Colonel Sibley, Pope had made his feelings clear: "The horrible massacres of women and children and the outrageous abuse of female prisoners, still alive, call for punishment beyond human power to inflict. There will be no peace in this region by virtue of treaties and Indian faith. It is my purpose utterly to exterminate the Sioux if I have the power to do so and even if it requires a campaign lasting the whole of next year. Destroy everything belonging to them and force them out to the plains, unless, as I suggest, you can capture them. They are to be treated as maniacs or wild beasts, and by no means as people with whom treaties or compromises can be made."[40]

Simply transporting the captives to Mankato had been fraught with challenges. While the army was moving the captured Sioux through the New Ulm area, the prisoners were attacked with clubs, knives, stones, and guns by a mob of New Ulm residents. One man's skull was badly fractured and others suffered broken bones. The soldiers had to resort to force to calm the mob. The *Record* stated, "While we sympathize with the people of New Ulm in their suffering, we cannot but condemn as unjustifiable their conduct in attacking prisoners strongly ironed and guarded and under sentence to atone with their lives for their misdeeds."[41]

It seemed to be a foregone conclusion that all of the captives being brought to trial would be executed. The Reverend Henry Whipple, Episcopal bishop of Minnesota, protested this rush to judgment and wrote to President Lincoln asking him to ensure these Indians receive a fair trial. The *St. Paul Pioneer* saw Whipple and other ministers as well-meaning, but naïve. "I would not say a word disrespectful of the intentions of Bishop Whipple and Mr. Riggs. They are intelligent and humane gentlemen, and whatever they do is dictated by an honest sense of duty. But I do not think they consider the whole question. Partial kindness is sometimes general inhumanity, and such, though well-intended, the effect of their action. The law of retaliatory war is the common law, and the law of the savage, which takes life for life, whether it be that of the offender or his relatives, and which would require a thousand more victims, demand that these prisoners should die."[42]

In the end, 392 Dakota were brought to trial, with as many as 42 tried in a single day. Most were charged with murder and a few were also charged with robbery and rape. According to historian Chomsky, the commission tried the Dakota for the wrong crimes. "Based on the historical and legal views prevailing in 1862 and the years that followed, the Dakota were a sovereign nation at war with the United States, and the men who fought the war were entitled to be treated as legitimate belligerents. The Dakota, therefore, should have been tried only on charges that they violated the customary rules of warfare, not for the civilian crimes of murder, rape and robbery. Judged by those standards, few of the convictions are supportable."[43]

Testimony against the prisoners was given by white women who had witnessed specific attacks or who, during their captivity, observed the men leaving and returning to camp. Most of the evidence that convicted the defendants, however, was provided either by the defendants themselves or by mixed-bloods who had been swept up in the war effort and who claimed they had been forced to participate in the fighting. Every defendant found to have participated in any fighting, whether against soldiers or against settlers, whether in a pitched battle or in a raid, was convicted and sentenced to be hanged. Those found to have participated only in plundering were found guilty and sentenced to terms of imprisonment ranging from 1 to 10 years. Of the 392 men tried, the commission convicted 323, of whom 303 were sentenced to be hanged and 20 sentenced to terms of imprisonment.[44]

According to the *Record,* the prisoners were brought into court chained, in some cases eight together. The charges were interpreted to them and they were told to tell the truth. At least two-thirds of the prisoners admitted that they fired, but in most instances insisted that it was only two or three shots and no one was killed.

The newspaper ridiculed their excuses and poked fun at their appearance:

> One day all the elderly men, who were in the vigor of their manly strength, said their hair was too grey to go into battle; and the young men, aged from eighteen to twenty-five, insisted that they were too young and their hearts too weak to face fire. Another frozen faced, shaggy haired, rank specimen of many winters, looked more like the Devil than anything human. I should have run from him in fright had he been a "good Indian" in times of peace. It is a reasonable probability that he was satanic—horns and a tail were all that were necessary to make the personification.[45]

President Lincoln was apparently torn between the cries for vengeance and his concerns about potential injustice to the accused. On December 1, 1862, he wrote to Judge Advocate General Joseph Holt, asking his legal opinion on whether, if he should decide to execute only some of the prisoners, would he have to choose or could he leave it to some officer on the scene? Holt replied that only the president could decide which prisoners to pardon.[46]

A telegraph from President Lincoln to General Pope declared that he required clear evidence of guilt before he would agree to execute any of the prisoners. His principal interest was in punishing the ringleaders. The *Record* was not sure who the president meant when he referred to "ringleaders" but reminded him that Little Crow and other leaders were still at large and "must be caught before they can be hung." It added, "The massacre was premeditated and simultaneous by the whole Sioux tribe; and it must indeed be a nice discrimination that can distinguish the 'ringleaders' from the followers. All alike are murderers and no punishment short of hanging will satisfy the citizens of Minnesota. If the Government will not execute them, the people must and woe to the men or set of men who interpose between the people and the savage murderers."[47] In its fervor to punish the Indians, the *Record* was endorsing not only mob rule but treason.

The *Record* made its attitude toward the fit punishment for the Dakota abundantly clear when it ran a parody of Alfred Lord Tennyson's "Charge of the Light Brigade" on its front page. It called its poem "Charge of the Hemp Brigade."

Charge of the Hemp Brigade

Hemp on the throat of them
Hemp round the neck of them
Hemp under the ears of them
Twisting and choking;
Stormed at with shout and yell
Grandly they'll hang and well
Until the jaws of death
Until the mouth of Hell
takes the Three hundred.

Theirs not to make reply
Theirs not to reason why
Theirs but to hang and die.
Into the valley of Death
Send the three hundred.

Hemp on the throat of them,
Hemp round the neck of them,
Hemp under the chin of them
Twisting and choking
Stormed at with shout and yell,
Where wives and children fell,
They that have killed so well
Come to the jaws of Death
Come to the mouth of Hell,
All that is left of them,
Left of three hundred.

When can their mem'ry fade?
All the sad deaths they made
All the State mourned.
Weep for the deaths they made,
But give to the Hemp Brigade
The Devilish three hundred![48]

There were rumors that Little Crow was gathering 2,000 warriors for a raid to free the prisoners and secret societies were springing up all over Minnesota to ensure that all the Indians were executed. A force of 75 to 80 men raised in New Ulm allegedly marched on Camp Lincoln where the prisoners were being held. They turned back when they learned that the army was prepared for their arrival. The *St. Paul Pioneer* stated that "secret societies are being formed throughout this State, the avowed object of which is to hang or shoot every Indian suspected of having a hand in the Indian massacres, should the government refuse to execute them. No less than 500 men at St. Paul have signed a pledge for that purpose."[49]

A letter to the *Record* from a group calling itself the "Sioux Exterminators Lodge #28" promised a certain fate for the Dakota, no matter what President Lincoln decided. "Rumor, double-tongued, brings to us much too frequently, words of doubt as to the fate of the red devils who have desolated our frontier. Shall we hold meetings and petition the President that justice be meted them? Nay! Let me tell you that I violate no secret when I say to you that all the Quakers this side of eternity cannot save a single red devil. If President Lincoln will not heed the petition that goes to him from five-hundred murdered whites, he will pay but little attention to the school-boy resolutions of the living. So we of the frontier watch and wait. No matter the how, or when, but sure as there is a living God, there will be a carnival of death, somewhere, among the Indians, even if from Washington come orders to let the miscreants loose."[50]

The *Record* reported on December 13, 1862, that President Lincoln had decided to hang 30 Indians. They were to be hung in installments of 10 each. After the first group was executed, if the people were satisfied, then the president would be satisfied. If not, then they would continue to the second group, but in no case would they hang more than 30. The newspaper criticized this decision as a wholly inadequate solution. "We might at least respect the firmness of the President if he had decided not to hang the prisoners after a calm, and impartial examination of the testimony; but to hang thirty for the mere gratification of the people, and not because they are guilty, is a doctrine so disgusting and repulsive to intelligent people that they cannot but loath and abhor the personage—even though he be President of the United States—with whom it originated."[51]

The *Record* was wrong. The president had decided, on the merits of each case, to pardon 264 and execute 39 men. At the last minute, a reprieve was granted for one of the condemned men and 38 men were scheduled to be executed on December 26, 1862.

Minnesota Senator Morton S. Wilkinson and Congressmen Cyrus Aldrich and William Windom wrote a letter of protest to Lincoln asking that he rescind his order to hang only 39 of the Dakota and instead execute the 303 that were condemned by the court. They cited the testimony of "90 women who were captured by the Dakota, witnessed the murders of their husbands and sons and were spared only to take them, into a captivity that was infinitely worse than death."[52]

> There was no war about it—it was wholesale robbery, rape, murder. The people of Minnesota, have been patient and stood by you and have not taken the law into their own hands because they believed the President would deal with them justly.
>
> We protest against the pardon of these Indians because if it is done the Indians will become more insolent and criminal than they ever were before. They will believe that the Great Father in Washington justifies their act or is afraid to punish them for their crimes.
>
> We protest against it, because if the President does not permit these executions to take place under the forms of law, the enraged people of Minnesota

will dispose of these wretches without law. We do not wish to see the mob law inaugurated in Minnesota, as it certainly will be if you force the people to it.[53]

Almost without exception the condemned men professed that they were innocent of any murders. Some were condemned because they had lied and boasted of deeds they had not done. Others were like *Ma-ka-ta-e-na-jin* (One Who Stands on the Earth), an old man who claimed he had not used a gun in years. He was at New Ulm but did not kill anyone. He had two sons killed and just wanted the truth told.[54]

Rda-in-yan-kna (Rattling Runner), in a letter to his father-in-law, Wabashaw, wrote, "You told me that if we followed the advice of General Sibley and gave ourselves up to the whites, all would be well—no innocent man would be injured. I have not killed, wounded or injured any white man or any white persons. I have not participated in the plunder of their property; and yet today, I am set apart for execution and must die in a few days, while men who are guilty will remain in prison. My wife is your daughter, my children your grandchildren. I leave them all in your care and under your protection. Do not let them suffer, and when my children are grown up, let them know that their father died because he followed the advice of his chief, and without having the blood of a white man to answer for to the Great Spirit."[55]

A reporter for the *St. Paul Pioneer* was present the morning of the hanging, as the Dakota prepared to be taken out to the scaffold. His vivid description of the scene gives us insight into their last moments. "While Father Ravoux was speaking to them, Old Tazoo broke out in a death wail, in which one after another joined, until the prison room was filled with an unearthly plaint which was neither of despair nor grief, but rather a paroxysm of savage passion, most impressive to witness and startling to hear, even for those who understood the language of the music only. During the lulls in their death-song, they would resume their pipes, and with the exception of an occasional mutter or a rattling of their chains, they sat motionless and impassive, until one among the older would break out into the wild wail, then all would join again in the solemn preparation for death."[56]

According to the *Pioneer,* the "death song" relaxed them and they all seemed resigned and unconcerned as they shuffled, loosely shackled hand and feet, out of the prison room toward the scaffold. White caps were placed over their heads and pulled over their faces. "There then ensued a scene that can hardly be described and which can never be forgotten. All joined in shouting and singing, as it appeared to those who were ignorant of the language. The tunes seemed somewhat discordant and yet there was harmony in it. Save the moment of cutting the rope, it was the most thrilling moment of the awful scene. And it was not their voices alone. Their bodies swayed to and fro and their every limb seemed to be keeping time. The drop trembled and shook as all were dancing. The most touching scene on the drop was their attempt to grasp each other's hands, fettered as they were. They were very close to each other and many succeeded. Three or four in a row were hand in hand and all hands swaying up and down with the rise and fall of their voices.[57]

The words they were chanting were not those of a final, defiant death song. "We were informed, by those who understand the language, that their singing and shouting was only to sustain each other." Each man was shouting his own name and calling out the names of his friends, saying, "'I'm here! I'm here!'"[58]

The Dakota who had not surrendered fled north and west. Colonel Sibley pursued them into Dakota Territory and defeated the Dakota and their allies in a series of battles. Little Crow fled to Canada but drifted back to Minnesota in the summer of 1863. On July 3, he was killed by a farmer near Hutchinson, Minnesota, while picking raspberries with his son. The farmer had shot him to collect the $25 bounty being offered by the state for the scalps of fugitive Dakota. When it was discovered it was Little Crow, the farmer was paid a $500 bonus. Little Crow's body was dragged through the streets of Hutchinson and children celebrated the fourth of July by placing firecrackers in his ears and nose. His body was dismembered and his skull and scalp were sent to St. Paul, where they remained until 1971.[59]

Between 1,300 and 1,700 Dakota were held near Fort Snelling, Minnesota, during the winter of 1862–1863. In April of 1863, the United States Congress abolished the Dakota reservation, declared all previous treaties null and void, and expelled the Dakota from Minnesota. More than 130 Dakota died in the camp or on the way to their new home. The Winnebago would also be expelled and both tribes were given small reservations in northeast Nebraska Territory.

A few scattered place names are all that remains to mark their passage.

CHAPTER 2

Sand Creek Massacre:
November 1864

The treaty of 1851 promised the tribes of the Great Plains that if they allowed free passage to settlers crossing their lands, they could continue their nomadic lifestyle without interference. The discovery of gold in Colorado changed all that. New treaties were sought with the tribes and conflict became more common. In the early 1860s, there were isolated murders of both whites and Indians.

John Evans, governor of the Colorado Territory, petitioned the federal government to send him more troops or at least allow him to keep local regiments in Colorado. He stated that rather than sending them to eastern battlefields, he needed them to thwart Confederate invaders from Texas and Indian raiders. Evans journeyed to Washington to plead his case, but the War Department did not share the governor's fears and continued to siphon off Colorado militia. According to historian Alvin M. Joseph Jr., Evans returned to Colorado determined to find an excuse he could use to justify military support and his pursuit of a war against the tribes.[1]

In April 1864, in response to allegations of Indians running off horses and cattle, Evans sent Colonel John M. Chivington and the 1st Colorado Calvary after the raiders. Not waiting to establish guilt or innocence, Chivington's men followed his orders to "kill Cheyenne wherever and whenever found."[2] For a time, the tribes were too shocked to respond. The *Daily Mining Journal* of Black Hawk, Colorado, declared, "The Indian War has blown over for the present. Col. Chivington says the Platte route was never more free from Indian insolence than at present."[3]

However, Chivington's raiders had killed many innocent Indian men, women, and children, and angry tribesmen soon retaliated with raids against settlers in Kansas and Colorado. In May of 1864, Nathan Hungate, his wife, and two daughters were murdered by a roving band of Arapahoe. When the scalped and mutilated bodies were discovered, they were brought into nearby Denver and displayed on a wagon for the populace to see. It enraged Denver's citizens and caused mass hysteria. It was just what Governor Evans had been waiting for. He announced a war against all Indians who refused to go to the reservations. Hoping to divide and conquer, he decreed that any Indian leaders who sincerely desired peace should take their people to designated forts where Indian agents would protect and feed them. Those Indians who did not comply would be declared hostiles. He called for civilian volunteers to help him enforce his plan. They would serve for 100 days and would be led by Colonel Chivington.[4] Comprising almost exclusively recruits from Denver's saloons and toughs from the streets, the Third Colorado Cavalry was designed to calm public fears and punish the Indians.[5]

That summer and fall, the issues of the Cheyenne and Arapahoe were not the only matters that Chivington and Evans had on their minds. They both had political ambitions, playing leadership roles in the attempt to earn statehood for the Colorado Territory. Evans wanted to be a senator and Chivington hoped to be Colorado's first congressman. The movement for statehood coincided with President Abraham Lincoln's wishes. He hoped that Colorado's entry into the Union could provide him with votes that would help to reelect him in the fall.[6]

Chivington had burst on the scene after his success in helping to defeat the Texans in the battle at Glorieta Pass. A former preacher, he was famous for his size and the fire-and-brimstone nature of his sermons. Historian Alvin M. Josephy Jr. described him as "Crude and overbearing, he had grown ruthlessly ambitious, as well as contemptuous of ethical or legal constraints."[7] Chivington had flouted local authorities when he arranged for the execution of six confederate prisoners even though he had earlier been denied permission. He claimed they were shot while attempting to escape. When he was not reprimanded, Chivington grew bolder. According to Josephy, he combined a drive for power with the fervor of a self-righteous religious zealot. Colonel John P. Slough, Chivington's former superior, described him as "a crazy preacher who thinks he is Napoleon Bonaparte."[8] Chivington's arrogance and the temporary nature of the Third Colorado Cavalry's volunteer force made for a volatile combination—one that was about to be unleashed on the Cheyenne and Arapahoe.

The *Rocky Mountain News* reported high levels of anxiety among Denver's citizens, who were concerned with the government's ability to quell the Indian outbreak. It reassured its readers that, according to its highly placed sources, everything would work out just fine. "Plans are working well and Mr. Lo [Lo the poor Indian] will soon find it quite hot down among the sand hills."[9] The *News* wrote the Cheyenne leaders said the trouble was the fault of 100 to 150 braves who were flouting the authority of their chiefs. The chiefs hoped that the "whites will kill these outlaws."[10]

Major Edward Wynkoop, the commander of Fort Lyon, led an expedition of 120 men against the Cheyenne as a show of force and to try and free captives. According to newspaper reports, he encountered a group of Cheyenne and Arapahoe numbering around 600. He held council with the Indians and offered them his protection if they would give up their captives and declare their peaceful

Bosse, Left Hand, White Wolf, Black Kettle, White Antelope, Bull Bear, Neva: Chiefs of the Arapahoe, Sioux, Cheyenne, and Kiowa tribes. Courtesy of Denver Public Library, Western History Collection.

intentions. Bull Bear, Black Kettle, White Antelope, and Little Robe agreed and released four white captives. They promised to accompany Wynkoop to Denver to meet with Governor Evans and Colonel Chivington and declare their desire for peace.

"Great credit is due to Major Wynkoop for his coolness and energy on the trip," wrote the *Rocky Mountain News*. "He has saved the lives of four whites, which in my estimation, were better than the lives of a thousand savages! He, with one hundred and twenty men, went into the heart of the Indian country in the midst of five thousand hostile Indians and it was a scratch that we ever got out of it."[11]

The same article reinforced some of Evans's fears when it wrote that the Cheyenne and Arapahoe reported they had been in contact with the rebels in Texas for some time. "They tell them that the whites in Colorado want their hunting grounds from them and will take their squaws and everything they have and if the Indian will join them they will go with them and take Denver and give the whole country to the Indian."[12]

Major Wynkoop made good on his promise and escorted the Cheyenne and Arapahoe chiefs to Camp Weld to meet with Evans and Chivington on September 28, 1864. The Indians were told to submit to the military authorities at Fort Lyon and they would be protected. Black Kettle was relieved and believed that he had secured peace for his people. He returned with them to Fort Lyon and the protection of his new friend Major Wynkoop.

It was all a sham. The same day he met with the Indians, Chivington had received a letter from General Samuel R. Curtis, commanding officer of the Department of Kansas. Curtis ordered him not to make any peace with the Indians. Chivington and Evans decided not to reveal the contents of the letter and to proceed as if nothing had changed. Both men readily agreed to the deceit. They did not tell Major Wynkoop until later, and when he objected to the treachery, he was relieved of his command and replaced by a Major Scott Anthony. Anthony quickly evicted the Cheyenne from the protective shadow of Fort Lyon and sent them 40 miles north to Sand Creek.

Historian George Bird Grinnell writes that Anthony, while hinting at peace to the Indians, was simultaneously writing to district headquarters and requesting additional troops to attack the Indians.[13] "This shows clearly that he told the Cheyennes to camp on Sand Creek only in order that he might have them within reach if he could get a chance to attack them."[14]

On November 9, 1864, Black Kettle reported to Anthony that the Cheyenne and Arapahoe were camped peacefully along the banks of Sand Creek. Anthony informed them they were to wait there until he was given permission by his superiors to accept them as prisoners. Then they could return to Fort Lyon, where he would feed them.

Meanwhile Chivington was secretly moving his forces south. His men had been taunted as the "Bloodless Third" because of the public's belief their enlistment would run out before they fought a battle. Chivington promised his men combat and a chance for glory. On November 28 they arrived outside of Fort Lyon, surprising Major Anthony. Seeking to maintain secrecy, Chivington threw pickets around the fort with orders to shoot anyone who tried to leave.[15]

Major Anthony told Chivington he was happy to see him and supported his efforts to punish the Cheyenne. This despite the fact the Indians were currently camped peacefully at Sand Creek following Anthony's express orders. According to testimony later given at a military inquiry, Anthony was almost alone in his initial support for Chivington. "Most of his fellow officers at the post were stunned, arguing that an attack on the Indians would violate pledges of safety that had been given them. Chivington lashed back at them furiously, damning 'any man that was in sympathy with Indians' and warning that such persons 'had better get out of the United States service.'"[16]

Shortly after dusk, the Third Colorado Calvary left the fort accompanied by around 125 of Major Anthony's garrison. Some 700 men in all, they took with them four 12-pounder mountain howitzers. Riding through the night, the soldiers arrived outside of the camp at Sand Creek just as the sun was coming up.

It was November 29, 1864, and the Cheyenne and Arapaho were waking and beginning to prepare for the day. Some of the women and other early risers, sighting the soldiers, raised the alarm. Black Kettle quickly raised a white flag along with the American flag given to him in 1860. He had to show these soldiers his camp was at peace. He tried to reassure his people that the soldiers would not harm them.

The sight of the flag did not stop Chivington's men. Their commander exhorted them to "Remember the murdered women and children on the Platte. Take no prisoners."[17] As they galloped across the creek, some of Major Anthony's men split off to round up the pony herd and the others flanked the camp on the left. The main body of the troops charged the center of the encampment. The soldiers fired indiscriminately, killing men, women, and children. The mountain howitzers rained grapeshot on the Indians frantically trying to flee the village. Black Kettle grabbed his family and rushed to escape the slaughter.

There was isolated resistance from some of the tribesmen, but it was unorganized and did not last long. Grapeshot ripped through the warriors trying to fight back and the few survivors scattered. The troops rode back and forth among the tipis shooting at anything that moved. According to historian Josephy, "For hours, the frenzied Coloradans, in an orgy of brutality and hate, went over the battlefield, murdering the wounded and scalping and mutilating the dead."[18] The Indians who had managed to escape huddled in whatever cover they could find and after night fell, they stumbled north to try and find refuge in the camps of the Sioux and other Cheyenne.

The next day Chivington's men remained in the camp, looting whatever they could find and finishing off any wounded Cheyenne and Arapahoe. Jack Smith, a half-breed trader's son they had captured earlier, was brought out and murdered. On the morning of December 1, 1864, the troops set the village on fire and headed out.

The soldiers' losses were 9 killed and 38 wounded. More than 150 Cheyenne and Arapahoe were slaughtered; two-thirds of the dead were women and children. Rather than marching north to try and intercept some of the Sioux and Cheyenne war bands, Chivington's men, flushed with triumph, headed south for easier pickings. Major Anthony informed Chivington a small band of Arapahoe was camped along the Arkansas River and should make an attractive target. However, warned of the soldier's approach, the small group had already fled. Chivington soon abandoned the chase and headed back north to Denver.[19]

The first news of Sand Creek was carried in the *Rocky Mountain News*. Under the headline, "Big Indian Fight," the brief story provided only basic information. "The 1st and 3rd regiments have had a battle with the Indians on Sand Creek, a short distance northeast of Fort Lyon. Five hundred Indians are reported killed and six hundred horses captured. Captain Baxter and Lieutenant Pierce are reported killed. No further particulars. A messenger is hourly expected with full details. *Bully for the Colorado boys!*"[20]

The Black Hawk *Daily Mining Journal* had its first Sand Creek story the next day. Referring to Chivington's failed attempt at running for Congress, the newspaper praised the Colonel's military prowess.

> The people of Colorado will see renewed cause of thankfulness that they did not send Col. Chivington to Congress since he appears to have again turned his attention to military matters. One more such blow, as of the avenging angel, inflicted upon the Devil's own sons of the Plains, will quite reconcile us to Col. Chivington. . . Two more such blows will make us warm admirers of the Methodist Colonel and if by any happy chance of fortune, he should be able to inflict three more, making in all a neat sum of 2,000 killed, the Journal will become his fast friend and support him for any office within the gift of the people of Colorado, at any time in the future for he will be worthy to be called her temporal savior.[21]

More details of the fight arrived in the next few days with reports in the *News* that Chivington and his men were pursuing other bands of hostiles. A letter from Captain J. C. Anderson, reprinted in the *News*, trumpeted, "We have met the enemy and they are ours. The 'Bloodless Thirdsters' have gained the greatest victory, west of the Missouri, over the savages."[22] The letter claimed that there had been around 900 Indians at the battle and that 500 to 600 had been killed, including Black Kettle and all the principal chiefs. "We have completely broken up the tribe and think the settlers will not be further molested by them. Tomorrow we leave here, whither I know not. Our boys are well supplied with Indian plunder and perfectly satisfied to renew the attack with any tribe."[23]

The December 14, 1864, edition of the *Rocky Mountain News* headlined their big story, "The Savages Dispersed! 500 Indians Killed!"[24] A report from Chivington echoed earlier claims of 500 Indians killed and the deaths of Black Kettle and other chiefs. He described his soldier's performance as heroic, stating, "All did nobly."[25]

Chivington was wrong on several counts. As later investigations would prove, the Indians numbered nearer to 500 than 900, around 150 Indians were slain and Black Kettle and several other leaders survived the massacre. In addition, rather than ending any Indian troubles, the Sand Creek Massacre inflamed the frontier and ignited a war far larger and bloodier than anything that had happened in Colorado before. Chivington promised to head north in pursuit of other hostile bands, but after a brief detour, he returned to Denver to raucous acclaim from most of its citizens.

The first criticism, although mild in nature, came from the *Daily Mining Journal*. It complained that "while it seemed a vigorous Indian campaign had been opened" and the public believed that "not a redskin between the Platte and the Republican could possibly escape," the campaign had been abandoned. It stated that Chivington and Colonel George Shoup had allegedly been on the way to

Sioux villages containing 8,000 warriors and there were high hopes that their actions would close a war lasting 170 years. "But alas for all these high-colored visions, the Indian campaign has been abandoned. Col. Chivington has returned to Denver and is there to be mustered out. . . . It may be too that the immortal blow of the 29th November will settle these fellow's coffee for a while."[26]

The *News* still championed the Colorado militia claiming, "Among the brilliant feats of arms in Indian warfare, the recent campaign of our own Colorado Volunteers will stand in history with few rivals and none to exceed it in final results." It praised the militia's efforts in marching hundreds of miles through a snowstorm and reported that in "no single battle in North America have so many Indians been slain." It concluded by stating, "All acquitted themselves well and Colorado soldiers have again covered themselves with glory."[27]

The last week of December saw the triumphant return of the "bloody Third-sters" to Denver. They paraded through the main streets of the town led by a regimental band. "As the 'bold sojer boys' passed along, the sidewalks and the corner stands were thronged with citizens saluting their old friends. The fair sex took the opportunity, wherever they could get it, of expressing their admiration for the gallant boys who donned the regimentals for the purpose of protecting the women of the country by ridding it of redskins."[28]

Historian Josephy describes the scene in a different way. "Indian earrings, rings, and other personal possessions some still attached to ears, fingers and other pieces of flesh, were shown off in the streets and scores of Cheyenne and Arapaho scalps were held up in theaters to cheering audiences or were hung as decorations on the mirrors behind bars in Denver saloons."[29]

The first rumblings that the events at Sand Creek may not have been accurately reported appeared in the *Daily Mining Journal.* "A good many of the Third Regiment boys are returning to their old haunts. Some of them do not scruple to say that the big battle of Sand Creek was a cold-blooded massacre. If so, it must be remembered that the individual who gave the order for its commission is alone to blame for it. 'Tis the soldier's part to obey without question and right nobly was it done on this occasion. Many stories are told and incidents related by the actors in the bloody scene, which are too sickening to repeat."[30]

The *Rocky Mountain News* reacted to the rumors quickly and strongly. "Letters received from 'high officials' in Colorado say that the Indians were killed after surrendering and that a large proportion of them were women and children. Indignation was loudly and unequivocally expressed, and some less considerate of the boys were very persistent in their inquiries as to who those high officials were, with mild intimation that they had half a mind to 'go for them!' This talk about 'friendly Indians' and 'surrendered villages' will do to 'tell it to the marines,' but to us out here it is all bosh."[31] The *News* continued to rebuke the rumors, using a sarcastic and threatening tone.

Probably those scalps of white men, women and children—one of them fresh— not three days taken—found drying in their lodges were taken in a "friendly," playful manner; or possibly those Indian blankets trimmed with the scalps of white women and with the braids and fringes of their hair, were kept simply as mementoes of their owner's high affection for the pale face. At any rate these delicate and tasteful ornaments cannot have been taken from the heads of the wives, sisters or daughters of these "high officials."

It is unquestioned and undenied that the site of the Sand Creek battle was the rendezvous of the thieving and marauding bands of savages who roamed over this country last summer and fall, and it is shrewdly suspected that somebody was all the time making a very good thing out of it. By all means let there be an investigation, but we advise the Honorable Congressional committee, who may be appointed to conduct it, to get their scalps insured before they pass Plum Creek on their way out.[32]

The *News* embarked on a strident and forceful campaign to clear the name of its hero Chivington and to accuse his accuser of being motivated either by greed or political spite. It lamented the mustering out of Chivington and praised his time of service. "In losing the efficient service of such a man as our own Chivington—whose name is now commensurate with the west, and whose force of character, civil, military and moral, was a tower to his friends and a terror to his enemies—we feel our District is deprived of a brave executive whose service to Colorado and New Mexico are imperishable—let 'sorehead' cowards say, or write to Washington, what they will!"[33]

In editorials, the *News* blamed the charges against Chivington on his political enemies. Calling the accusations "contemptible" and "outrageously false" it lamented that "Colorado is saddled with a lot of uneasy spirits, among them these 'high officials,' who would drag her down to hell, if by so doing they could further their own political ambition, or put money in their pockets. Their hate is as vindictive as their consciences are unscrupulous. They will take desperate chances upon forever damning themselves, to work a temporary injury to those who differ with them upon questions of public policy. . . . They would blast the prospects of the Territory for years to come, and for what? Solely and simply to vent their spite upon two or three men against whom they have personal animosities, or whose power and popularity they envy and fear."[34]

Deciding that political spite may not be seen as a sufficiently powerful motive for betrayal, the editors of the *News* also accused Chivington's accusers of greed. They hinted that "high officials" had been accustomed to earning a good living off of supplying the Indians with overpriced goods. The recent conflict had driven away their best "customers." "No wonder, then, that there are 'soreheads' in that camp, who chatter about 'peaceful Indians,' and what not, when it deprives them of the privilege of having those lazy, lousy red-skins lying around, eating Uncle Sam's provisions and experiencing the maxim that 'there is more pleasure in being cheated, than to cheat.'"[35]

The *Daily Mining Journal* took a more balanced approach to covering the controversy. They were in favor of an official investigation as the only way to get the truth. "We do not feel sufficiently posted to say much with regard to Chivington's action; only an official investigation will bring out the facts amidst so many clashing rumors and reports." They cited the testimony of officers at Fort Lyon who considered the Indians at Sand Creek under the protection of the government and the attack on them to be a betrayal. However, they offered no sympathy to the Cheyenne and Arapahoe. "On the question of killing these miserable, cruel fiends of hell, who murder and mutilate our women and children, who steal our stock, burn our homes and destroy us by cutting off our communication with the States, the people of Colorado are united as one. The Sand Creek Indians were guilty of all of the above."[36]

The *Journal* also speculated that some of the accusations may only be a weapon used by Major Wynkoop and his allies to discredit Chivington. "The Wynkoop faction is by no means idle; hence this outrageous stench, which, while chiefly intended on their part to destroy Chivington, is becoming unbearably offensive to other men who have no interest in those gentleman's quarrels or aspirations."[37]

The *Journal*'s biggest fear was that the controversy would inhibit efforts for future conflicts with the Indians. "Furthermore, the men who are raising this disturbance, arresting all present and discouraging all future operations against the Indians, perhaps making it impossible to raise men even for the protection of our homes, if their actions spring from purely personal motives, deserve the same fate as their friends at Sand Creek. In the minds of the people, they are doomed to that fate already."[38]

The local newspapers both had their points of view on the controversy. The *Rocky Mountain News* sarcastically suggested that "high officials" should pacify the Indians. "Since it is a settled fact that the friendly—peaceable-surrendered—high-toned—gentle-minded—quiet—inoffensive savages are again 'on it' down the Platte, we respectfully suggest that a small and select battalion of 'high officials' be permitted to go down instanter to pacify the devils."[39]

In contrast, the *Daily Mining Journal* claimed that the Cheyenne and Arapahoe had offered themselves as potential allies against the hostile Sioux, but Chivington's attack had now made them bitter enemies and the resulting Indian war was going to be far worse than anything the frontier had yet experienced. It blamed the ambitions of Chivington and Governor Evans for igniting this maelstrom. "If it be honest to plunge a whole community into an Indian war to make of one man a Brigadier General, and of another a Senator; if it be honest to prostitute the military service in the person of its officers and the use of its stock to personal electioneering; if it be honest to steal, destroy, alter and make up outright election returns, then these men are honest."[40]

On January 9, 1865, Senator James R. Doolittle, the head of the Senate Committee on Indian Affairs, rose to address his colleagues. He described in brutal detail the massacre at Sand Creek and introduced a resolution to demand an investigation of the tragic affair. Under pressure from newspapers and politicians, General Henry W. Halleck ordered General Samuel R. Curtis to investigate what had happened at Sand Creek.[41]

The *News* wrote that it welcomed the investigation and assumed it would be held in Denver and staffed by officers from the local military. "If nothing happens to prevent it, we will soon be informed who committed ruthless murders upon the friendly Indians; stole from them the scalps they had stripped from the heads of white men, women and children and committed other similar outrages upon the peaceably disposed aborigines. And last, but not least, we will find out who the 'high officials' are without the chance for a mistake. We are in favor of investigations. They are a bully good thing."[42]

The *News* continued to champion Chivington in its pages. It admitted he was not a perfect man, but averred that his qualities outweighed his faults.

> Colonel Chivington, like all of us, has faults that tarnish his noble qualities; many of which he possesses. Could we divide a man into one hundred parts, and find him in possession of ninety good parts and with only ten bad ones; we would then have found a good man. This we believe Colonel Chivington, the rough diamond of Colorado, possesses. . . . While we have had reasons to not always feel towards Col. Chivington as we would like to feel towards our friends, yet we believe in "fair play and equal rights," and think for killing Indians he deserves the praise and not the censure of Colorado.[43]

As the investigation got under way, in February 1865, the *News* expressed surprise that Major Anthony's testimony at the Sand Creek investigation did not match his original battle report. The paper speculated that his change in testimony may have been prompted by a change in public sentiment. It also criticized the tendency to excuse recent Indian raids as justifiable responses to the Sand Creek "Massacre." It reminded its readers of the "murders, house burnings and train and mail robberies of last summer." It criticized public officials saying, "They see only the present and they justify the savages for their acts, because it is in revenge for the 'massacre' by Col. Chivington."[44]

The *News* seemed frustrated by the willingness of some public officials and eastern newspapers to criticize Chivington's actions. It felt his attack on the Indians had been totally justified.

> How long, O God should we have endured and suffered in silence? Day by day the murderous tomahawk and rifle were thinning our sparse settlement; night after night the flames of burning homesteads and moving trains of goods, lighted up the eastern horizon, or gleamed along the Platte and Arkansas. But they tell us it was wrong to strike a blow in return. The first punishment given to the enemy—not half or quarter equaling their own barbarity—is called a

"massacre." The officers and men who did it were maligned. High Officials misrepresent the facts, to blot and disgrace the fair name of our territory, and yet we are commanded to "suffer and be still."[45]

A joint resolution was passed in the Senate condemning Sand Creek as a massacre and it recommended withholding the pay of Chivington's soldiers. However, the resolution was defeated in the House of Representatives. The *News* took the resolution's failure as vindication for the paper's stance on Chivington and Sand Creek and a defeat for their political foes. "They went into the session to remove the Governor [John Evans], implicate the Secretary [Secretary of State Samuel H. Elbert] and disgrace the Colonel [John M. Chivington] commanding; they came out of it as meek as sucking doves and gentle as lambs."[46]

Throughout the spring of 1865, the *Journal* and the *News* continued to bicker with each other in their editorial pages. The *News* reprinted excerpts of an article from the *Journal* that accused the *News* of propping up Chivington and attempting to intimidate anyone testifying against him. The article implied that the *News* was at least partly responsible for two attempts on the life of Captain Silas Soule, a witness against Chivington. Soule had held his men back at Sand Creek and not allowed them to participate in the slaughter of the Cheyenne. He was accused of cowardice by Chivington.

The *Journal* stopped short of accusing the *News* of actually calling for Soule's killing, but it blamed the *News* for stirring up sentiment against Soule. "We do not say that Chivington or the *News* have instigated this extreme proceeding, but taken in connection with the daily fulminations of that press against what it deems the 'inquisition,' and the 'menagerie,' it looks as though these men not only did not want investigation, but were determined there would be none."[47] The *News* vehemently denied the accusation and reiterated that it fully supported an investigation.

A little over a month later, on April 23, 1865, Soule was assassinated by a former soldier in the 3rd Cavalry. He said it was in revenge for Soule having once put him in the guardhouse, but the *Journal* theorized it was in revenge for Soule's testimony against Chivington and his men.[48]

In a story headlined, "The Responsibility for the Indian War," the *Rocky Mountain News* [Denver, Colorado] attacked the *Daily Mining Journal* [Black Hawk, Colorado] for its stance on Sand Creek and the resulting Indian war.

The Journal set out to think the Indian right. It is ever ready to excuse, justify or apologize for their acts. It prefers to believe their reports. It thinks their stories repeated from mouth to mouth, through half-breeds, Indian traders and sympathizers like itself, are far more reliable by the time they reach Black Hawk than can be statements of a respectable white man, or the official reports of a sworn officer. There is the difference. Our sympathies are upon the side of the white

man, and between the two stories, we incline to believe his. The Journal is exactly against us. It favors the Indians, excuses the Indians, justifies the Indians,
believes the Indians.[49]

The *Journal* did not necessarily see itself on the side of the Indians, but its
editors did think that an investigation was needed to determine the facts of the
case. "We demanded an investigation into the conduct of Indian affairs because
we believed it would appear that an Indian war had been encouraged rather than
averted, and because the Indian war brings ruin to us, the nearest way to peace
was the removal of those men who had brought it on, and in whom the Indians
have lost confidence."[50]

The *Journal* made it clear that it wanted to defend the good name of the men
who had helped to protect the homes of Colorado settlers and that it was only interested in finding out the truth. It defended the right of men like Soule to testify
against Chivington even though some thought it better to just let the furor fade
away. "We would be willing to let Sand Creek rest, because the more it is disturbed
the worse it stinks, but we cannot stand by in silence and see as honorable men
with whom we have risked our lives in several well-fought fields to protect this
people and territory from invasion, loaded with the most foul and disgusting epi-
thets because they dare to be right."[51]

The report of the "Joint Committee of the Conduct of the War" on the Sand
Creek Massacre was released May 30, 1865. It wasted no time in condemning the
actions of Chivington and his men and also criticized Governor Evans for his role
in the tragic affair. Beginning with a description of the event that led up to November 29, 1864, it described in graphic terms what happened on that bloody day.

And then the scene of murder and barbarity began. Men, women and children
were indiscriminately slaughtered. In a few minutes all the Indians were flying over the plains in terror and confusion. A few who endeavored to hide
themselves under the bank of the creek were surrounded and shot down in
cold blood, offering but feeble resistance. From the sucking babe to the old
warrior, all who were overtaken were deliberately murdered. Not content with
killing women and children, who were incapable of offering any resistance,
the soldiers indulged in acts of barbarity of the most revolting character; such,
it is to be hoped, as never before disgraced the acts of men claiming to be
civilized. No attempt was made by the officers to restrain the savage cruelty
of the men under their command, but they stood by and witnessed these acts
without one word of reproof, if they did not incite their commission. . . . It is
difficult to believe that beings in the form of men, and disgracing the uniform
of the United States soldiers and officers, could commit or countenance the
commission of such acts of cruelty and barbarity as are detailed in the testimony.[52]

The joint committee strongly criticized Chivington, accusing him of executing a "foul and dastardly massacre" and condemned him for gratifying "the worst passions that ever cursed the heart of man." The report speculated that Chivington may even have been prompted by political ambition, believing that this massacre would be looked upon favorably by the citizens of Colorado. Nor did the report spare Governor Evans. It characterized his testimony as "prevaricating and shuffling" and stated it seemed designed to try and show that he did not know the Indians were under a flag of truce and therefore protected.[53]

The report finished with a powerful call for justice and retribution. "In conclusion, your committee are of the opinion that for the purpose of vindicating the cause of justice and upholding the honor of the nation, prompt and energetic measures should be taken to remove from office those who have thus disgraced the government by whom they are employed, and to punish, as their crimes deserve, those who have been guilty of these brutal and cowardly acts."[54]

Most of the major players in the Sand Creek Massacre were haunted by the experience. President Andrew Johnson called for and received the resignation of Governor Evans. General Henry W. Halleck called for the court martial of Colonel Chivington, but Chivington had already resigned his commission. As a civilian he was beyond the reach of military authorities. He was disgraced and his political ambitions were crushed. He ran for congress again in Colorado and later ran for the state legislature in Ohio, but the ghosts of Sand Creek doomed both campaigns. Black Kettle met his fate on another cold November morning, along another river. He was killed on November 27, 1868, near the Washita River in Indian Territory, when his village was attacked and burned by Lieutenant Colonel George Armstrong Custer.

CHAPTER 3

Fort Laramie Treaty:
1868

By 1868, the United States had been making treaties with Native Americans for almost 200 years. However, there was a renewed urgency for treaty-making with the end of the Civil War and the clamoring for western lands. The policy of removing Indian tribes to remote areas called reservations became a popular solution. It opened the Indian land for white settlement and removed the former landowners to a distant locale where they could not object or interfere.

> For several years after the Civil War, the policy of concentration was extremely popular. Settlers who wished the removal of neighboring Indians enthusiastically welcomed the scheme, and there were few at the moment to object to post-war treaties which provided for locating tribes either in the Indian territory south of Kansas or in the newly established Sioux reservations to the north. Senate ratification of these agreements during the late sixties provided legislative support for policy, which was applied successfully in removals of the Osage, Kaw, Otoe, and Pawnee tribes from Kansas and Nebraska to the Indian Territory.[1]

The isolated U.S. army posts on the western frontier were charged with the duty of making sure that Indians stayed on the reservations that had been created for them. It was often a difficult job.

The years 1866 and 1867 had not been easy for Colonel Henry B. Carrington and his garrison at Fort Phil Kearny in Wyoming Territory. In December 1866, Captain William J. Fetterman and his entire command of 81 men had been killed and Carrington and his men had been besieged inside the fort by the Sioux, Cheyenne, and Arapaho for over a year. In September 1867, a group of peace commissioners arrived at the end of the Union Pacific tracks in western Nebraska to seek an end to what was being called "Red Cloud's War." This group of commissioners included Nathaniel Taylor, John Sanborn, John Henderson, Samuel Tappan, General Alfred Terry, General William S. Harney, and General William T. Sherman. The commissioners summoned the tribes to meet with them at Fort Laramie on September 13, 1867.

The commissioners were informed that the northernmost bands of Sioux, waging war on the Powder River, would be unable to meet at Fort Laramie at the time indicated. The commissioners postponed the meeting at Fort Laramie until November 1 and met instead with the tribes of the Southern Plains. Here they negotiated the Medicine Lodge Treaty of October 21–28, 1867.[2]

When they returned to Fort Laramie, the commissioners found a few friendly Crow Indians waiting for them, but Red Cloud, of the Oglala Sioux, refused to meet them. He sent word that "his war against the Whites was to save the valley of the Powder River, the only hunting ground left to his nation, from our intrusion. He assured us that whenever the military garrisons at Fort Phil Kearny and Fort C. F. Smith were withdrawn, the war on his part would cease."[3]

Later that winter, Red Cloud agreed to meet with the peace commissioners the following spring. The commissioners returned to Fort Laramie in April 1868 to begin talks with Red Cloud and the allied tribes of Sioux, Cheyenne, and Arapaho. On February 5, 1868, the *Omaha Weekly Herald* wrote about the hopes for the Fort Laramie Treaty. It blamed much of the current animosity on the violent actions of Colonel John M. Chivington and his Colorado Volunteers during the Sand Creek Massacre of November 1864, in Colorado Territory. The editorial declared:

> The *Rocky Mountain News* and other organs and echoes of Chivington and his piety will be pained to learn that the authorities of Fort Laramie are in receipt of messages of peace from the most powerful Indian warrior of the West.
>
> A son and nephew of the "dusky chief" came to the Fort with a message wondering if the government would give him protection if he came in. This overture means peace with the Indians.
>
> We hope that the bloody-minded Chivington exterminators will be patient under the prospect which offers a fair promise of no more massacres of White people. We remember the time when, for more than 10 long years, the lives and property of White people were safe on these plains against Indian attack. . . . We remember when the lives of defenseless White women were as safe on Indian hunting grounds as they are in Omaha today. What caused the change need not be recounted here but we may say that every White life lost or captive child or woman taken by the Indians in the last four years has been due alone to such diabolisms as the Chivington massacre and the continued wrongs practiced on the Indians. We hope the messages of Red Cloud presage the return of old-fashioned peace with the Indians.[4]

In this short article on the Fort Laramie Treaty, the *Weekly Herald* employed several stereotypes. First, its language in describing Red Cloud as the "dusky chief" and "the most powerful Indian warrior of the west," were reminiscent of James Fennimore Cooper and his "noble red man." Second, its author assumed that Red Cloud was acknowledged leader of all the allied tribes and implied that he should be the focus of the peace commissioners' efforts. While Red Cloud was certainly an important leader, he was but one of several leaders.

In addition to its adversarial relationship with government authorities, the *Weekly Herald* was also careful to point out that the eastern press simply did not understand what was happening on the frontier. In March the newspaper wrote about the progress of the Fort Laramie peace talks. "We see by an Eastern paper that the commission was a 'grand success.' All the warrior tribes are at last pacified and the Indian war is closed. My God! What lies! Every man here, soldiers, citizens and officers, consider powder given to Indians to have elected some of them for a wooden overcoat."[5]

After its initial euphoria about the prospects for peace, the *Weekly Herald* was becoming more cautious with its hopes for reconciliation. While the newspaper still held out hopes for a settlement, it expressed uncertainty about the pace of the peace talks. In a later issue of the *Weekly Herald,* the paper reiterated its accusation that the eastern press was blind to what was really happening in the frontier West.

This time the *Weekly Herald* listed some other villains, including unscrupulous Indian agents and beef contractors. "Throwing chaff into the eyes of the Eastern press is not only done by the Indian agents but also by beef contractors and others who hope to sell goods to the Indian department for 'those poor peaceable Indians.' Discharge lying agents and put Indians under the control of the War department. Every citizen of the country will be satisfied and help whip the Indians to a good peace if necessary."[6]

Newspapers throughout the region were concerned about the Fort Laramie Treaty. The *Rocky Mountain News Weekly* wrote that although the commissioners had arrived weeks earlier they were still waiting for most of the Indians to show up. They were not certain what good it would do if they did. "It is the opinion of the oldest settlers that the treaty will be a farce. . . . While the commission is waiting, their 'children' are making some very friendly demonstrations in the way of stealing stock and scalping the whites when they have a good opportunity."[7]

The peace talks had been in full swing for over a month and the *Weekly Herald* was growing impatient with their progress. While it had earlier used the stereotype of the "noble red man," the newspaper now utilized the stereotype of the "murdering redskin" to describe the situation on the frontier. "We believe in the wisdom of making peace and removing Indians to far reservations. But why sit idly by and talk of peace whilst your neighbor and friends are being murdered by these red devils? Why not declare war and wage it? We are for war, if we cannot have peace, because that is the only alternative. We are for anything and everything that can stop or lessen these accumulated outrages upon our people."[8]

One of Red Cloud's primary demands was that the United States abandon its three forts on the Bozeman Trail: Fort Reno, Fort Phil Kearny, and Fort C. F. Smith. Admitting partial defeat, President Andrew Johnson, on March 2, 1868, ordered that the forts be abandoned. The blow was somewhat softened by the fact the Union Pacific Railroad had, by this time, built its lines farther west. This meant that the Bozeman Trail was no longer the primary access to the mines of Montana and Idaho. The forts were not actually vacated until transportation was provided in August of that year. However, it was a rare occurrence in Indian–white relations when the Indians forced the whites to abandon land or property via a treaty.

The *Rocky Mountain News* still held little hope for a successful treaty, but it at least had some empathy for Red Cloud and his people. "A gentleman told us the other day that he had helped to make 12 Indian treaties, not one of which had ever been fulfilled in a single item. We do not want the forts dismantled and the road abandoned through the Powder River country, but we cannot blame Red Cloud for putting no faith in the government or its agents."[9]

Red Cloud agreed, in principle, with the provisions of the Fort Laramie Treaty in May 1868. However, he refused to sign the treaty until the three forts on the Bozeman Trail were abandoned. When it heard the news, the *Weekly Herald* reversed its belligerent stand:

Generals Harney, Sherman, Tappan *et.al.* have concluded a treaty with the northern Indians who have agreed to go on reserves. Red Cloud will come in as soon as the Powder River country is abandoned. If true, and we do not doubt it, this is glorious news.

We believe, and have long maintained against the idle clamor and natural Spirit of revenge aroused amongst our people by Indian massacres, in an ultimate and enduring peace with the Red Man.

It has been the White Man, and not the Red Man, who has violated agreements under which the former has nearly crushed the latter out of existence. We are, as we have been, for peace with these savages.

Captive Whites in Indian lodges exposed to horrible lusts and cruelties were unknown in this country for ten long years. Until the red-handed Chivington and their Colorado backers and apologists made worse than savage war on bands that were friendly, we had no real war, and now these men lament a peace.

Peace is not yet. It will come. The Indians will go on reserves and live out the remainders of their days in a state of semi-civilization like the Cherokees. Settlements will advance without fear of the tomahawk and scalping knife as they did in years gone by; commerce will go unvexed to the mountains; lives will be safe from the Indian incursions; millions will be saved by the government.

These and other blessings will fall on the heels of an enduring peace with the Indians just as certainly as effect follows cause.[10]

The *Weekly Herald*'s principal competition, the *Omaha Republican,* had provided limited coverage of the treaty proceedings. During this period, it had focused its columns on the coverage of the impeachment proceedings against President Andrew Johnson. However, when General Alfred Terry visited Omaha and praised the efforts of the peace commissioners, the *Republican* portrayed his optimism as naive and misplaced:

> They are no doubt such views as every man with General Terry's experience of Indian affairs and knowledge of the Indian would form from the facts which came under observation. We think, however, they are not in all respects such conclusions that are formed upon the same facts by the men of the plains and the mountains, who have a much more extended knowledge of Indian affairs and a more intimate acquaintance with the Indian character than the General can lay claim to, we believe. It has to be confessed that they put very little faith in the peaceful indications on which General Terry lays so much stress. They know the Indians well and put no faith in Indian professions. They hold to the belief that Indians are "bamboozling" the commission and that belief is born of their experience and knowledge of Indians and Indian deception.[11]

The *Republican* had softened its stand somewhat within a week However, it still urged caution regarding the proposal to place different tribes within the same reservation. It quoted the *Cheyenne Leader* as predicting that this "attempt to 'corral' the Indians within this reservation will be productive of bloody wars among themselves."[12]

The *Republican* went on to say that the Oglala and the Brule would be moving to their reservations shortly and that the Cheyenne and the Arapaho had a month to decide if they would move south to the reservation on the Arkansas River or north with the Brule and Oglala Sioux to the reservation in Dakota Territory. They also added that not all the tribes had come to terms. "The Indians known as the 'Bad Faces' have not yet come to terms, and if they don't behave they are to be 'cleaned out' by Spotted Tail and Man-Afraid-Of-His-Horses, who have engaged to undertake the job provided the government will furnish them with arms and ammunition." The claim by the *Republican* that Spotted Tail and Man-Afraid-Of-His-Horses, would be given arms and ammunition to "clean out" Red Cloud and his recalcitrant Bad Faces if they did not "behave" is ridiculous and inaccurate. It shows a lack of understanding or "judgment" on the part of the *Republican.* The two Indian leaders would never have been strong enough to attack their fellow tribesman; in fact, they would probably have found the idea repugnant.

The *News,* surprisingly for a paper that had encouraged genocide just a few years earlier, seemed to also be willing to give the Fort Laramie Treaty a chance. It even admitted some culpability on the part of the white settlers for the Indian troubles. "They admit . . . they have occupied the hunting grounds of the Indians, and in various ways made game scarce and that an Indian must eat to live. . . .

They will admit further, though they deprecate the policy, because of its failure to secure peace, that the making of treaties with the Indian is a recognition on our part of their right to the country."[13]

In the end, though reluctantly, the *News* gave its blessing to the treaty effort. "As this [Peace] is the settled and determined policy of the commission and the government, and we might add, of national public opinion. . . our people must wish to see it speedily and fairly tried, and also that it shall succeed in giving them peace and security. This they may do with ever so little faith in it."[14]

It was expected, however, that Red Cloud would soon come in and make terms. "If the terms of the treaty are only kept, both by the government and the Indians, we shall have peace and prosperity, and no longer be troubled by Indian outrages."[15]

True to his word, once the forts on the Bozeman Trail had been abandoned, Red Cloud came in and signed the treaty on November 6, 1868. It was ratified by the U.S. Senate on February 16 and proclaimed on February 24, 1869. Despite all the high hopes, the Fort Laramie Treaty lasted only until 1874 before it was violated, and the lands it had created to preserve for the Indians were subsequently opened to white settlement.

The coverage of the Fort Laramie Treaty by the *Weekly Herald* and the *Republican* was uneven. The *Weekly Herald* fluctuated between hopes for peace and tough talk about waging war. In its edition of May 20, 1868, the *Weekly Herald* stated that it had always been for peace and yet, just two weeks earlier, in those same columns, it had called for war rather than "sit idly by" while neighbors and friends were being "murdered by red devils."[16]

In this early coverage of Indians, the Omaha newspapers had not yet fully developed the stereotypes they would later use so frequently. At this time Native Americans were usually referred to simply as Indians without a descriptive qualifier before or after the word *Indian*. The *Weekly Herald* did evoke the stereotype of the "murdering red skin" several times in its coverage of the treaty process, but it also blamed "bloody-minded" Chivington for instigating much of the conflict and stated that whites bore more responsibility for violating agreements than the Indians did. The *Weekly Herald* also used romantic language in describing Red Cloud as the "dusky chief" and "the most powerful Indian warrior of the west."[17] The *Weekly Herald* summed up its position when it said, "We are, as we have been, for peace with these savages."[18] Yes it was for peace, but the use of the denigrating term "savages" reveals that the newspaper did not consider the Indians to be the equals of the whites.

The *Republican* did not cover the Fort Laramie Treaty as extensively as did the *Weekly Herald*. However, it was more consistent in its approach to the coverage. It did not fluctuate between optimism and pessimism. It remained cautious and skeptical about the success of the treaty. The *Weekly Herald* did assign responsibility for a good deal of the conflict to the whites, singling out Chivington and his Colorado militia for the lion's share of the blame.

The *Republican* fared a little better than the *Weekly Herald* when it came to prediction. It was very cautious in assessing the ultimate success of the Fort Laramie Treaty. The newspaper felt it could work but this was said without great conviction. The *Weekly Herald* on the other hand was effusive in its praise of good that would come from the treaty, with bloodshed at an end and commerce expanding.

The *Rocky Mountain News* was initially very critical of the possibility of success, but in the end it too succumbed to the wave of public opinion and gave a reluctant endorsement to the Fort Laramie Treaty.

Unfortunately, the treaty did not even meet the newspapers' limited expectations. Within a few years, it was being ignored. It was shattered by Lieutenant Colonel George Armstrong Custer's flagrant violation of the treaty during his exploration of the Black Hills in 1874. Miners and settlers swarmed the Sioux's sacred *Paha Sapa,* inflamed by Custer's claim of finding gold "from the roots down."[19] In the end, the treaty that was to last forever lasted less than six years.

CHAPTER 4

The Little Big Horn Campaign:
January–July 1876

No single battle in the history of the American Indian Wars resonates with more power than the Battle of the Little Big Horn, June 25, 1876. It features several mythic elements that have made it legendary. First, there were a high number of casualties. Every man under Lieutenant Colonel George Armstrong Custer's immediate command was killed. The number of casualties, for a single battle in an Indian war, was second only to Little Turtle's defeat of General Arthur St. Clair in 1791 (900 total casualties, 630 killed).[1] Second, the defeat took place on the eve of the United States' centennial celebration. Third, the death of Custer, who had become a larger-than-life figure, truly made the battle of the Little Big Horn legendary. He had gained notoriety during the Civil War and had added to his reputation during the Indian Wars. Historian Robert M. Utley described the shock felt at the news of Custer's defeat: "Custer dead? To the generals as well as all who read the papers that morning, the story seemed preposterous. For more than a decade George Armstrong Custer had basked in public adulation as a national hero. . . . By 1876 the public saw him as the very embodiment of the Indian-fighting army. . . . Even to hard-eyed realist like Sherman and Sheridan, the vaunted Custer could hardly fall victim to a calamity such as the newspaper reported."[2]

The response of the Omaha newspapers was predictable. They were as shocked as the rest of the country. The *Omaha Daily Herald* said that the news "created a profound sensation throughout the entire city, and a deep feeling of pity was manifested for the brave men who had been thus ruthlessly destroyed."[3] The *Omaha Bee* wrote, "The shocking intelligence of terrible disaster which has overtaken Gen. Custer and his ill-fated command in a deadly encounter with the hostile Indians of the Yellowstone region, cannot but produce the most profound sensation that has in many years been experienced in this country."[4] The *Omaha Republican* stated that the news of the Custer defeat "carried a thrill of horror through the heart of every reader. It was the absorbing topic of conversation through the morning."[5]

While the battle occurred on June 25, the first published word of the defeat did not appear until E. S. Wilkinson's special edition of the *Bozeman Times* on July 3, 1876. This "extra" became the initial source for the rest of Montana's newspapers.[6] The remainder of the country heard about the battle after July 4. The country was just catching its breath from the raucous centennial celebration when the news of Custer's defeat became headlines. Following closely on the heels of a celebration of the nation's progress, the defeat and killing of a national hero by the Sioux and Cheyenne was a shock to the nation.

After the initial jolt, the reaction to Custer's defeat was mixed. For example, some of the Democratic papers in Montana criticized the Grant administration for pursuing a foolish course of skimping on frontier troops while keeping sufficient troops in the Reconstruction South to influence upcoming national elections. Some newspapers in the South even accused President Grant of misplaced priorities. The *Charleston Journal of Commerce* wrote, "The President cannot escape severe condemnation for suffering such a disaster to occur in the West while he is planning to control Southern elections by the bayonet."[7]

A few Republican papers in Montana criticized the Quaker policy and advocated "extermination" of the Sioux.[8] In contrast, R. N. Sutherlin, of the *Rocky Mountain Husbandman,* believed the Indians had been mistreated by the Indian Bureau and that the Indians' uprising was justified.[9] The *Western Home Journal,* of Detroit, Michigan, also felt the Indians were justified in their armed resistance. In an editorial published on July 8, 1876, it criticized the military expedition led by Generals Alfred Terry, John Gibbon, and George Crook as leading to a "bloody, fruitless and expensive war." The newspaper contended that the Sioux were only defending the land that was rightfully theirs and added that "our troops have long looked on the killing of a red skin with the same nonchalance as a street boy on the killing of a wharf rat."[10]

The news of Custer's defeat was not merely a regional disaster; it engulfed the whole nation. Many southern newspapers seized upon the defeat as a means to make a political point and especially to embarrass the Grant administration. The *Charleston Journal of Commerce* wrote that the "tragic events" on the Little Big Horn were "hardly more than the logical results of the scandalous mismanagement of the army by our military President and the infamous frauds, peculation and inefficiency which flourished in the Indian Bureau of the interior department." It added that "The Indian policy of General Grant's administration has been simply to pamper the Indians with the left hand while robbing them with the right hand."[11]

In "The Southern Response to Custer's Last Stand," historian Brian W. Dippie writes that the Wilmington, North Carolina, *Daily Journal* raised the question of race in criticizing the Republican Party and the North in general. It opined that the North did not treat the Indians any better than the South treated blacks. "It added that the only logical reason for the Republicans' interest in the Negro and indifference to the Indian was simply that, 'the one could be made a voter and the other could not.'"[12] Dippie wrote that the Southern line was "to emphasize that the army was of sufficient strength to defeat the Sioux if the troops were correctly distributed. Once again, therefore, Grant was held responsible for Custer's death. In his obsession to secure a Republican victory in November, he had neglected the army on the frontier in order that bayonets might preside over Southern ballot boxes."[13]

Custer made the perfect foil for southern editorialists. He had been a dashing leader of northern cavalry who was in sympathy with the South before and after the Civil War. He also was in disfavor with President Grant, for accusing Grant's brother Orville of corruption in his involvement with selling of operating licenses to Indian traders.[14] All of these factors made Custer a worthy tool with which to hammer the Republicans and the Grant administration.

The *Richmond Whig* raised Custer to heroic status in its editorial pages by declaring, "The North alone shall not mourn for this gallant soldier. He belongs to all the Saxon race; and when he carried his bold dragoons into the thickest of the ambuscade, where his sun of life forever set, we behold in him the true spirit of that living chivalry which cannot die, but shall live forever to illustrate the pride, the glory and the grandeur of our imperishable race."[15] In contrast, the *New York Herald* painted a more balanced portrait of Custer: "Rising to high command early in life he lost the repose necessary to success in high command. . . . but you see we all liked Custer and did not mind his little freaks in that way any more than we would have minded temper in a woman. . . . Custer's glorious death and the valor of his men will become a legend in our history. . . . We all think, much as we lament Custer, that he sacrificed the Seventh Cavalry to ambition and wounded vanity."[16]

Ironically, unlike their brethren to the East and the South, the story of the battle of the Little Big Horn soon faded from the pages of the Montana newspapers. Historian Rex C. Myers wrote that "At a time when it was attracting major attention elsewhere in the nation, the region most affected by the outcome relegated the actual engagement—and Custer—to a place of relative insignificance."[17] Coverage of the battle and its aftermath by the newspapers in other parts of the country, including Omaha, kept the controversy and the stories alive and turned the Battle of the Little Big Horn into "Custer's Last Stand."

The Omaha newspapers also held contrasting views concerning the Custer battle and who was ultimately responsible for his defeat. Because of the hysteria surrounding Custer's death, the Indian question was shoved once more to the forefront. Editors were trying to discover how a modern army, led by one of the nation's most famous officers, had been so utterly defeated by the Sioux and Cheyenne. It seemed beyond belief that the Indians could have destroyed Custer, and the nation's newspapers led the charge to determine who was ultimately responsible for this defeat.

Some of the theories expounded in the nation's press were incredible. They ranged from speculation that Confederate officers had led the Indian warriors, to the claim that Sitting Bull, attending as a student nicknamed "Bison," had been a graduate of West Point![18] John William Howard, a reporter for the *Chicago Tribune*, wrote that Sitting Bull had learned French from the Jesuit missionary Pierre-Jean De Smet and had read, in French, the history of Napoleon's campaigns, modeling his generalship on Napoleon.[19] No matter what theory was advanced, it all came down to stereotypes and long-held beliefs about the Indians. While they might be fierce, brave, and sometimes even noble in a fair fight, it was believed that they could not defeat a well-armed, well-trained army of white men. It was the firm belief in these stereotypes that sent the nation's editors scrambling to find an answer for this almost unprecedented defeat.

Only one reporter was known to have been with Custer at the Little Big Horn. His name was Mark Kellogg and he had worked as an assistant editor for the *Council Bluffs Democrat* in 1868.[20] By 1873 he was a correspondent for the *Bismarck Tribune* and the *St. Paul Daily Pioneer Press*, writing under the nom de plume of "Frontier." In August of 1875, Kellogg made his opinion on the "Indian question" clear when he wrote about the killing of a homesteader by an Indian raiding party: "And thus they go, making raids here and there, killing inoffensive White citizens, raiding off stock, and doing pretty much as they please, with the utmost impunity—and yet the present Indian policy calls out for 'Peace! Peace!— Christianize the poor unfortunates, treat them with kindness,' and all that sort of bosh. Bah! I say, turn the dogs of war loose, and drive them off the face of the earth, if they do not behave themselves."[21]

In the spring of 1876, Kellogg was in Bismarck. His friend Clement Lounsberry, correspondent for the *Bismarck Tribune,* was to join Custer on his summer campaign against the Sioux and their allies. When his wife became very ill, Lounsberry decided not to accompany Custer on his military expedition. Kellogg was an enthusiastic substitute and rode out with Custer's troops on May 17, 1876.[22]

In addition to working for the *Bismarck Tribune* on this campaign, Kellogg also was a correspondent for the *New York Herald.* He described the day and Custer in his first dispatch of the Sioux campaign of 1876: "Gen. George A. Custer, dressed in a dashing suit of buckskin, is prominent everywhere. Here, there, flitting to and fro, in his quick eager way, taking in everything connected with his command, as well as generally, with the keen, incisive manner for which he is so well known. The General is full of perfect readiness for a fray with the hostile red devils, and woe to the body of scalp-lifters that comes within reach of himself and brave companions in arms."[23]

Kellogg used a diary format to write about Custer's march to the Little Big Horn. In a prophetic dispatch written on June 21, 1876, aboard the steamboat *Far West,* (which transported some of Custer's supplies), Kellogg wrote, "We leave the Rosebud tomorrow, and by the time this reaches you we will have met and fought the red devils, with what results remains to be seen. I go with Custer and will be at the death."[24] He was with Custer "at the death," but probably not the way he intended. His body was not found with the others on Custer Hill. Historian Utley writes, "Undiscovered until the next day was the body of Mark Kellogg, the correspondent who was to report Custer's great victory over the 'hostile red devils.'

In unintended irony the 'scalp lifters' he had ridiculed on the eve of the campaign had repaid the compliment. Except for cutting off an ear, they had not mutilated him. They had only lifted his scalp."[25]

A wire story from the *Chicago Times* that appeared in the July 8 edition of the *Daily Herald* mistakenly claimed that Kellogg's body was not touched and speculated it was out of respect for journalists. It declared that, "Kellogg lay in the field as he fell undisturbed. Perhaps even the Indians who had learned to fear and respect Custer had also realized the power of the lead pencil and had come to respect those who wield it."[26] By the time Kellogg's last dispatch was published in the *Tribune,* he had been dead for more than two weeks.

It was left to Lounsberry to complete Kellogg's work. He developed the first major story of the battle: "Lounsberry's article was transmitted—a complete account of 15,000 words—the last message of the day sent by the weary operator twenty-two hours after he had begun."[27] It had been forwarded to the *New York Herald* at an estimated cost of $3,000. "Starting with the material Kellogg had prepared, he wrote the lead story, running about 7500 words as it appeared in the *Herald,* in the first person."[28]

Lounsberry also found time to compose a story for his own *Bismarck Tribune.* "The single sheet extra came out the next morning. The oversized single-word headline, followed by ten subheads, read: MASSACRED."[29]

With his "heroic" death, Kellogg rose from obscurity to become a martyr to his journalistic contemporaries. The *New York Evening Post* editorially eulogized Kellogg: "The brave civilian should not be forgotten while we honor the brave soldiers who fell in that great butchery on the banks of the Little Big Horn River. . . . If it is heroic to face danger and meet death calmly in the discharge of duty, then Mark Kellogg, the correspondent of the *New York Herald,* who died with Custer, was a hero. . . . His heroism is a credit to his profession as theirs is to theirs."[30]

Kellogg's death was also mourned by the *Omaha Daily Herald,* but it was more straightforward homage. It wrote, "Mark Kellogg, the *Tribune* correspondent who was victim in the Custer slaughter, was a former resident of Council Bluffs, and was connected with the *Democrat* when [Alf S.] Kierolf was the editor. We knew Mr. Kellogg well and met him at Bismarck on our visit there three years ago when he was printing the *Tribune* of that place. We join his numerous friends in this part of the country in regretting his tragic fate."[31]

While the three Omaha newspapers' coverage of the battle of the Little Big Horn began in July, their coverage of the Sioux war of 1876 had begun several months earlier. The scene was set with a report about the ongoing problems with rations at the Red Cloud Agency in the January 15, 1876, edition of the *Omaha Republican*:

> The rations for the Indians at Red Cloud Agency have almost given out and will not last beyond the first proximo; an appropriation of $150,000 is asked for to continue the good work of feeding these idle beggars until the end of the current fiscal year, [June 30th]. This is to say for 14,000 Indians . . . for five months, the

cost of subsistence will be only $150,000, or a daily average of not quite seven cents for each Indian present. . . . We ask for information; does the Indian bureau mean to say it can procure these rations and deliver them for the infinitesimal sum of seven cents? There is a manifest disproportion between the end in view and the means of attaining it. . . . For seven years money has been squandered like water to pay for the support of idle lubbers simply because their skins happened to be red; this extravagance is a gross imposition upon the poor working-men of our nation, who cannot get food. It has not been productive of good as our constantly recurring account of Indian depredations will conclusively prove, and its discontinuance is demanded by the voice of every honest and disinterested person in the country.[32]

The *Republican* criticized the Indian Bureau for being deceptive and for either overreporting the number of Indians in its care or underreporting the amount of money being spent on them. In the end, it called for a halt to the subsidizing of the Indians. Of course, this would have been a gross violation of treaty terms, but that did not seem to come into play in the *Republican's* analysis of the issue. The paper continued its criticism of the Indian Bureau in an editorial on January 22: "If the Indian bureau were capably and honestly managed, a much better state of things might be chronicled. . . . Peace will come to our frontiersmen with the day when idle vagabondage shall no longer be tolerated on the reserves, and when every Indian shall feel that he is accountable to a powerful tribunal for every delinquency of which he may be guilty."[33]

In the same issue, the *Republican* examined the "absurdity" of making treaties with Indians as if they were sovereign nations. It declared that, "It is wrong in morality to treat him with brutality; it is wrong in policy to let him remain in ferocity and barbarism; but to rescue him from his present degradation, moral persuasion is inapplicable and incapable. Force must be introduced to make him feel that he is the pupil of the nation and not its master; that he has now to accept the alternative of extinction or work and education."[34]

Likewise, problems with rations contributed to the unrest on the reservations. There was also the example of the "free" Indians under chiefs like Sitting Bull. A February issue noted that, "A gentleman just in from Montana states that Sitting Bull's band of outlaws from all of the Sioux tribes, has been at work lately attacking straggling parties of travelers, hunters and occasionally a miner and prospector's camp. . . . Our informant states that the impression is general that unless these renegades are promptly checked, their numbers will be so great that much difficulty will be experienced in them, and that if allowed to get a start they will extend their operations far to the southward and accomplish no end of mischief."[35]

According to historian Robert M. Utley, the basic aim of the government was to neutralize the "hostiles" by forcing them to merge with their more "dependent brethren" on the reservation. To mask their plan and soften their naked aggres-

Sitting Bull, Lakota Chief. Courtesy of Denver Public Library, Western History Collection.

sion, the Indian Office decided to notify all of the hunting bands and request that they report to the agencies. Runners were sent to all of the winter camps to tell the free Indians to come to the agency by January 31, 1876, or soldiers would march against them.[36] The *Omaha Republican* saw this ultimatum as actually encouraging depredations by the Indians. It stated, "Although these Indians have been killing settlers and stealing stock for some time past, this renewal of all their old deviltries on a more extended scale is said to have been prompted by the notice recently served upon them by the Indian bureau that they must get inside reservation bounds by a certain time or submit to a thrashing."[37]

The deadline came and went. Although most of the Indians had heard of the ultimatum, according to Utley, it probably puzzled the tribes more than it angered them. "They had no impending sense of war with the Whites and thus did not understand the ultimatum as portending war. In Indian conceptions of time, moreover, a deadline such as January 31, 1876, carried no urgency and indeed no meaning. In truth, the chiefs simply did not know what to make of this missive, delivered at such peril by couriers braving deep snow and bitter cold."[38] Most of the runners brought back no reply, but one who did said the tribes were peaceful but were hunting buffalo just now. They would come in to trade in the spring, just like always, and they would discuss things then. They certainly had no intention of fighting the whites.[39]

While the Indians may have had no intentions of fighting the whites, according to the *Republican,* the whites certainly intended to fight the Indians. "It seems quite probable that there is a movement in contemplation to punish Mr. Sitting Bull, the bad, for the murders which he has been committing during the winter and for a long period previous. The object undoubtedly is to strike this old sinner and his band of scalpers, before he can be reinforced by the braves from Red Cloud and Spotted Tail. A combination of all the warriors which the Indians can muster would make a powerful force almost too great to be resisted by the small army which can be brought against them. The Indians are better armed than most people suppose."[40]

It is interesting to note that the *Republican* accurately predicted the gathering of the tribes that would occur the following summer and the awesome power of the Indians that would emerge from this alliance, four months before the battles of the Rosebud and Little Big Horn.

The *Republican* continued to offer solutions to the "Indian problem" in the months leading up to the battle of the Little Big Horn. It even offered an opinion about General George Armstrong Custer in its pages. In an interview, Custer had suggested that William Tecumseh Sherman, his superior, would make a good presidential candidate. The newspaper added, "Speaking of running reminds us of the Indian; and him Custer declares as 'everywhere simply a brute.' Sherman's Indian policy he thus sums up: 'There would be one grand Indian war, and then there would be no more Indians.'"[41]

A little over a week later, the *Republican* again weighed in with advice on how to handle the Indians. Using two separate stereotypes, it cautioned that it did not want to tame the "savage nomad" only to have him turn into the "lazy loafer." The *Republican* wrote, "Every care should be taken that they are not converted from savage nomads who support themselves to lazy loafers who are a burden to the country forever. . . . We may confidently look forward to a policy firm and just toward the Indians, but having for its cardinal point their education in the art of earning their own bread, as other people do, by the sweat of their brows."[42] Under the headline, "Lo! The Poor Indian," the *Omaha Bee* wrote about the upcoming campaign against the Sioux and their allies: "it indicates lively times ahead for Sitting Bull and his band of red-faced cutthroats. Nothing but quick decisive action will satisfy the Indians that the government now means business. General Crook's experience with the Comanche will be useful in the present contest."[43]

The *Republican* also wrote about the early stages of the Sioux campaign of 1876. "This is an undertaking full of hazard, and it must be expected that accidents, and maybe reverses, may occur to such a formidable undertaking. The General has but a handful of men; the number of the Indians is unknown. Besides the Indians are on their own familiar ground and chosen battle-field, every inch of which is known and has been fought over many and many a time. The advantages are all in favor of the Indians. . . . General Crook is acknowledged to be the best Indian fighter in the United States today. He is just the man to meet the old untamed Sitting Bull and thrash him into obedience."[44]

Just a few days later, the *Bee* ran a story about a successful attack that Crook had made on the village of Crazy Horse. According to the *Bee*, Crook had "fought with Crazy Horse and completely annihilated his force of 500 men after a five hour fight. Four soldiers were killed and eight wounded. The Indians not killed will starve as their provision, stock and equipage was destroyed."[45] The *Bee*'s story was far from accurate: there were four soldiers killed and most of the Indians' supplies were destroyed; everything else was inaccurate.

According to historian Robert M. Utley, the village Crook attacked was not Crazy Horse's but an allied camp of Northern Cheyenne under Two Moons and some Oglala under He Dog, as well as a few Miniconjou. All together the camp contained 735 people, including 210 fighting men. Far from being annihilated, the Indians suffered only light casualties, including two dead and several wounded. While half of the Indians' pony herd was stolen, it was retaken from the soldiers the next day. The most grievous loss was the supplies that were destroyed. Short on food, shelter, and clothing, the Indians stumbled through the snow and bitter cold until they reached the haven of Crazy Horse's camp.[46]

The *Republican* also believed that Crook had defeated Crazy Horse. It wrote, "Crazy Horse has now been whipped, his partner in crime will have his turn next, and although we claim the most earnest sympathy for such well disposed Indians as may be on the reservations, we say for this bad fellow: 'Off with his head; so much for Sitting Bull.'"[47]

The attack did two things to the hunting bands; it stunned them and it made many of those Indians who had professed peace now hunger for revenge and war. Utley writes, "Even if they fully understood the government's ultimatum, they had not taken it seriously. They thought they were at peace, but now, unmistakably, the soldiers had declared war. . . . Chiefs previously opposed to war now harangued their young men to attack undefended trading posts and obtain the arms and ammunition needed to wage all-out war."[48]

The *Republican* continued to focus on the "Indian question" in its editorial pages. It criticized the treaty of 1868 and the failure to get the Sioux to sell the Black Hills:

We take the position that the treaty of 1868, which ceded this country to the Indians, was a bad bargain on our part and that on the part of the Indians it has never been observed. There are no good reasons why we should be compelled to observe a treaty that has been broken by the other party to the contract over and over again, and to purchase a country a second time that we already own. Our government, by the Louisiana Purchase, has the title in fee to the soil, while the Indian, if he has any right at all, has simply a usufructory right.

The sooner the people of the nation learn that the Indian is no better than a White man, and that he should earn his daily bread by the labor of his hands, the better it will be for all. The Indians have got to learn to work, and that is all there is of the Indian problem.[49]

The Crook expedition continued into the heart of Sioux territory and the *Republican* said that the expedition's movements proved that the "number of Indians as hostile must have been over-estimated by persons interested in having exaggerated reports of their strength sent abroad through the country." The *Republican* claimed that it had been proved beyond doubt that during the winter there had never been more than five hundred warriors under Sitting Bull and Crazy Horse.[50]

The *Republican* continued to attack the treaty of 1868 in its editorial columns throughout March 1876. It declared that, by treaty, the Sioux had only tenant's right to much of the land they occupied, and that the Sioux had violated the treaty many times, therefore making it invalid. It added, "An erroneous impression prevails in certain quarters regarding what are called 'the rights of the Indian.' An Indian has no rights which do not involve a reciprocal obligation. . . . A failure by one party to observe its agreement necessarily released the other from any compliance with its proper obligations."[51] For the *Republican,* these alleged multiple violations of the treaty of 1868 by the Sioux and their allies justified the 1874 invasion of the Black Hills and the Crook expedition.

The *Omaha Bee* was happy to join its competitors in offering advice in how to deal with the Indians. In an editorial headlined, "How to Fight Indians," it laid out its views:

The only cheap and effective way to fight Indians is to put 3,000 to 4,000 men in the field. With such a force General Crook would not be long in reversing the normal order of things. We would soon find Red Cloud, Sitting Bull and other kindred chiefs begging to be led to a reservation. The theory of Indian ownership has long been exploded. When the government purchased this western land from the French it admitted French title to the territory.

Experience of the past 10 years has however, amply demonstrated that human savages, like brutes, must be taught that force exists before they are made to respect it.[52]

In late June, news of Crook's battle at the Rosebud on June 17 began to appear in the Omaha newspapers. The *Daily Herald* was the first with the news, although it offered few details. It confirmed that the Sioux had attacked in force and that Crook had lost nine men killed and more than 20 wounded. However, it feared that the battle was not decisive. "The *Daily Herald,*" it said, "desired a decisive battle, if any was to be fought, because it is well aware of the probable effect of such a battle upon the Indians engaged in it. If defeated and severely punished, they would skulk back to their reservations, become more tractable, and be more willing to return to their reservations."[53]

The *Bee* echoed the *Daily Herald*'s call for a decisive battle and recommended that a large force be sent against the Sioux and their allies. It claimed that the Rosebud battle

has demonstrated conclusively that our Army is altogether too weak in numbers to cope with the overwhelming force that confronts it. It is self-evident that the national government must either reinforce Gen. Crook with at least ten thousand well equipped men, or this intrepid commander will be compelled to abandon the campaign and leave the Indians masters of the situation. Such a withdrawal would not only prove disastrous to the settlers in the Black Hills and in the Big Horn region, but it would inevitably surrender Western Nebraska, Wyoming and portions of Dakota to the bloody rule of the Sioux.[54]

The *Daily Herald* published an extensive report on the Rosebud battle in its June 28, 1876, issue. It reprinted a story filed by a special correspondent of the *New York Herald*. The *Daily Herald* erroneously reported that 2,500 hostile Sioux, "under Sitting Bull of the North," attacked General George Crook's command of 1,300 men and 250 Indian allies (mostly Crows and Shoshones). "The fight lasted five hours and resulted in the discomfiture of the savages although not before they had inflicted on the troops a loss of ten killed and twenty wounded. On their own side they sacrificed by the bold attack which they made about one hundred warriors and an equal number of ponies."[55]

The *Daily Herald* praised Crook's Indian allies for their bravery and said that Crook's forces had pursued the fleeing Sioux for three miles until "the country appeared so dangerous that General Crook determined to fall back to the point where the battle began."[56] It claimed that Crook's forces had taken 13 Sioux scalps while losing only one scalp to the Sioux. The *New York Herald*'s correspondent, who had accompanied a "Captain Andrews" into battle, singled him out for praise, saying that he "manipulated his men under the difficult and conflicting orders from his superior with consummate skill, although he could not prevent unnecessary sacrifice of life without risking the penalty of disobedience." It added that the Sioux "were too much demoralized to trouble the column while withdrawing."[57]

Historian Robert M. Utley disagrees with Crook's claim of victory in the battle of the Rosebud. He writes that "the true victory, both tactical and strategic, lay with the Indians. They had attacked a force twice as large or larger than their own, kept it off balance and largely reactive for a day, inflicted serious casualties, and sent it in a stunned retreat back to the security of the base camp. . . . That counted him out of the strategic equation for six weeks, by which time the crucial events of the campaign had run their course."[58] Utley adds that "The Indians knew they had won. On the way back to their village, while mournfully burying their dead, they also feasted in triumph."[59]

Crook's claim of victory was also questioned by the *Daily Herald* in a story that ran the same day as the first coverage of the Little Big Horn battle:

> The serious check experienced by General Crook's column in its recent battle with the warriors of Sitting Bull and which was described by our special correspondent, has shaken public confidence in our ability to conquer the Sioux as quickly as was anticipated at the outset of hostilities.
>
> The most able and renowned of Indian fighters has discovered that the contract to whip, saying nothing of the more difficult contract to exterminate, even a small portion of the Sioux nation of Indians is proving a very dangerous thing to execute.
>
> We were right on this subject. The war that was opened upon the red men last winter by Gen. Crook was a wicked war on the principle of the thing, but it was also a war upon ourselves which means the destruction of our best interests. . . . We say to Governor Thayer of Wyoming, that when he urged these military operations against the Indians he cut the commercial throat of the entire western country, and put back gold developments and the progress of settlement more years than we shall be willing to count until we hear more from a field of war that promises to be occupied much longer than many suppose.[60]

The *Daily Herald* criticized General Crook again three days later and said that it was generally believed that he was "badly whipped" by the Sioux even though he occupied the field at the end of the battle. It said, "For all practical purposes of the campaign, Gen. Crook, in being compelled to retire, was defeated, but it appears to be true nevertheless that he was not defeated in the battle. We must not forget that this is a war with savages in which civilized codes have no part and every white soldier captured or wounded is mercilessly massacred, there must be more caution than in a civilized war."[61]

Crook's battle with the Sioux and their allies was a precursor of the major battle to come, eight days later, when Lieutenant Colonel George Armstrong Custer would meet these same Indians in the valley of the Little Big Horn. The story of that battle would have a resounding effect on the psyche of a young nation celebrating the centennial of its founding. The first reports of the battle of the Little Big Horn did not appear in the Omaha newspapers until July 6, 1876, 12 days after Custer and his men were killed near the river the Indians called the "Greasy Grass."[62] The *Daily Herald* headlined their story "The Savage War," with subheads that included "The Army of the North Who Were to Sweep the Indians from the Field Meet With Fearful Disaster," and "Three Hundred Soldiers Killed and Fifteen Wounded Strew the Battle Ground, Presenting a Sad and Sickening Sight." It briefly described the battle:

> Gen. Custer found the Indian camp of about 2,000 lodges on Little Horn, and immediately attacked the camp. Custer took five companies and charged the

thickest part of the camp. Nothing is known of the operations of this detachment only as they trace it by the dead. Major Reno commanded the other seven companies and attacked the lower portion of the camp. The Indians poured in a murderous fire from all directions, besides the greater portion fought on horseback. Custer, his two brothers, nephew and brother-in-law were killed and not one of his detachment escaped. Two hundred and seven men were buried in one place, and the killed is estimated at 300, with only 31 wounded. . . . The Seventh fought like tigers and were overcome by more brute force. The Indian loss cannot be estimated as they bore off most of their killed.[63]

While it was certainly a huge gathering of Indians, the *Daily Herald*'s report exaggerated the size of the village. Historian Utley writes, "Over a span of only six days Sitting Bull's village more than doubled, from 400 to 1,000 lodges, from 3,000 to 7,000 people, from 800 to 2,000 warriors."[64]

The *Omaha Bee* featured the same wire story about the Little Big Horn battle as had the *Daily Herald* in its July 6 edition. It described the battle ground as a "slaughter pen, as it really was, being in a narrow ravine. The dead were much mutilated. The situation now looks serious." It also included a column of the "very latest" information provided specially for the *Bee* by the Atlantic and Pacific Telegraph Company. It reported on rumors that Major Marcus Reno's command of seven companies had also been massacred. It wrote, "The most intense excitement prevails, and some doubts are yet felt as to the authenticity of the reports. A report is in circulation, though not authenticated, that the seven companies supporting Custer were afterwards massacred."[65]

The *Bee,* while still questioning the news from the Little Big Horn, was inclined to believe it was true. "The shocking intelligence of terrible disaster which has overtaken Custer and his ill-fated command in a deadly encounter with hostile Indians in the Yellowstone region cannot but produce the most profound sensation that has in many years been experienced in this country. Although the distressing news, transmitted from the scene of horror by the way of Bozeman and Salt Lake, still lacks confirmation, we have every reason to fear that the intelligence concerning Gen. Custer's fate is only too true."[66]

The *Bee* expressed surprise at Custer's attack on the large Indian village but explained it by praising Custer in a backhanded way: "That any experienced military man would attack a body of well armed savages advantageously posted and numerically three times as strong as his own force, would at first blush seem highly improbable."[67] It added that Custer's "impetuous temper" and dashing courage, along with his previous success in fighting Indians, may have led him to believe he was invincible. The *Bee* concluded: "It is to be hoped that the report of General Custer's death may yet be contradicted. The country and particularly the defenseless people on the western frontier can hardly, just now, spare such an intrepid and experienced Indian fighter. If Custer has really fallen, he and the gallant men who died with him must be avenged. If the Indians have really won such a bloody victory, the country must prepare to conquer a peace with the Sioux which shall make them harmless for all future time."[68]

The *Republican* did not publish the wire story on the battle until July 8—two days after the story had run in the *Daily Herald* and the *Bee*. It added that the news of the "massacre of Custer and his command by the hostile Sioux carried a thrill of horror though the heart of every reader. It was the absorbing topic of conversation throughout the morning, and when the news came just after the meridian that a courier arrived in the forenoon at Bismarck, bringing information that Major Reno and the remaining seven companies of the Seventh cavalry had shared Custer's fate, the excitement was intense, and nothing else was heard on the streets except the Indian news."[69]

The *Republican* also reported: "If anything was needed to add to the excitement it was the report that General Terry had also fallen into the hands of the savage red men. That report followed the rumor about the Reno massacre. It was stated that Gen. Gibbon had telegraphed to Gen. Sherman the fact of Terry's death."[70] The *Bee* and the *Republican* were wrong about the massacre of Reno and his men. He certainly suffered casualties, according to historian Utley. His charge cost him 40 dead and 13 wounded.[71] As for the *Republican*'s speculation about the fate of General Alfred Terry, he was not killed by the Sioux and their allies. In fact, he did not even arrive on the scene until June 27, two days after the battle.[72] The *Daily Herald* also heard the rumor about General Terry's death and had one of its reporters investigate by contacting army headquarters. There it found out that the rumor was unfounded.[73]

Stories about Custer and the Little Big Horn battle dominated the news columns of the three Omaha newspapers for the next few weeks. In its July 7 edition, the *Bee* confirmed that Custer had indeed been killed. It added, "No doubt Custer dropped into the midst of no less than 10,000 red devils, and was literally torn to pieces."[74] Doubts about Custer's judgment were already starting to circulate. "The movement made by Custer was censured to some extent at military headquarters. The older officers say it was brought about by foolish pride. . . . The commission of Indian affairs is of the opinion that this victory will have a disastrous effect upon the agency Indians who will be attracted to the field by the glory the warriors have won."[75]

The *Daily Herald* also reported the rumor that Major Reno and his men had been wiped out. It stated that while it would not rush to print the news until it was authenticated, its "heartfelt fear is that this heart-sickening news is but too true." It added, "This war was begun in wrong; only disaster has followed it thus far—disaster to our troops and our commerce. Still greater dangers confront us, and if the men who are responsible for them are not driven from their murderous imbecility to prompt action to arrest the progress of our calamities, only wreck and ruin to every trans-Missouri interest will be the certain consequence."[76]

The same edition of the *Daily Herald* claimed that General Sherman himself must now admit that the Sioux were capable of much more than a simple "scalp hunting war." It added, "we say that the Government will prove itself as craven and cowardly as it has already shown itself to be corrupt and imbecile, if it does not instantly call for ten thousand volunteers for two years service to put an end to it." It chastised critics for not believing its warning that the "Sioux extermina-tors were a set of dunces," and claimed the officers and men of Custer's command "sold their lives dearly, and that at least twice their number of savages fell in the same battle."[77]

According to the *Daily Herald,* rumors flew in the aftermath of the news of Custer's defeat. It claimed that the newspaper and telegraph offices were "besieged by crowds of men who were anxious as to the fate of Army friends who are sup-posed to be near the scene of the late fight."[78] The paper rejoiced in squelching one of those popular rumors with its announcement that Major Reno and most of his command had indeed survived. Ironically, the man who many (including Elizabeth Custer) would later call a "coward"[79] was singled out as a hero. "The real hero of the battle on Little Horn is the valiant Reno. God bless him facing that storm of death when surrounded by the blood-thirsty savages, all hope of succor gone, he led his men and cut his way through the murderous lines by which he was hemmed in, and saved his command. Such is real heroism. . . . If there is a man in all the Army who deserves the star which dazzled Custer into that 'valley of death' on the Little Horn, that man is Reno."[80] Though later tried by an army court of inquiry, Reno was judged to not be at fault during the battle.[81]

Newspapers from around the country tried to find interesting angles on the battle of the Little Big Horn. The *Helena Herald* headlined its July 15, 1876, story "The Valley of Death" and promised to tell the "Unwritten Chapter." They had an exclusive interview with "Curley," who had been one of Custer's Crow Scouts and had been with him in the early part of the battle. He was described as "the only survivor of the battle." "Curley says the field was thickly strewn with the dead bodies of the Sioux who fell in the attack—their number considerably more than the force of soldiers engaged. He is satisfied that their loss will exceed 300 killed, beside an immense number wounded. Curley accomplished his escape by draw-ing his blanket about him in the manner of the Sioux, and passing through an interval which had been made in their line as they scattered over the field in their final charge. He says they must have seen him, as he was in plain view, but was probably mistaken by the Sioux for one of their own number or one of their allied Arapahoes or Cheyennes."[82]

While Curly was probably still with Custer when he began his descent into the valley of the Little Big Horn, it is all but certain that he left the troops well before the fiercest of the fighting began. He may have observed the action from a dis-tance, but it is highly unlikely that he slipped away from the battle with a blanket over his head. Historian Evan S. Connell wrote that at a reunion of Little Big Horn survivors in 1886, Sioux Chief Gall called Curley a liar and claimed there was no way he could have escaped the battle as he claimed.[83]

The search for answers and justifications for Custer's defeat began almost im-mediately. Under the headline "The Lesson of the Massacre," the *Bee* offered its advice:

Every calamity teaches its lesson. The tragic fate of General Custer and his brave men carries with it a lesson that cannot be lost upon the American people. It demonstrates conclusively that the Quaker peace policy, under which the government has been furnishing the Indians with annuities for the purchase of long-range rifles, ammunition and horses, and under which these murderous vagabonds and their families have sheltered in the winter season, to enable them to wage merciless war upon us in the summer, must be abandoned. . . . The massacre of Custer's command teaches us that we have underestimated the strength and fighting qualities of the Indians, who flushed with their recent victory, will be more than a match for any equal number of white men. . . . To insure the chastisement of these savages the government should organize and put in the field a corps of at least ten thousand volunteers recruited among the hardy frontiersmen of the trans-Missouri region.

Such a corps can be mustered in thirty days. Under experienced leaders such a force would be more effective than our entire regular army. In order to effectually prevent all future Indian wars, every Indian should be promptly disarmed and dismounted.[84]

While the *Republican* looked for lessons to be learned, the *Daily Herald* looked for scapegoats. Perhaps motivated by political allegiances, it found what it was looking for in the Grant administration. It claimed the war had been "instigated by Grant and the gang of thieves who have robbed the Indians and the government of hundreds of millions of dollars. The lives of Custer and his men, and of all who have been lost in this bloody business, are upon the hands of Grant and his corrupt and imbecile administration, and the country will soon understand the fact."[85]

The formation of the Custer myth began within days of this death. The *Bee* published a poem entitled "Custer's Death," written for William F. Cody, by his friend Captain Jack Crawford. It glorified Custer while demonizing the Indians and blaming the Quakers for the disaster:

Did I hear the news from Custer?
Well, I reckon I did, old pard;
It came like a streak of lightnin'
And, you bet it hit me hard.
I ain't no hand to blubber,
And the briney ain't run for years;
But, chalk me down for a lubber,
If I didn't shed regular tears . . .

But little we knew even then, pard
(And that's just two weeks ago)
How little we dreamed of disaster,
Or that he had met the foe—

That the fearless, reckless hero,
So loved by the whole frontier,
Had died in the field of battle
In this our centennial year . . .

They talk about peace with these demons
By feeding and clothing them well;
I'd as soon think an angel from heaven
Would reign with contentment in hell.
And some day these Quakers will answer
Before the great judge of us all
For the death of the daring young Custer
And the boys who around him did fall . . .

Perhaps I am judging them harshly,
But I mean what I'm telling ye, pard
I'm letting them down mighty easy,
perhaps they may think it is hard.
But I tell you the day is approaching—
The boys are beginning to muster,
That day of the great retribution,
The day of revenge for our Custer.[86]

The *Bee* added to the Custer legend with a report on Custer's death allegedly brought to them by some agency Indians who heard it from their relatives who had fought in the battle. According to this report, Custer had shot three Indians with his pistol and killed three others with his saber before he was killed, shot through the head by the Sioux warrior Rain-in-the-Face. The paper described the fighting as hand to hand, and it claimed the Indians had lost 70 warriors killed, many of them prominent chiefs.[87]

A slightly different approach was taken by the *Daily Herald.* It felt that while the war was caused mostly by the miners' illegal occupation of the Black Hills, the military disaster that the whites had suffered at the Little Big Horn made it imperative that "a war with the northern Sioux must be prosecuted until they shall be driven into subjection."[88] Styling itself the "friend and defender of this perishing race,"[89] the *Daily Herald* opined that hand in hand with the war policy toward the "hostile Sioux" should go a peace policy toward the friendly tribes. The paper claimed that Red Cloud and Spotted Tail and their people were ready to leave their reservations in the Dakotas and move to the Indian Territory. It wrote, "Negotiations should be pressed for the removal of Red Cloud's and Spotted Tail's people, at whatever cost, to the Indian Territory. Peaceably if possible, forcibly if necessary."[90]

The *Daily Herald* believed that it had the "best welfare of the Indians," in mind in recommending this policy. In an unusual admission, the paper wrote, "Admitting, as we do, that such a policy is grounded in wrong and injustice in the abstract, when all the circumstances are fairly weighed, we hold it to be wise, if not right, in the concrete. The Indians can never have security on these borders, and they should be persuaded or compelled to abandon the chase within civilized confines, and accept their fate."[91]

While their editorial columns were philosophical, the *Daily Herald*'s front page joined most other newspapers in praising Custer as "The Dead Hero." It added a detail to the story regarding Custer killing six Indians before he himself was killed by Rain-in-the-Face. "Rain-in-the-Face cut the heart from Custer's dead body, put it on a pole and a grand war dance was held around it."[92] Both the claim that Custer was killed by Rain-in-the-Face and the alleged mutilation are controversial. Custer biographer Evan S. Connell believes that Rain-in-the-Face could have killed Custer, but so could hundreds of other warriors. The whites seemed obsessed with discovering who had actually killed Custer, so in 1909 the Indians had a council to "put an end to the matter. They themselves had no idea who killed Custer, but after discussing several possible candidates they elected Chief Brave Bear of the Southern Cheyenne. He had been with Black Kettle at the Washita. . . and done his part at the Little Big Horn. Therefore he was as qualified as anyone."[93]

Most accounts of Custer's death say he was not mutilated except for having the tip of one finger cut off. Some accounts add that his ear drums were pierced by two Cheyenne women so that he could hear better in the next world.[94] This refutes the story of Rain-in-the-Face dancing with Custer's heart on a pole. Almost every account agrees that he was not scalped, although the reasons given vary. Some accounts say it was a token of respect given by the Indians to a brave enemy. Some say his hair was cut short and receding and made a poor scalp, and still others claim his corpse was guarded from mutilation by various Indians.[95]

A contemporary account in the *Bee* mirrored the *Daily Herald*'s account of Custer's heart being cut out and displayed. The difference is that the *Bee* claimed it was Captain Tom Custer's heart and not his brother's heart that was cut out. Both of these claims were attempts to portray the savagery of the Sioux. The article also claimed that "The loss of the Sioux is estimated at 500, though it is hard to tell how many were killed, as they carried them off."[96] Connell writes that the number of Indians killed could not be determined, but whatever the exact body count, it must have been shockingly low by white standards. He notes that "David Humphreys Miller, who consulted dozens of old warriors, produced a list of thirty-two dead."[97] Historian Utley cites a similar figure. "The Indians never accurately counted their own losses, but their estimates suggest that White Bull's enumeration of 27 falls short of the true total by no more than a dozen. Many more, of course, were wounded."[98] Both Connell and Utley's estimates of Indian casualties are far below the *Bee*'s. Perhaps it was difficult enough to deal with the fact of Custer's annihilation without also admitting he and his men had been outfought by the Indians.

The same edition of the *Daily Herald* that touted Custer as "The Dead Hero" on page one had an interesting synopsis of the Indian situation on page two. It left no doubt that the army could "whip Gen. Bull" but suggested that an army composed of "plainsmen and frontiersmen" could do a better job since they already knew what it would take raw recruits months or years to learn. It urged the President and Congress to call for volunteers "speedily."[99]

Coming on the heels of the strong calls for revenge that were featured in the other Omaha newspapers, the *Daily Herald* carried a more philosophical editorial in its July 13, 1876, edition:

> The next settlement of the Sioux should be made final by their removal from a country which they will never be allowed to live in peace. We are confessedly a nation of mercenaries and land thieves, and have been since the nation was born. The African is the only being of an inferior race whose rights a majority of the people of this country ever felt bound to respect, all because he had no land to steal. The blacks simply had votes to give to a political party. The Reds have land but no votes, and hence their best interests require they should follow the Cherokees and the Creeks, and Pawnees to homes and peace in the Indian Territory.
>
> We must accept the facts of the situation. The brave men of a dying race who guide in its councils must be made to see, and many of them already see, that this conflict is hopeless as the results are inevitable for them. An enlightened regard for their own welfare demands that they should yield to their fate and make the best terms possible with their enemies. No adjustment can be permanent that is not based upon their removal from the country they have inhabited. This done, the best welfare of the red man will be gained, the future civilization of the continent ensured, and the Indian, hunted down no longer by the merciless spirit of the superior race, will be allowed the poor privilege of perishing in peace.[100]

Even though the *Daily Herald*'s obvious agenda was to remove the Indian from western lands, it is still remarkable that the newspaper would condemn the whites in such a direct manner. While placidly stating that the sad fate of the "inferior race" was inevitable, it at least did not describe the white man in glowing terms while demonizing the Indian, as its competitors did.

The *Republican*'s description of a dead Custer, featured in a *New York Herald* wire story, was more typical. Its correspondent found Custer, "near the top of a little knoll in the center of a plateau. . . it touched my heart to see the savages, in a kind of human recognition of heroic clay, had respected the corpse of the man they knew so well. Other bodies were mutilated; Custer's was untouched—a tribute of respect from such an enemy more real than a title of nobility. He lay as if asleep, his face calm, and a smile upon his lips."[101] Historian Utley disputes this claim of the Indian's instant recognition of Custer. He writes that, "Almost certainly no Indian recognized "Long Hair" in the smoke, dust, grime, and excitement of the battle, or indeed even knew they were fighting his soldiers." [102]

In contrast to its heroic portrait of Custer, the *Republican* ridiculed Sitting Bull as "not at all modest in committing to posterity the story of his great deeds. Whether scalping of a soldier or the sly theft of a mule, he brags equally of his prowess."[103] In the same edition, the *Republican* joined the *Daily Herald*'s call for a volunteer force of frontiersmen to fight the Indians. It suggested that the government accept the myriad offers of volunteers and "throw a body of frontiersmen at least 10,000 strong into the field and give Crook and Terry opportunity and means to wipe out the whole horde of unnatural enemies of our people as they annihilated Custer's gallant three hundred."[104]

On the same day, the *Daily Herald* wrote in its columns that no one, including the military, the *Herald*'s editors, and especially not Custer, expected the Indians to stand and fight. "Gen. Custer thought when he charged into that 'valley of death,' 'into the mouth of hell,' that he was to repeat that of a few years ago on the Cheyenne village [Black Kettle's village on the Washita] and his own destruction and that of his command, and all of the disasters that have befallen our army since the Crazy Horse failure, have been the direct results of these fatal estimates of the fighting qualities of the Sioux." The *Daily Herald* went on to predict that there would be no final great battle with the Indians unless they believe they again had the advantage of numbers. It stated that the tribes would scatter and the soldiers embark on a "wild goose chase" unless some way could be found to "conquer them by starvation."[105] This proved to be a remarkably accurate prediction.

The *Daily Herald,* continued to take a different tack than the other newspapers in its portrayal of the battle of the Little Big Horn. Even a poem, written expressly for the *Daily Herald* to honor Custer, included a stanza that justified the Indians' actions:

> Dead!
> All Dead!
> Oh how is wept!
> Through the domain! Three hundred souls . . .
> Distorted and rent by demons ferocious
> On the wretches, be thou merciful O God!
> But ye on earth powerful haste not revenge.
> Wert thou oppressed, and with enmity gall'd
> Wouldst not thou strike thine foe
> Nor deem it offense?
> And the Red Man, swarthy
> And gaunt, and distain'd
> Has a claim
> To the common right of man![106]

Custer and his men were more often portrayed as glorious heroes and the Indians as "demons" in other poems about the battle. A poem titled "George A. Custer," which was featured in the *Republican* three weeks after Custer's defeat, is a good example:

> No flinching no failing, each man at his best,
> With sabre uplifted and carbine aimed low,

Those men would have charged all the Reds of the West,
Without stopping to count the cost or the foe.
Theirs not to take heed!
Theirs only to follow where Custer might lead!
A captain of legions, denuded of power,
His blood turned to lava at thought of the plight,
But his not the soul of craven to cower;
With many or few, he must lead in the fight,
And prove to them all
He knew how to fight as he knew how to fall!

As the hot breath of battle fanned his brown cheek,
Bronzed with kisses of south wind and sun,
His long-swinging sabre with red blood did reek,
He knew he was charging a hundred to one,
Yet what cared he then?
He often won victory a thousand to ten!

They fled far and fast, but like tigers at bay,
And knowing their strength and his weakness full well,
They turned like the tide and bare-armed to the fray,
As demons might charge from the centre of hell,
Fought all the day through,
Fought only as fight the savage and Sioux.

He knew he was doomed, that no aid was near,
Yet of all his soldiers not one turned to fly,
In hearts of such heroes there's no room for fear,
Room only for courage to struggle and die!
When night came, the pall
Of death and of silence had settled o'er all.

There's a sob in the Platte, there's a sigh o'er the plain
For the heart of the west is pulse less and dead.
There's a patter of tears in the soft falling rain,
Soft tears that the angels in pity have shed,
But no tears have we!
The barb that brought death gave immortality.[107]

The poem is filled with inaccuracies, such as Custer flailing away with a saber, as well as the line about not one soldier fleeing the battlefield. They are both vivid pictures, though grossly inaccurate. According to Connell, while sabers were issued, they were cumbersome and were left at the Powder River depot still packed in boxes. Only two soldiers were known to have retained their cavalry sabers for use in the battle and neither was Custer.[108] Connell also refutes the story of Custer's men standing resolute. He writes, "That Custer's elite regiment fell apart in a most unprofessional manner seems to be substantiated by the testimony of whites. The entire battleground was studied by officers from the Terry-Gibbon army and by survivors of the Reno-Benteen command in an effort to learn what had happened. Capt. Myles Moylan said he could find no evidence of organized resistance anywhere on the ridge with the exception of Lt. James Calhoun's L Company. Lt. Camilius DeRudio was surprised to see so few expended cartridges. Lt. George D. Wallace also noted very few shells: piles of twenty-five or thirty at various places where Calhoun's men fought, otherwise not much indication of a battle."[109]

While the other Omaha papers were lamenting Custer's fate, the *Daily Herald* was looking to place blame for the debacle on President Grant's administration:

> The imbecility and rottenness of Grant's administration cannot be better illustrated than by the way he has mangled our Indian affairs. There has been no fixed, determined policy visible, but all the time some makeshift arrangement by which some pimp or relative could fatten off the government, or Indians, or both, and at the same time, nothing done. The Indian question is no nearer a settlement today than it was twenty years ago.
>
> Does any sane man suppose that we would not be suffering the pangs of an Indian war, if the Indians had been turned over to the management of the war department twenty years ago? As it is now, neither justice is done to the hardy pioneers nor to the half-starved Indians who are barely kept within the bounds of their agencies, by a system of promises that are only made to be broken.[110]

After firmly attaching the blame for Custer's defeat to the Grant administration, the *Daily Herald* moved on to speculate about the Indians' next course of action. There was widespread fear that, emboldened by their recent success, the Sioux and their allies would go on a rampage. The *Daily Herald* reiterated its call for an army of frontiersmen and noted, "The boys are fairly itching for a chance to avenge our Custer, and if the government only says the word, will march on very short notice." The *Daily Herald* promoted the idea of an army of frontiersmen because they believed that the regular army was not up to handling the Sioux:

> You see, the Sioux are different from southern Indians, and the regular army officers are apt to underrate them. They are magnificent men and physically are well-armed with Henry rifles and have abundant ammunition which they have been storing up for years past. They are unequaled in horsemanship, and are really equal, man to man, with the whites.
>
> The Sioux can put 10,000 well-armed warriors in the field; Cheyenne are good for 600 more; the Arapahos for 500, and if those south of the road join in, which is very likely, you can add nearly 2,000 to the above—making altogether an effective army of 12,000 to 15,000. To cope with these, at least 6,000 whites are needed—probably more, that is if the intention is to make a finish of the business, and by subduing the Sioux that object will be attained, for they are the only real stumbling block to civilization now left among the aborigines.[111]

The *Daily Herald* added that with an army of 10,000 experienced frontiersmen, Generals Terry and Crook could surround the Standing Rock, Red Cloud, and Spotted Tail Indian agencies and "every red skin found outside of the limits should be sent to the happy hunting grounds at once."[112] A letter sent to the *Daily Herald,* from a correspondent at the Red Cloud Agency, complained that following Custer's defeat the Indians at the agency were becoming "sassy" and were very eager to get arms and ammunition. The correspondent claimed that Sitting Bull, "Grant's pet Indian," had left the agency on the "morning of the 18th," ostensibly to get his gun and to "bring his friends back with him."[113] This claim of Sitting Bull's perfidy is ridiculous, since Sitting Bull did not reside at the agency and had been roaming freely long before June 18, 1876.

Another correspondent from the agency painted an even grimmer picture of the situation. "Everybody here at the agency is nearly frightened to death at the insolence and independence of the Indians since the news of the Custer massacre. The Indians do not seem to have any idea of when it will end, and express themselves freely in regard to the slow actions of the government. We hope that some energetic young officer with sufficient command will be placed at the head to show the Indians are not the rulers of this country."[114]

The rumors were driven to a new height at the report that General Crook had been attacked by Indians on Goose Creek, nearly 300 of his men had been killed, and his command had been driven across the creek in disarray. The *Daily Herald* quoted an Indian named Lame Deer as saying more soldiers were killed than were lost at the Little Big Horn. It added that "the Indians now have full sweep of the northern country and propose, after driving miners out of the Black Hills, to make a clean sweep of the agency."[115]

Unfortunately for the *Daily Herald,* there was no battle between Crook and the Indians at Goose Creek. The only confrontation of any size following Little Big Horn was the inconclusive battle at Slim Buttes fought on September 9, 1876,[116] long after the alleged battle on Goose Creek. Contrary to the reports in the Omaha newspapers, the mass exodus from the reservations had occurred before the battle of the Little Big Horn, not after it. Utley maintains that "Buffalo, not soldiers, governed the movements of the Indians after the Little Big Horn. When none could be found, they moved rapidly."[117]

Solutions to the Indian problem continued to be offered by the Omaha newspapers. The *Bee* suggested that the answer was to kill all of the Indians' horses and set them afoot. It claimed that had this policy been followed earlier, the warrior chiefs such as Sitting Bull, Crazy Horse, and others would have only had a "scant following" and their "operations could have been circumscribed within very narrow limits."[118] However, the *Bee* offered no specific plan for exterminating the Indian horses. The *Bee* also predicted that the Indian campaign was "likely to degenerate into protracted guerrilla war, which will finally terminate when winter sets in. . . . When the Indians are compelled to seek shelter in their villages and when their ponies are reduced to mere skeletons, then will be the time for Gen. Crook to strike the decisive blow from which the hostile Sioux will never be able to recover."[119]

Unable to admit that their hero Custer was overwhelmed by "primitive savages," supporters created a legion of fanciful theories to explain his defeat. One of the earliest theories appeared in the August 1 edition of the *Omaha Bee*. Purporting to be the latest news of the Custer fight, this story claimed that Custer was betrayed by a scout and that the Indians were aided by renegade white men:

> A special from Bismarck says: A new version of the Custer fight has just been learned, being a story related by a sergeant of the 6th Infantry. He asserts that Custer was led in a snare by the treachery of a Crow scout, named Cross. This scout, with the guides Girard and Jackson, were all who escaped from the massacre. It is said that Cross was sent out to reconnoiter by Custer the night before the battle, and that he returned in the morning and reported the Indian village a small one, and one that offered an easy victory. Then followed the disastrous charge and wholesale massacre.
>
> The Indians were fully informed and aware of Custer's intentions, and had made every preparation to give him a warm reception. Everything was done and breastworks of willow were thrown up, behind which the Indians could pick off the soldiers without being seen themselves. Further evidence has been obtained proving that white men were with the Indians. Reno's men say they heard English being spoken frequently in the Indian ranks. During the fight one of the Indians shot by Reno's men was found to be a white man with a long gray beard and wearing an Indian mask. A bugler who was honorably discharged from the Second Infantry in 1869 is also believed to have been with the Indians during the fight. He blew the calls on the trumpets several times.[120]

The theories expounded in this article are easily disproven. Utley says that despite the numerical odds against him, Custer could have won the battle. He claims that Custer came close to surprising the Indians and they had little time to prepare.[121] This certainly would not have been the case if Custer had been betrayed by a scout and the Indians had time for massive preparations. In addition, no evidence of a willow barricade has been reported in official accounts. The description of a white man with a long gray beard wearing an Indian mask seems to be an interesting anecdote added for flavor, but hardly realistic. It seems unlikely that he or any other white man would have survived long in that maelstrom of allied tribesmen.

The speculation of how Custer met his death continued in the papers for some time. Over a year later the *Daily Herald* reported that a scout who had interviewed Sitting Bull claimed that the Sioux Chief, "gave the following facts":

> Many of Custer's men were run down and over by mounted Indians, who dispatched them with their knives as they fell, and, while the Indians admit the lives of many wounded and killed, they assert the troops were annihilated within about 30 minutes from the time the attack commenced. Custer, with a

few men, retreated some distance, and Sitting Bull admits, could have escaped, but he suddenly reversed and ordered a charge, the devoted remnant rushed to a certain death, discharging their revolvers into the ranks of the savages.

Custer killed five himself, and after his last shot, beat in the skull of a Sioux who grappled with him, with the butt of his pistol, receiving his own mortal wound as his last victim tumbled from his horse. At first he was not recognized, being regarded merely as a scout, but was soon identified by Sitting Bull himself, his body was placed in a sitting position by the side of two dead soldiers, and left unharmed.

It has always been imagined that Custer sacrificed himself rather than meet the criticism probably to follow the movement ending so disastrously, or that in a moment of desperation he determined to die with his command, when he recognized the mistake he had made. These ideas receive support from the stories Howard brings, and prove that Custer and perhaps other officers might have escaped to tell the tale.[122]

This account seems largely concocted to satisfy the growing legend of the heroic Custer. It is doubtful that Sitting Bull could have identified Custer, since they were not well acquainted and the report that Custer and some of his men could have escaped but returned to give final battle is not supported by any existing evidence.

In recent years there has been much archeological study of the Custer battlefield, which supports the contention that the Indian forces at Little Big Horn were well armed and ready to fight. According to an article in *Military History Quarterly*, "Even more important, it now seemed likely that a series of opportune tactical movements by the Sioux and Cheyenne, rather than a simple imbalance of forces, were crucial factors in the Custer fight."[123] This is not the sort of thing readers would have found in the columns of Omaha newspapers in 1876. It flew in the face of their long-held stereotypes regarding the military prowess of Native Americans. The *Bee* and the *Republican* looked for scapegoats or blamed the defeat on overwhelming force. The *Daily Herald* was alone in its contention that the fighting prowess of the Sioux had been underestimated, but even it did not claim that Custer had been outfought.

All of the Omaha newspapers seemed to understand the ultimate significance of the Little Big Horn battle. While they may have differed on the immediate effect it would have on the nation, they knew it meant that one final effort to pen the free Sioux and their allies on reserves was crucial and inevitable. While there were to be occasional Indian wars in the years to come, never again would there be gathered a force of Indians as powerful as the allied tribes at the Little Big Horn.

CHAPTER 5

~

The Flight of the Nez Perce:
March–October 1877

Historian Richard H. Dillon called the Nez Perce war of 1877 "the saddest and most unnecessary of all Indian wars."[1] With their long history of peaceful relations with whites, the Nez Perce seemed to be unlikely candidates for a war. The first Nez Perce contact with whites occurred when they befriended the Lewis and Clark expedition in 1805, and for 70 years they remained at peace.[2] The trouble began when the tribe split into pro- and antitreaty factions over the Nez Perce Treaty of 1863. The original Nez Perce reservation was situated in the Salmon River valley in Idaho and the nearby Wallowa valley in Oregon. It encompassed the ancestral lands of the Nez Perce and had been guaranteed by the treaty of 1855 but was to be opened to exploration by miners.

Lawyer, leader of the pro-treaty faction, became frustrated with his attempts to get Old Joseph and other leaders of the antitreaty faction to sign the new 1863 treaty. He recruited a list of allies from protreaty bands and had them sign as substitutes for the antitreaty faction. The 1863 treaty was quickly ratified by Congress and signed by President Abraham Lincoln. All of the Nez Perce bands that had lived on the newly ceded land were told to move onto the new Lapwai Reservation in northwest Idaho Territory. Old Joseph and the antitreaty faction successfully fought their removal through passive resistance. They tore up survey stakes and argued with government officials that they were autonomous bands and had never signed the 1863 treaty and that therefore its provisions did not apply to them.[3]

Old Joseph and the other antitreaty leaders continued to protest that the treaty was illegal. In 1873, President Ulysses S. Grant declared in an executive order that Old Joseph, who had died two years earlier, was correct. However, the outcry of land hungry Oregonians forced the revocation of the executive order in 1875.[4] Following a council in May 1877, the Nez Perce antitreaty bands were ordered to leave their ancestral lands and move to their new reservation by June 15, 1877.[5]

Chief Joseph, Nez Perce, wearing embroidered band across chest. Courtesy of Denver Public Library, Western History Collection.

Chief Joseph (the son of Old Joseph) and White Bird were peacefully moving their bands toward the new reservation when an incident occurred that would change everything. Two young men, Wahlitits and Sarpsis Ilppilp of White Bird's band, became drunk and sought out a white man who had murdered Wahlitits's father. Having been unable to find their intended victim, they killed four other whites. They then returned to camp and recruited 17 other young men and continued their raid, killing several more settlers.[6]

The first Omaha paper to report the story was the *Republican*. Under the headline "Startling News from the Walla Walla—Massacre of Whites by the Savages," the *Republican* reported that there had been an uprising of Indians 60 miles from Lewiston, in Idaho Territory.[7] It added that "several settlers living on Cottonwood Creek have been massacred by Indians, and the messenger who brought the intelligence to Lapwai was wounded, being entrapped by savages. Gen. [Oliver O.] Howard, who is beyond Walla Walla, has just telegraphed to Adjutant General [H. Clay] Wood in this city [Portland] to forward all available troops to the scene of trouble. Great excitement prevails."[8] The *Daily Herald* reported the same story on June 20, 1877, and the *Bee* on June 22, 1877.

The *Republican* expanded on the story the next day, introducing its accounts with headlines that read, "Men, Women and Children Being Brutally Massacred by the Savages," and "A General Uprising of the Savages and the Whole Country Wild with Alarm." It added that settlers were fleeing in all directions and that the Indians in the region could gather about 2,000 warriors.[9] On the same day, the *Daily Herald* reported that 1,500 savages were destroying life and property in Idaho. The paper claimed that 29 whites had been killed and that the whites had killed the Nez Perce Chief White Bird and his family.[10]

In response to the action by the Indians, General Howard sent Captain David Perry, a veteran of the Modoc campaign, and 93 men to prevent any further attacks by the Nez Perce. Perry found the Nez Perce under White Bird and Joseph near White Bird Creek on June 17, 1877. Joseph intended to talk peace with the soldiers, but a force of volunteers who accompanied Perry opened fire on Joseph and his men despite the flag of truce. The Indians were unprepared for this attack but soon responded with a heavy return fire, driving their attackers back.[11]

The *Bee* reported that the Indians soon repulsed the attacking soldiers.

> Upon the first fire of the Indians the soldiers broke ranks and retreated. The officers could not rally them and make them face the fire. The Indians pursued them about sixteen miles, firing upon them constantly. [A scout named Williams] stated that the Indians had better guns than the troops and their aim was deadly from the first attack. There were one hundred and twenty-five Indians in pursuit. . . . Some of the men who have returned have estimated the loss in killed and wounded at sixty men.[12]

The *Republican* wrote that the Indians killed six soldiers and that the soldiers had killed Joseph and his "squaw."[13] The actual loss was 1 officer and 33 enlisted men slain, with 4 others wounded. Joseph and his wife were unharmed.[14]

Perry's defeat by the Indians earned scorn from the editors of the Omaha papers. The *Daily Herald* reported that the soldiers broke and ran for shelter and "refused to face the murderous fire of the redskins."[15] The *Republican* stated that it was "another engagement in which the soldiers made a cowardly retreat." It added, "The dusky savages, flushed with victory, held a grand war dance on the prairie."[16] The *Bee* was a bit kinder, stating that after battling the Indians for three hours, Captain Perry was "compelled to retreat, losing about sixty men."[17]

The news from Idaho prompted the *Bee* to weigh in with an editorial regarding the "moral status of the average Indian":

> The recent Indian outbreaks in the far west demonstrate to a fineness that is an impossibility to improve, to any great degree, the moral status of the average wild Indian after he has grown up with all his aboriginal customs and traditions engraved into his nature. As early as 1835 missionaries settled in the Nez Perce country and gave the natives of that region all the church and school advantages

that could be desired. . . . Through the labors of their white brethren the tribe was in many ways benefited, and today there are a great many well disposed and sensible old men among the Nez Perces and the Indians in the immediate vicinity; but most of the young men are bigoted, insulting in their manners towards the whites, and have more the appearance, when away from home, of the wildest Sioux and Blackfeet, than of Indians who have had the advantages of moral training.

It is not surprising to hear that many of these young braves are now the allies of their rebellious neighbors, aiding in the murder of settlers and soldiers since it is a part of Indian nature to first attack those who have done them the greatest favors. Doubtless this small band of apparently insignificant Indians that engaged in this first uprising, have found aid in their evil-disposed brethren among the Nez Perces, Koutanais and others in the adjoining valleys. . . . Having been heretofore classed with the friendly and Christian Indians, and regarded as harmless, has given them the privilege of buying all the arms and ammunition they desired.[18]

The *Bee* did not specifically describe what behavior by the young Nez Perce toward the whites branded the Indians as "bigoted and insulting in their manner."[19]

The *Daily Herald* and the *Republican* both reported that the Nez Perce had not killed the women and children they had captured but had escorted them to a white settlement. In addition, they reported that the Indians had not burned or destroyed any property. However, they did not expect the Indians to continue to refrain.[20]

In a story headlined, "The Camas Scalping Ground," the *Daily Herald* expressed concern that some of the other tribes in Idaho Territory would join with the Nez Perce despite their protestations of neutrality. "Whether the protestations of these Indians [Bannock and Shoshones] will be fulfilled will depend upon the success of the Nez Perce and their allies. The situation is critical and the influences to which these Indians are exposed are adverse to the safety of the settlements."[21]

In contrast to the wire stories, which blamed the Indians for the uprising, the *Daily Herald* placed the blame on white men: "It turns out, as we predicted it would turn out when the Indian outbreak of the Nez Perces was first announced, it is all due to the systematic robbery of the poor Indians, who, driven from their homes by Christian gunpowder, are plundered of the pittance which they were compelled, by the same merciless power, to receive for them. It is the same old, old story. Bishop Whipple has told it, over and over again, with the crushing eloquence of the truth, and no man can go amiss who predicts in any given uprising of the red men that it is the fruit of wrongs and outrages heaped upon them by the white men until these hopeless and helpless beings are reduced to despair."[22]

In reply, the *Bee* referred sarcastically to the *Daily Herald*'s views of the Nez Perce war when it wrote, "A collection for the patriotic Idaho Indians, who are just now being scalped and butchered by the atrocious white settlers, will be taken up by the *Omaha Herald*."[23]

The *Republican* reported that the Nez Perce were removing their women, children, and property across the Salmon River so that the warriors would be free to raid the settlements in the Walla Walla valley. It claimed the news had been obtained from a "reliable Indian" who had come directly from the Indians' camp and that the news had been corroborated by word brought in by whites.[24]

There was an increasing fear that other tribes in the area would join the Nez Perce in their uprising against the whites. A council held with chiefs from the Umatilla, Cayuse, and Walla Walla tribes revealed that many of the Indians were "dissatisfied"[25] with their treatment by the whites. According to Father Jim [Mesplie], a missionary working among the Nez Perce and other allied tribes in the area, almost 8,000 warriors could be raised.

> The Indians represented their reservation as being continually trespassed upon by the inhabitants adjoining the White settlements, who would sell the Indians whisky and otherwise injure and demoralize them. If required to remain there, they would find themselves compelled to fight. From some cause this wish of the Indians received no attention at Washington. Some two months ago Howlias Wampoo, one of the chiefs who had been present at the council, who is principal chief of the Umatillas, passed through Boise city. The chief told Father [Jim] Mesplie at this time that the Umatillas were dissatisfied and had made up their mind to leave, as the silence and neglect of the government left nothing to hope from that quarter, and that they would join Chief Joseph in Wallowa valley, who was already resolved to go to war.[26]

The *Bee* echoed the report of the *Daily Herald*. It reported that "an old missionary among the Nez Perce says the war has been contemplated for some time, and probably twelve thousand Indians will take part. Troops are rapidly going forward, although there are very few troops to draw upon. Every post in this neighborhood is completely stripped."[27]

Reports of other tribes allegedly joining the Nez Perce continued to make the news in the Omaha newspapers. The *Republican* reported that there were between 99 and 400 warriors with Joseph, and that "a great number of renegade Indians from different bands have joined Joseph on the Salmon River."[28] The *Republican* added that while several tribes professed friendship for the whites, it was certain that some of their young men would drift away to join the Nez Perce.[29]

The *Bee* said that Winnemucca, chief of the Paiutes in Silver City, assured the governor that he had no intention of breaking the peace with the whites and that he would remain friendly if there was an Indian outbreak. However, it added, Winnemucca said if he decided to fight he would give fair warning.[30]

The Nez Perce were not without their supporters. The *Daily Herald* quoted Peace Commissioner A. C. Barrow as saying that there were about 3,000 Nez

Perce, of which half were living peacefully on their reservation while the other half, the nontreaty Indians, were occupying the old lands guaranteed to them by the treaty of 1855. According to the *Daily Herald,* Barrow claimed that the nontreaty Nez Perce did not assent to the later treaty of 1863, in which nine-tenths of their property was "ceded" to the whites and that there had been "bad blood ever since between them and the Oregonian squatters." It added, "But Mr. Barrow asserts that, 'until the present outbreak the Indians have been the sufferers, the life of no white man having been sacrificed by them.'"[31]

Under the headline "A Kind Word for the Indians," the *Daily Herald* reported a recent interview it had with a Jesuit priest who had spent 17 years as a missionary to the Nez Perce. The paper quoted the missionary as saying: "I do not doubt that these troubles, as many others, have been the result of misunderstanding between the Indian agents and the Indians. The aborigines have been cruelly outraged and slandered. They are not, as represented, treacherous and unfeeling. They have been duped, deceived and swindled by the government agents, and General [William S.] Harney, one of the best of Indian agents, and an honest man, said to me nearly a quarter of a century ago, that in nine cases out of ten, when there ensued trouble between the Whites and Indians, it was the fault of the United States Government. It is natural for the red man, when driven about, maltreated, swindled and even spit upon, to resent the insult."[32]

It seems out of character for General Harney to be quoted as blaming the whites for trouble between them and the Indians. This is the same General Harney who was said to have hated all Indians since he was forced to flee in his underwear by the Seminoles during the Second Seminole War in 1836. It was also the same General Harney who attacked the Brule Sioux at Ash Hollow, Nebraska Territory, in 1855 and killed over 100 men, women, and children, thus earning the nickname "Butcher."[33]

Talk that other tribes would join the Nez Perce continued to be reported in the Omaha newspapers. In a story that also was featured in the *Daily Herald,* the *Republican* reported that a Nez Perce Indian "who talks good English" had said the Nez Perce were coming into the Bitter Root valley and were going to "clean it out." It added that the Nez Perce warned the Flatheads that if they did not join in the uprising, the Nez Perce would "clean them out too." According to the *Republican,* the Flatheads were expected to join the Nez Perce by July 1, 1877. In the same edition the paper reported that "the number of murders thus far ascertained is one woman, two children and fifteen men in addition to the thirty-three soldiers of Perry's command killed and missing in the late fight. Details of the murders are horrible in the extreme. There are several women at Mount Idaho, wives of settlers who narrowly escaped or were rescued after suffering terrible outrages."[34]

The *Bee* reported the same basic story but added: "If the Indians remain in their present position an engagement will take place tomorrow or Friday at the latest. . . . No intelligence is received of any outbreak among other Indians in the vicinity." It also reported that General Howard had overtaken Joseph at the mouth of White Bird Creek and that Chief White Bird was in charge of the entire united bands and Joseph was the "fighting chief." It claimed that "The Indians are bold and waiting for the United States to engage them."[35]

In an extensive editorial, the *Bee* elaborated on the relationship between the whites and the Flathead Indians that was being threatened by the movements of the Nez Perce. It illustrated the fragile nature of the relationship between even the friendliest of Indians and whites:

> The heretofore friendly-disposed Flatheads have removed their families and stock to a place of security, and the young braves have buckled on their war-pelts and left the Bitter Root, possibly to avoid a conflict with the Indians of the Camas Prairie; but by the settlers, this sudden stir among the Flatheads is regarded as a foreboding of evil. This is all the more striking when it is remembered that the Flatheads and whites have dwelt together in peace and harmony from the first settlement of the valley by the whites, over twenty years ago.
>
> Although the Flatheads boast that no white man ever perished at their hands and that they befriended Lewis and Clark on their visit to their country in 1805, yet for some years many of them have exhibited a spirit of restlessness that their white neighbors feared might, under favoring circumstances, develop into un-friendly relations with them. More than twenty years ago the Flatheads entered into a treaty with the government in which it was stipulated that in 1873 the tribe should remove to the Jocko, a reservation set apart for them about 100 miles northwest of the Bitter Root and on which the whites could not settle. . . . They said the Bitter Root was the home of their fathers and they would prefer to live and die there. They have even gone so far as to declare that they would prefer war and death than removal to the Jocko. . . . This has all wrought dissatisfaction among the Indians and the settlers feel they have good reasons for anticipating a war with their red neighbors. With the three tribes mentioned, constituting the Flathead confederacy, there are probably 1,000 able-bodied, well-armed war-riors, and if they should decide to join the Nez Perces, a war of the very ugliest kind would be the result.[36]

The rumors of an alliance of tribes that would rise in one concerted effort to throw out the whites continued to grow. Duncan McDonald, a half-blood Nez Perce who covered the Nez Perce campaign as a correspondent for a small Montana newspaper,[37] alleged that while Flathead chiefs Michell and Arlee were peaceful, they did not feel they could control their young men. McDonald claimed that "preparations have long been progressing for all Indians to fight Whites."[38] A wire story, run by both the *Republican* and the *Daily Herald,* also claimed "Indians have advices that the Crows are to make peace with the Sioux and ally against the Whites. They had word that the Crow chief would this spring refuse to go with the soldiers, but would ostensibly go out alone to fight the Sioux. When near the

Sioux camp he would send ten men to treat with Sitting Bull for peace and alliance in an offensive war."[39]

Historian David Lavender claims that General Oliver O. Howard enlisted the help of a Jesuit missionary, Father Joseph Cataldo, and Bill Craig, the son of a mountain man, to help keep the Indians of Northern Idaho from joining the Nez Perce. Howard later praised both men for their success. Lavender adds, "But grant some credit to the northern Indians. Joining the beset Nez Perce rebels to give vent to their own dissatisfactions seemed short-sighted to most of them. In fact, some of them actually took care of the ranches of settlers who had bolted at the first breath of trouble."[40]

The July 6, 1877, edition of the *Republican* also carried a brief article describing an attack by Captain Steven C. Whipple on the Looking Glass band of the Nez Perce. "Four Indians were killed and left on the field dead. Many others were wounded. Squaws and children took to the river and several were drowned. Fighting was still going on when the courier left. The Looking Glass band is estimated by scouts to number about four hundred."[41]

The paper seemed to judge the incident as insignificant, but it was to have larger implications in the months to come. There had been rumors that Looking Glass had been sending recruits and supplies to the fugitive Nez Perce. These rumors, which may have been planted by whites hoping to profit from the ensuing confrontation, were not investigated by General Howard. Instead, Howard sent Whipple to move the Looking Glass band out of the way. Accompanied by civilian volunteers, Whipple's force confronted the Indians and demanded their surrender. Confused, the Indians asked why, but in reply an unnamed volunteer fired his rifle and a barrage of gunfire erupted.[42]

Lavender writes, "The terrified inhabitants, most of whom had been in their tipis unaware of the whites' intrusion, fled in disorder, some into the forest, some across the adjoining stream. A few were killed or wounded. The troops burned several tipis, swooped up some plunder and drove off a reputed seven hundred horses. But the band remained intact—and enraged."[43] Until the attack by Whipple, Looking Glass's band had been neutral. Now Howard had driven them into the arms of Chief Joseph.

Just as they had in previous wars between the Indians and the army, some Omaha newspapers were calling for a volunteer army to deal with the Nez Perce once and for all. "It is evident that volunteer cavalry in large force ought to be put into the field to reinforce Gen. Howard and stop this uprising before it assumes larger and more definite proportions. Such a force under his command will do the work." [44]

The *Bee* echoed the *Republican*'s call for enlisting volunteers:

Gen. McDowell has been authorized to call for two hundred volunteers to take part in the western Indian war, with the power of extending the call to five hundred if it should be necessary. This is the first instance in many years where the federal authorities have originated and sanctioned a call for volunteer troops to suppress Indian raids. The policy of the government could not be more effectual in its treatment of the frontier difficulties than by the employment of western frontiersmen to fight the Indian savages.

Our regular army, as constituted at present, does not comprise the vigor and intelligence which usually goes to make up an effective military corps. The average regular is either the unfortunate victim of some evil circumstance, or an indolent person who lacks energy or ability to succeed in any civil enterprise. The western frontiersmen are men who have interests at stake, and who have come west to build up a competency. They not only know how to use a gun, but also how to fight the treacherous savage. The government can pursue no more popular and effectual policy to crush out the savage warfare in the west than by the use of the western volunteer.[45]

Considering the disastrous role that volunteers had played in both the defeat of Captain Perry by the Nez Perce and in Whipple's attack on the Looking Glass band, it seems ironic that the Omaha newspapers would clamor for more assistance from volunteers who had twice proved their ineptitude.

The headlines in the July 14, 1877, edition of the *Omaha Bee* shouted, "Thirty-one Heathen Chinese Sent to the Happy Hunting Ground by Joseph's Band," and "The Massacre Claimed to have Been Inhuman and Without Provocation." The story claimed that the Nez Perce had killed 31 "Chinamen as they came down the Clearwater in canoes. The massacre was inhuman and without provocation."[46] It might have been "inhuman and without provocation" if it had happened, but it appears to have been a fabrication. The *Colorado Miner*, of Georgetown, Colorado, repeated the same story even to the detail of 31 miners being killed. It claimed that the Nez Perce "cheerfully slew the whole party for recreation."[47] There is no record of it in accounts by Lavender or other historians. It seems clear that an incident of this nature, if true, would have earned more than a mere footnote in the history of the Nez Perce campaign.

In contrast to the story in the *Bee* and *Republican,* a little over a week later, in the July 22, 1877, edition of the *Daily Herald,* that paper stated that 150 Chinese miners arrived in Walla Walla, in the Washington Territory. It claimed that the Indians had entered the miners' camp and taken all of their provisions, blankets, and some of their clothing. The paper added "After taking all they possessed the Indians told them to leave, which the Chinamen lost no time in doing."[48] There is no mention of even one miner being killed by the Indians, let alone 31.

Looking Glass, following the attack on his camp by Whipple, joined Joseph near the Clearwater River. Their combined forces were then attacked by General Howard on July 10, 1877.[49] The headlines from the *Republican* read, "The Savage Hordes Utterly Routed and Scattered in All Directions with Considerable Loss," and "Gen. Howard Now in Fine Condition to Make Quick Work of the Latest Uprising."[50] The paper claimed that the Indians had 13 killed and "a large number wounded." They quoted General Howard as saying, "The Indians fought as well as any troopers I ever saw, and so did ours, not one man failing in his duty. I now believe that I am in fine condition just as soon as [Col.] Green appears from Boise to make thorough work with these Indians." It added, "The Indians fought in a recumbent position and kept up a steady fire from behind rocks, trees and every advantageous rise in the ground like skirmishers and sharp shooters."[51]

The *Republican* claimed that Joseph had wanted to fight to the finish but was persuaded to retreat. "A squaw who fell into our hands says that seven Indians were killed outright and the number wounded was very large. She says the chief wanted to fight and die at the river but the woman prevailed upon him to retreat."[52] The Indians had made the mistake of letting the soldiers get too close to their camp, but they did not panic. Historian Dillon states that the Indian sharpshooters were no match for the howitzers and Gatling guns, even though the Nez Perce had captured General Howard's pack train and, temporarily, some of his artillery. The Nez Perce retreated and Howard's forces were too "bloodied to pursue." He had lost 15 men killed and 25 wounded to Joseph's 4 dead and 6 wounded.[53] Howard had claimed a victory, but it was a Pyrrhic victory at best.

The *Republican* reported that Joseph had offered to surrender to General Howard following his "defeat" at the battle of the Clearwater. Howard wrote in a July 19, 1877, dispatch, published by the *Republican,* that "Joseph may make complete surrender tomorrow morning. My troops will meet him at the Ferry. He and his people will be treated with justice, their conduct to be completely investigated by a court composed of nine of my army selected by myself."[54] The *Republican* believed that Joseph's proposition was merely a ruse to gain time.[55] According to historian Lavender, Joseph's offer was never more than an unsubstantiated rumor.[56]

The *Denver Daily Times* was confident that Howard had won a crushing victory. It wrote that since the "rough handling" Joseph and White Bird had received at the hands of Howard, the "war was virtually over."[57]

Howard indeed felt that the campaign was all but over. The *Daily Herald*'s three headlines on their July 22, 1877, story on the Nez Perce campaign read: "Howard is Happy," "Having Thoroughly Walloped the Redskins, He Returns to More Peaceful Pursuits," and "The Settlers Once More at Rest, and Returning to Their Homes."[58] Howard believed the Nez Perce would be met by either General George Crook or General Nelson A. Miles as they crossed into Montana and would be captured by these forces.

"The Nez Perce war is practically over . . . troops will march through the Spokane country for the moral effect it will have upon the Indians. Colonel Green's cavalry, upon its arrival, will be kept here to prevent a return of the hostile Indians this way. Another force of Indians with a flag of truce, are now coming in to surrender."[59] Howard's confidence that the Nez Perce campaign was over was misplaced. It would continue for almost three more months.

The *Omaha Bee* agreed with General Howard that the war was almost over. In an editorial it laid out its version of who was responsible for the troubles. It laid all the responsibility at the feet of an "arrogant, insulting" Chief Joseph:

When the Indian war first broke out in Idaho, the Chief Joseph was represented as the instigator of hostilities. In this respect he occupied the same attitude towards his followers that Sitting Bull did to the Sioux. He was arrogant, insulting and boastful in speech, and expressed a determination not to be reconciled until he had driven the Whites out of the country. Knowing this much of his character, it will not be surprising that he misrepresented his intentions to General Howard. When he heard that the offenders in his band were to be held to an accountability for their crimes, it was apparent to him at once that to surrender was to become a prisoner, who had to undergo trial and be held for punishment if found guilty. The information was not palatable, and Joseph from that moment was anxious to get away. His excuse to General Howard's messenger, that he was compelled to move at that time, but would meet the General at the river crossing the next morning for a parley, was so transparent that it would have hardly deceived General Howard who held himself in readiness for any emergency.

It is thought that the flight of Joseph has virtually brought the war to a close. The prediction may prove to be premature. The uneasiness of the Indians everywhere on the frontier gives a denial to the thought. Not until he and his band are subdued will it do to indulge so flattering a thought. In that event the discontented savages would be taught that they can never muster a force of warriors sufficiently strong to cope with the power of the government and that their overthrow would only be a matter of time.[60]

The *Bee* was right about at least one thing. It was premature to think that the war was over. Following the Battle of the Clearwater, the Nez Perce slipped out of Idaho Territory into Montana Territory, bypassing a fort that guarded the Lolo pass, which was later derisively called "Fort Fizzle." The *Republican* reported that the Nez Perce had assured the settlers in the area that they would pass through the country "without destroying life or property. The citizens therefore did not care to fight."[61] The Nez Perce had left General Howard far behind and Looking Glass convinced Joseph that the people needed to rest. Meanwhile, unbeknownst to the Nez Perce, a small force of 206 soldiers and volunteers under Colonel John Gibbon was approaching them from the east. They caught the Indians by surprise near the Big Hole River on August 9, 1877. Convinced of their safety, the Indians had not even posted sentries.[62]

Gibbon's force was outnumbered by the Nez Perce, and after some initial success, his men were repulsed with heavy losses. The *Republican* headlines trumpeted "Gallant Conduct of Colonel Gibbon's Soldiers Against Overwhelming Odds." It claimed that while half of Gibbon's command was killed or wounded during fierce fighting, "one-hundred hostiles are made to bite the dust." A dispatch from the front listed Gibbon's casualties as 7 officers, 50 men, and 10 citizens. One of the wounded was Gibbon himself.[63]

The *Daily Herald* described the fighting between the Nez Perce and Gibbon's men as "desperate." It added:

> The soldiers charged across the stream and into the Indian camp before the Indians had time to escape from their lodges. The attack was a complete success, but these shots had aroused the Indians, who were sleeping on their arms and watchful. Still the suddenness of the attack surprised them. The Indians rushed out in the wildest confusion, the men with guns, boys with knives and squaws with pistols, all fighting desperately. The Indians were well-armed and with plenty of ammunition. Among the lodges desperate hand-to-hand fighting was carried on for an hour and a half. By this time the Indians had recovered from their surprise. They outnumbered the soldiers largely, and now began to fight with desperation.
>
> The above is an imperfect account of one of the most desperate Indian fights on record. They were a brave band, with a gallant leader, that charged and defeated the Indians at Big Hole pass. They were only a handful of men, and outnumbered almost two to one; but Gibbons had been ordered to strike, and it was a fierce and terrible blow he struck the Indians—such a blow as he never before received.[64]

The *Bee* echoed the story in the *Daily Herald* and added a few of its own details. It described the Indians as "yelling like demons and swarming from their tents." It added that when the Indians counterattacked, it "staggered the body of whites, and when the red devils, outnumbering them two to one, charged with the knife and tomahawk, there was no alternative to retreat. . . . Charge after charge was made by the infuriated and desperate savages [, who] fought like panthers, and the noble little band of whites was at last compelled to seek refuge in the timber."[65]

The Nez Perce lost 87 people. Some were women and children, but most were warriors. The Nez Perce were forced to withdraw when Howard began to approach the battlefield.[66] Unlike the whites, the Nez Perce had no reinforcements to replace the fallen warriors. It was a grievous blow to the Nez Perce. However, after initial claims of victory for Gibbon, it was acknowledged that the Nez Perce had won the battle. According to a *Daily Herald* editorial, Gibbon and his men were sacrificial lambs:

> It is not merely a shame that such soldiers as Gibbon and [James] Bradley, and other brave men of the army, are ordered with disgracefully inferior forces to fight Nez Perces Indians and Sioux Indians. It is a crime, and somebody is responsible for it. Upon whose shoulders does the responsibility rest? Gen. Gibbon [the paper used his Civil War rank] is ordered to pursue and attack Joseph and his trained band of sharp-shooting soldiers. That brave Indian is known to

have a well-armed force of from 300 to 400 men. Every one of them is so skilled in the use of the rifle from boyhood that they may be called sharp-shooters. They shoot with deadly aim and seldom miss their mark or man. Gen. Gibbon had a force of only 132 regulars—183 men, all told. He encounters Joseph in his camp. He must have known the disparity of force and the danger of defeat, but he was under orders to attack, and there was no alternative. . . . The escape of the Nez Perce chief would have been certain without attack, and of course Gen. Gibbon must fight. He took all the advantages doubtless which the circumstances permitted, and led his little band of heroes to terrible slaughter and defeat.

It is barely possible, nay is it not more than probable, that the old infatuation that one U.S. soldier equals to four or five Indians in battle has something to do with the latest slaughter of our little army. If this be so, how long is it going to take the great Sherman and Gen. Sheridan to have this costly delusion dispelled. Might not the Rosebud and Little Big Horn suffice? What do these distinguished soldiers mean by this criminal trifling with the lives of the gallant men of the army? We are not soldiers, and we have every confidence in the commanders of our military forces, but if there is a man of ordinary sense in all the land who can not see the cruel and wanton sacrifices that are made in these Indian wars, they ought to go to a hospital for the blind until he can be made to see.[67]

The *Republican* claimed that the Nez Perce had outnumbered Gibbon's force 10 to 1 and, "though decisive advantages were gained by Gibbon in the earlier stages, retreat was necessary at last to save the troops from complete demolition."[68] The *Bee* wrote, "The disaster that befell Gen. Gibbon's command of 183 men a few days since, fell like a thunderbolt on the people. The reports previous to this were that Joseph desired to pass peaceably through Montana, and it would appear that he was honest in his assertion, as he had already passed through the Missoula settlements without a collision and had crossed the mountains and camped on the eastern side."[69]

Following the news of Gibbon's defeat, the *Bee* weighed in with its view of the Indian policy:

After years of mismanagement of our Indian affairs, it begins to look as though the government was about to make a change that will solve this complicated Indian question. The President's recent order prohibiting the sale of arms and ammunition to the Indians and instructing the army officers throughout the Indian country to see that the order is enforced, is a step in the right direction, and one that should have been taken long ago.

The Indian nature cannot be softened with kindness. That has been demonstrated years ago; he must be awed into obedience. . . . Until the Indian is disarmed, dismounted and made subservient to the will of military power, we will have the usual trouble with him and a rehearsal of the bloody scenes that are now being and have been enacted in years past.[70]

According to historian Lavender, Gibbon was at first treated as a conquering hero, but as time passed doubts began to creep in. Lavender asked rhetorically: "After having achieved the enormous advantages of surprise, how did it happen that Gibbon had finished the battle pinned down ignominiously and precariously by untrained Indians—Indians who were also said to have lost the Battle of the Clearwater but obviously hadn't. Clearly, the critics went on, the Nez Perce war was being mismanaged, one more example of the inadequacies of America's Indian-fighting army."[71]

The *Bee* took the stance that while the Battle of the Clearwater was a disaster; things were not as bad as they were first thought to be:

> Gibbon lost seventeen soldiers and five citizens killed; and five officers wounded [including himself], and thirty-six soldiers and five citizens wounded. The disaster, although great for the number engaged, is not so bad as was first reported. But sixty-seven killed and wounded out of 183, is nearly two-fifths of the number engaged, and shows how desperately the men fought, for this time for a wonder they were not ambushed . . . but the odds were too much in favor of the Indians. . . . It is more than likely Joseph's journey will not be a pleasure trip to the buffalo country, and his chances of being gobbled up are better now than before the battle. The Indian losses were great in killed and wounded, as many as forty dead being counted on one portion of the field. Two or three days more will decide the fate of Joseph for better or for worse.[72]

In contrast to the accusations of incompetence leveled at Gibbon by the press and the local civilians, Gibbon felt that he had been mistreated by having the blame for the defeat of the Battle of the Clearwater laid solely at his feet. He placed the blame for the defeat on some of the same citizens who were accusing him of ineptitude. "Colonel Gibbon reflects severely on the inhabitants of Montana, who sustained the red-handed plunderers and murderous Nez Perce by trading off provisions for stock stolen by them from the whites, and thus prolonging their fight and adding to the danger of pursuit."[73]

A council was held in late August of 1877 for many of the tribes of the Northwest. It was expected that over 100 chiefs and headmen, representing over 5,500 Indian men, women, and children, would attend. While these tribes had remained peaceful, they were "uneasy" and "many instances of impudence on their part was reported by settlers."[74] The whites were wary of the Indians and suspected the worst. "There is no doubt that all Indians in this section are and have been in direct communication with Joseph and have been posted several days ahead of the whites of every movement of General Howard's army, and in case of Joseph's success hundreds of young men would undoubtedly have joined him, although old Indians, who have stock and farms in the country, have manifested a desire to remain at peace.[75]

Chief Joseph and the Nez Perce now swung through the newly created Yellowstone National Park and headed back north into Montana Territory. The *Republican* criticized General Howard with headlines stating: "But Howard Manages to Keep a Safe Distance to the Rear," and "While the Warriors of Joseph Jog Leisurely Along, Apparently Unconcerned."[76] The Nez Perce raided Howard's camp and ran off about 100 of his pack animals and 30 horses belonging to civilian volunteers. The Indians were reported as numbering between 400 and 500 total and were thought to be heading to the country of the Crow Indians.[77]

Under headlines such as "Slaughtering the Innocents," and "The Wandering Joseph and his Followers Murdering Settlers by the Dozen," the *Daily Herald* described encounters between settlers and the Nez Perce. However, it listed reports of only 11 actual deaths, instead of the dozens mentioned in the headlines, and it reported that the Indians actually released three of their captives unharmed.[78]

In addition to the fear of local Indians joining Joseph's forces, there also loomed the specter of Sitting Bull and his Sioux warriors just over the border in Canada. "Serious apprehension is felt by the government that the reappearance of Sitting Bull and his band south of the Canada border is part of the combined movement on part of Sitting Bull and Chief Joseph to join their forces and conduct war on a larger scale."[79]

A brief story in the *Republican* refuted the *Bee*'s claim that Sitting Bull had crossed the border. It contradicted the report of Sitting Bull's presence in Montana and said he was still in Canada.[80] The fear that Sitting Bull would unite with Chief Joseph continued throughout the campaign and up until the surrender of Chief Joseph.

There was also a fear that other tribes of the Northwest would join with the Nez Perce. The *Pueblo Chieftain* wrote, "In the case of Joseph's success, hundreds of young [Indian] men would join him."[81]

According to the *Republican,* despite the defeats that Joseph had inflicted on them, General Howard's command was confident that the whites would triumph. The paper reported that Howard believed the Indians were "badly demoralized" and had no more than 200 fighting men with them. It added, "Howard and command are having a severe campaign, but are all in good spirits, hoping to finish the hostiles in a short time."[82]

The *Colorado Transcript,* from Golden, Colorado, had less faith in Howard than did the *Republican.* "As General Howard no longer makes bulletin board of the daily papers for the announcement of victories over the Indians, it is fair to assume that he is not winning victories. He and his accomplished aide have not been slow in reporting any successes, however trivial . . . The latest dispatches, apparently reliable, are to the effect that Chief Joseph, as soon as he puts his squaws, children and stock in a safe place, is going to hunt up General Howard and fight him."[83]

Meanwhile, the Nez Perce were moving fast and continued to encounter small groups of settlers. The *Republican* reported that the Indians had met two small groups and that "Joseph and other hostile Chiefs again commenced their bloody work." It added that seven men were killed in one party and two women and one man were made prisoners but were later released. The same edition of the paper also carried a brief report that the council held with the representatives of the "Northern Indians had been very successful. Inspector [E. C.] Watkins [of the Bureau of Indian Affairs] has in his possession a written agreement from the chiefs that they will go on the reservations designated. The Indians seem peaceably disposed and express kind feelings toward the whites. It is thought there will be no further occasion for apprehending hostilities from these tribes."[84]

In his book, *Let Me Be Free,* historian David Lavender wrote that the Nez Perce scouts had actually captured two parties of tourists, numbering 19 altogether, as they moved through Yellowstone National Park. Lavender claimed that the raiders killed two of the men and wounded two others. He added that several captives escaped and others, including two women, were released unharmed. He stated that the stories of the Nez Perce invasion of Yellowstone National Park were exaggerated and helped to lead to the creation of the Chief Joseph myth.[85] "White survivors of the escapades poured out their stories to eager journalists, some of them from the East. The tales, most of them exaggerated, made fine reading. The West, the last free-roaming Indians, Yellowstone—such images had a resonance to them. Injustice, endurance, a cunning David outmaneuvering the bumbling Minions of Goliath—those were magic topics. . . . A myth was on its way to incarnation."[86]

The *Daily Herald* was one of the newspapers that featured the story of the Yellowstone captives in its editorial columns. It quoted from a story by a correspondent from the *New York World* that was based on an interview with Frank Carpenter, one of the captives. It told of how he and his sisters, one of whom was Emma Cowan, were taken to Joseph, whom they described as a "tall, finely-built Indian, 45 years old with a thoughtful and intelligent face." Carpenter was told his sisters would be freed but he would be killed. Carpenter credits White Bird with favoring their release and says the Indians voted on their fate by sitting in a circle and passing a pipe around. "Then White Bird filled and lit his pipe and took a few whiffs at it, thus voting for their release. . . . How eagerly the captives watched his actions, and what silent heartfelt prayers of gratitude ascended to heaven when the stoical savage placed the mouthpiece of the pipe to his lips and the merciful wreath of bluish-white smoke slowly came out upon the air!" Carpenter claimed that four of the seven chiefs voted for their release and they were provided with horses to get them safely away.[87]

Despairing that General Howard would ever catch up with the Nez Perce, the *Daily Herald* reported that the Indians were to be "pushed to the wall" with the entry of General Wesley Merritt in the chase.[88]

Leaving Howard far behind, the Nez Perce continued northward into Montana Territory, disappearing from their pursuers and from the pages of the Omaha newspapers for two weeks. It was not until September 13, 1877, that the army again encountered the Nez Perce at a place called Canyon Creek, near Billings, in the Montana Territory. Colonel Samuel D. Sturgis, with six troops of Custer's rebuilt 7th Cavalry, followed by Merritt's regiment, joined up to attack the Nez Perce. Sturgis lost 2 men killed and 11 were wounded.[89] Sturgis vowed to continue his pursuit of the Nez Perce despite his losses.

However, according to historian Lavender, the Nez Perce did not even consider the Canyon Creek encounter a battle. No warriors were killed and only three were slightly wounded. Lavender states that the Nez Perce "abandoned thirty or forty lame and exhausted animals that they might otherwise have tried to bring along."[90]

Contrary to the *Bee*'s claim that the Indians were driven from the field, a report in the *Republican* stated it was Sturgis who was successfully held at bay by the Nez Perce rearguard while the rest of the tribe continued north. Sturgis was forced to stop and rest. "We have just had a hard fight with the Nez Perce, lasting all day. We killed and wounded a good many and captured several hundred head of stock. Reports are not in yet, and cannot say what our loss is, but it is considerable—several killed, good many wounded—nothing to eat for two days; marched sixty miles to strike the horses and our horses are worn out."[91]

After weeks of flight and relentless pursuit, the Nez Perce were weary. A series of easy victories by the Indians that Lavender called "psychologically unfortunate,"[92] combined with the Indians' exhaustion, made them succumb to advice that they should slow down. The Indians were sure they had left all the soldiers far behind. Lean Elk, war chief of the Nez Perce, wanted the people to continue north at a quick pace because Canada and refuge with the Sioux was close. Looking Glass, who had just recently been deposed as war chief, argued that the people needed rest. His eloquent arguments overpowered Chief Joseph and the majority of the council. They were reluctant to stop but they knew the people were very tired. The Nez Perce slowed the pace of their march. Near the Bear Paw Mountains, just 42 miles from the Canadian border, they stopped to rest and prepare a feast of buffalo meat.[93] After nearly 1,700 miles, they stopped less than 50 miles from the Canadian border and safety.

It was a fatal mistake. Unbeknownst to the Indians, Colonel Nelson A. Miles had crossed the Missouri River and was approaching them from the southeast. Miles's biggest fear was that the Nez Perce would link up with Sitting Bull and his Sioux. The Sioux were still conducting occasional hunting forays into Montana Territory because Canada lacked sufficient game to feed Sitting Bull's band. The government feared that the Sioux would unite enough unhappy tribesmen from other tribes to form a confederation that could pose a serious challenge to the army. Miles was determined to catch Joseph and the Nez Perce before they could form an alliance with Sitting Bull.[94]

There was speculation that the Nez Perce had already joined Sitting Bull. The *Bee* stated that "Jaunting Joseph" was beyond the control of the U.S. government and had "skipped" across the Canadian border with a large number of horses.[95]

The *Bee* also reported that it was "probable they have ere this joined Sitting Bull." It added, "Gen. Sheridan thinks Joseph has probably escaped to the British territory by this time. . . . The general believes that Howard and Sturgis have probably done the very best they could. He said it has simply been a race, and to use his own words, "When it comes to a race for life, the fellow who is being pursued can always go a little to the fastest."[96]

General Miles's Sioux and Cheyenne scouts found the Nez Perce camp on the morning of September 30, 1877. Despite having been victimized by surprise attacks in the past, once again the Nez Perce had failed to post sentries. A few hundred Nez Perce fled north immediately after the initial charge by the soldiers. The remainder of the Indians dug in on a ridge and began an effective return fire. After two unsuccessful charges against the Nez Perce, which cost him 53 dead or wounded soldiers, Miles realized his assault had failed. He decided to use his soldiers to lay siege to the Indian camp and hope that Sitting Bull would not appear with his warriors before reinforcements could arrive from Sturgis and Howard.[97]

The first report of the battle, in the Omaha newspapers, appeared in the October 8, 1877, edition of the *Bee*:

> The enemy were met and surprised in camp on the 30th ult., and Miles's force captured the larger part of their herd, about 600 horses, mules and ponies. The engagement was quite severe, the Indians losing 17 killed, including Looking Glass and Joseph's brother [Ollokot], three other chiefs and forty wounded. Gen Miles says that this band fights with more desperation than any other Indians that he has ever met, and he believes there is a communication between this camp and Sitting Bull, and he has used every effort to prevent a junction.[98]

According to historian Lavender, Miles was in real danger of being defeated by the Nez Perce, just as Howard and Sturgis had been before him. He had suffered heavy casualties in his attack on the camp and now had to sit back and wait for help.[99] However, in a letter from Miles to General Alfred H. Terry, published in the *Republican,* Miles sounded a confident note: "Dear Friend: We have had our usual success. We made a very direct and rapid march across the country, and after a severe engagement and being kept under fire for three days, the hostile camp of the Nez Perces, under Chief Joseph, surrendered at 2 o'clock today."[100]

Miles need not have worried about Sitting Bull. Although Joseph sent a message to the Sioux chief asking for aid, the latter did not supply it or even answer the message. At one point, Miles seized Joseph under a flag of truce but had to exchange him for one of his own lieutenants who had wandered too close to the Nez Perce lines. After a five-day siege and several parleys, Joseph asked to meet with the soldiers. He surrendered his rifle to Miles and shook the hand of General Howard, who had just arrived on the scene. Of the approximately 800 Nez Perce that had started on this flight of 1,700 miles, 120 had been killed during the journey, another 300 had slipped north to Canada to join Sitting Bull, and the remaining 400 surrendered with Joseph.[101]

The *Bee* called it the "first victory over the redskins in the past two years." It reported that while Joseph and his 60 remaining warriors surrendered their arms to Miles, 40 more disabled warriors were forced to remain behind in the rifle pits but were later taken to the army doctors for medical attention. The paper added, "When the history of the unparalleled march of the Nez Perce is written, they will be accredited with great gallantry in the field and a wonderful humanity. Their defense cannot have been excelled by any body of men nor their generosity; seven wounded men lying under the entrenchments during the entire battle live to corroborate this. They took away the guns and ammunition from the disabled troops but did not offer to molest them."[102]

The *Boulder News* wrote that Joseph had offered to surrender four times but each time with conditions. It was only when he agreed to an unconditional surrender that Miles accepted his offer. "Joseph raised the flag and advanced to the front of the line and shook hands with him [Miles] . . . . The glory of the fight rests with Miles."[103]

In an editorial printed in the same edition as the wire story about the surrender, the *Bee* added its own voice to the praise that was being heaped on Joseph and the Nez Perce. It claimed that "It was only by doubling teams on Joseph that he was at last captured, for he has proven himself more than a match for an equal number of soldiers." The paper added "The Great Father may make up his mind at once that he will have to feed, and well feed too, all his red children of the North this generation and the next. But it will be cheaper to wear their stomachs out with nick-knacks than to perforate their digestive organs with bullets."[104]

The *Daily Herald* also weighed in with its opinion of the Nez Perce campaign and the performance of Colonel Nelson A. Miles: "Gen. Miles telegraphs that he has captured Joseph and his band. Does that mean a 'star' on the shoulders of one more brigadier! The dispatch of Col. Miles is marked by the modesty of a soldier evidently conscious of his exploits and of the energy of a pursuit that made it possible. Now let the government persecute the brave Indian who was hunted down by the mercenaries of a Christian nation. Let it be consistent in its iniquities towards a perishing people, whose heroism in the face of a dreadful fate has not been less conspicuous than that which finds them the bravest of the brave in war."[105]

The *Colorado Miner,* in a sly reference to the distance the Nez Perce had traveled and a tribute to their conqueror, composed a brief rhyme—"Song of Chief Joseph":—Miles I have travelled—many miles more, but the last Miles of my jour ney, I couldn't quite get 'oer."[106]

The war was over. The chase was done. All that remained was the creation of the myth of Chief Joseph. The simple eloquence of his oft-quoted surrender speech was the crowning piece: "I am tired of fighting. Our chiefs are killed. Looking Glass is dead. . . . It is cold and we have no blankets. The little children are freezing to death. I want to have time to look for my children and see how many of them I can find. Perhaps I will find them among the dead. Hear me my chiefs, my heart is sick and sad. From where the sun now stands, I will fight no more forever."[107]

Ironically, according to historian Lavender, it was a speech written by Lieutenant Charles Erskine Scott Wood. Wood wanted more drama and pathos in the surrender speech, so he took the bones of Chief Joseph's words and fleshed them out with his own. When Wood and General Howard were interviewed by a reporter in Bismarck, Dakota Territory, Wood had his version of the speech completed and almost certainly handed a written copy of the speech to the reporter. It first appeared in the *Bismarck Tri-Weekly Tribune* on October 26, 1877. Shortly after Wood and Howard arrived in Chicago, a news story on the "Bible Chief" by the *Chicago Tribune* also included a copy of the surrender speech. Soon *Harper's Weekly* and other newspapers across the country reprinted the speech and it passed into legend.[108]

The military leaders and the frontier press portrayed Joseph as a brilliant tactician and war chief. In actuality he was neither. He was a "camp chief" and was in charge of making sure that the camp was properly organized while it was moving from place to place. While not a military position, this certainly involved no easy task during a fighting retreat of 1,700 miles. However, Lavender states that General Howard failed to understand this distinction, and being a warrior himself, tried to make a war chief out of Joseph. Howard was not content to make Joseph an ordinary war chief, he made him an exalted kind of war chief that never existed among the Native Americans. The press and others were also unable to understand this distinction and so, before the war was ended, Joseph had attained legendary proportions.[109]

Even the legendary Joseph was not immune from the portrayal of the Indian as savage. The *Bee,* which would praise Joseph at the end of the Nez Perce war, initially called him "arrogant and insulting."[110] The *Daily Herald* used headlines such as "Slaughtering the Innocents," and "The Wandering Joseph and His Followers Murdering Settlers by the Dozen."[111] It called the Indians, "red-handed plunderers and murderous."[112] The *Republican* reported in a headline that, "Joseph and the Other Hostile Chiefs Again Commence Their Bloody Work."[113]

It was not until the end of the campaign that the stereotype of the "noble savage" became prominent and subsequently was most often used to describe the Nez Perce, and particularly Joseph. The *Bee* praised the fighting skills of Joseph and the Nez Perce when it stated that they had proven themselves more than a match for an equal number of soldiers and were defeated only by "doubling teams" on them. It added that the history of their "unparalleled march" would feature the "gallantry in the field and wonderful humanity" of the Nez Perce. The *Daily Herald* echoed those sentiments when they described Joseph as a "brave Indian hunted down by the mercenaries of a Christian nation" and the Nez Perce as "a perishing people, whose heroism in the face of a dreadful fate has not been less conspicuous than that which finds them the bravest of brave in war."[114] In addition, the forced removal of the Nez Perce to their new reservation, which had not elicited journalistic cries of outrage when it first occurred, was now the focus of many stories justifying the resistance of the Nez Perce.

When Joseph surrendered, he was told that he and his people would be sent back to the Nez Perce reservation in Idaho. Instead, they were sent to Oklahoma.

In 1885, two bands of the Nez Perce were allowed to return to the Pacific Northwest. One band was permitted to return to their former reservation in Idaho. The other group, led by Joseph, was forced to settle on the Colville Indian Reservation in northern Washington State. Joseph died there in 1904. He was never allowed to return to his beloved Wallowa valley.[115]

CHAPTER 6

❧

The Cheyenne Outbreak:
September 1878–January 1879

It had been a year since the great victory of the Sioux, Cheyenne, and Arapahoe at Little Big Horn. It was a year when everything changed.

The army was out in force and had hounded the starving remnants of the Sioux and Cheyenne into flight or surrender. Sitting Bull chose flight and had taken his people north into Canada, the "Grandmother's Country." After a cold and desperate winter, Crazy Horse surrendered at Camp Robinson in northwest Nebraska in the spring of 1877. Several bands of Cheyenne, including those led by Chiefs Little Wolf and Dull Knife, joined Crazy Horse in his surrender.

The Cheyenne were certain they would be given a reservation in their northern homeland. They did not know that this visit to Camp Robinson would not be their last.

They expected to live on the Sioux reservation in accordance with the Fort Laramie Treaty of 1868. Instead, they were sent to Indian Territory [present-day Oklahoma] because of a little-known clause in the treaty specifying that the Northern Cheyenne could also be sent to join the Southern Cheyenne. When the Northern Cheyenne left Camp Robinson, they numbered 972 men, women, and children; but when they reached Oklahoma in August 1877, only 937 remained. Some of the old people had died on the journey and some of the young men had slipped away and headed back north to the land they knew and loved.

The Northern Cheyenne did not adapt well to Indian Territory. They were forced to move from the cool, dry, high country of the Montana and Dakota Territories to the hot and humid south, where they would be susceptible to fevers and shaking chills. Matters were made worse by the lack of food. There was little wild game, and the agency beef provided for them was skin and bones. The people began to wither and die; the old and the very young died first. Colonel Ranald S. MacKenzie wrote to General Phil Sheridan that the government was starving the

Indians in direct violation of the 1868 treaty it had signed. By 1878, the Indian agent for the Northern Cheyenne described the tribe in a government report by saying, "They have lived and that is about all."[1] Some did not do even that; 41 died the first winter.

A Cheyenne warrior named Wild Hog, in an interview with the *New York Herald,* said "They gave us cornmeal ground with the cob such as a man feeds his mules, some salt and one beef for forty-six persons to last for seven days. We ate it in three and starved on four days."[2]

The Cheyenne were unhappy with the government's Indian policy, so a council was arranged with General Nelson A. Miles and the agent for the Cheyenne, John D. Miles. Little Wolf acted as spokesman and asked that the Northern Cheyenne be permitted to return to their traditional homes in the northern plains. He said his people were dying every day. If they waited another year as their agent wanted, they would all be dead. He said he feared there would be no one left to speak their names when they were gone.

Agent Miles, following orders from Washington, refused to let them leave. For the Cheyenne it was a simple choice. Stay in Indian Territory and starve or head north to the land they knew, the land in which they had lived for generations. Some, fearing the journey, decided to stay. When dawn broke on September 10, 1878, a total of 297 Cheyenne men, women, and children, less than one-third of them warriors, headed north with Little Wolf and Dull Knife.

Agent Miles wired army headquarters that the Cheyenne were gone and heading north. Troops began to mobilize while the frontier newspapers assured their readers that there was nothing to worry about. Both the *Omaha Herald* and the *Omaha Republican* carried a brief wire story that said, "it is learned that the renegade Cheyenne will be captured. They have been arrested by our troops at a point about twenty miles distant from the fort [Camp Supply, Indian Territory]."[3] The newspaper account was unduly optimistic. In fact, the Cheyenne under Dull Knife were not captured until over a month later, and more than 100 miles farther north. Those under Little Wolf eluded capture for several additional months.

Keeping to the countryside and traveling mostly by night, the Cheyenne fled northward across Indian Territory. The first encounter between the escaping Cheyenne and the army occurred shortly after the Indians crossed the Cimarron River near the southern border of Kansas. The Cheyenne scouts kept an eye on the advancing soldiers while the rest of the tribe dug rifle pits for the warriors. The unsuspecting soldiers advanced into firing range and the Indians trapped them in crossfire. The Cheyenne warriors sniped at the soldiers for most of the day, pinning them down, while the women and children continued to move steadily northward.

The *Wichita Beacon* romanticized the encounter. "The officer in command before the fight twice demanded their surrender, but the savages replied that they had come back to have a fight and they were hungry for it."[4]

The progress of the Cheyenne through western Kansas started a panic among the area settlers. The *Herald* reported that there had been rumors that the Indians were burning houses near Dodge City. However, the paper expressed confidence that the Indians would be "corralled" quickly and stated, "there is no danger of any real problem."[5]

Initially, the Cheyenne outbreak was viewed as an isolated instance that posed no real danger to peace on the frontier. While many people felt that it was unfortunate, they also believed it would soon be over and would serve as another damning illustration of the failure of the government's Indian policy.

The *Herald* bemoaned the fact that this "single Indian scare" would cost "thousands of dollars" and added that these conflicts "make the borderline between civilization and barbarism a scene of carnage and a cause of irritation and anxiety to the entire country." They held the government responsible, claiming, "These wards of the nation have been subjected to plunder, rapine, murder and whatever abuse a dominant and unprincipled race was pleased to inflict upon them. . . . The faults lie with its [the government's] creatures, which it does not punish or destroy, though corrupt in the extreme. It is not too much to say that the Indian ring is the most corrupt organization that this country has ever seen."

The paper went on to say that the regular army was simply a police force for the Indian Bureau. It added, "Then accounts of Indian depredations reach us, most of which are lies, and the troops are called upon to pursue and capture or destroy the treaty-breaking savages. After more or less effort, the Indians are quieted and returned to the parental care of the Indian Agent, until nearly dead with hunger and then the same old story is repeated. So it is now. So it has been in the last hundred years. . . . Criminal abuse will continue until the unfortunate victims of them pass away, leaving a blot on the history of their nation that time will never obliterate."[6]

So far, any damage inflicted by the Cheyenne had been limited to military casualties. In fact the *Dodge City Times,* fearful that the news of the Cheyenne's journey would panic settlers, proclaimed the whole thing a hoax.[7] That would all change when the Cheyenne passed through the Sappa Valley in northwestern Kansas.

The *Omaha Bee* reported that the Cheyenne, moving across the Sappa and Beaver Creek valleys, had "murdered every man they came across who was unarmed."[8] It described the Cheyenne as "Mounted Murderers" and claimed the " 'Noble Reds' are Gathering Scalps and Stock by the Hundred," and that the settlers were fleeing their homes for places of safety. It reported that 60 people were killed, with 17 bodies already found. It added that all those killed so far had been men except for one woman and one child, and that the Indians did not seem to be going out of their way to kill settlers but were simply killing everyone who crossed their path.[9] The *Bee* expressed its hope that "every one of these warriors big enough to raise a gun or draw a bow will be killed by the troops now awaiting them along the line of the Union Pacific."[10]

The Kansas newspapers echoed the *Bee*'s call for revenge. The *Dodge City Times* wrote, "It is about time that the Border States and territories took a contract for missionary work, in which a few companies of frontiersmen should civilize or exterminate Government pets." It also took this opportunity to aim a blow at the eastern press, charging, "Every day or two we read accounts of how some phil-anthropic . . . ass in Boston or New York dishes up a lot of slush concerning the nobility of the savages."[11]

According to Mari Sandoz, in her book *Cheyenne Autumn,* the Cheyenne killed 19 men during their raid in northwest Kansas. Sandoz claimed they were under express orders from Little Wolf to avoid killing women or children. She added that the Indians were avenging a brutal massacre of the Cheyenne that had oc-curred in the Sappa Valley three years earlier in 1875.[12]

The Cheyenne were now over 100 miles north of their reservation. With the exception of the killings in the Sappa Valley, they had encountered few civilians or soldiers. No one was really sure where they were or what they planned to do. The *Herald* feared they would link up with the Sioux under Red Cloud and warned of the danger of a "general outbreak of the Northern tribes."[13] The *Herald* claimed that Red Cloud and Spotted Tail had actually taken their warriors out on the "warpath," and that a "universal Indian war" was now expected in the northern plains.[14] The *Republican* reported that Spotted Tail was heading north, possibly to circle around and join the Cheyenne. It added, "Some of the Indians still have Sitting Bull on their brain."[15]

It was all just newspaper speculation, designed to sell papers and inflame the populace. Spotted Tail and Red Cloud remained secure on their reservations. Whatever yearning they had to supply aid to the fleeing Cheyenne was tempered by the knowledge of the price they would pay for helping their friends.

In fact, the Cheyenne, rather than gaining allies, had actually split into two bands after they crossed the North Platte River in Nebraska. Little Wolf headed north to winter in the Niobrara River valley and Dull Knife and his band headed west toward Camp Robinson and the Red Cloud Agency.[16]

The editorial battle between two of Omaha's leading newspapers on the Chey-enne outbreak reflected the two conflicting views on the "Indian question." The *Bee* accused the *Herald* of assuming "the championship of the bloody scalpers who are murdering western settlers, ravishing their women, stealing their stock and burning their dwellings." It mocked its rival saying, "According to the *Herald,* these red-handed murderers are waging a holy and patriotic war for their homes, their families and their firesides."[17]

The *Bee* declared that contrary to the *Herald*'s claim that the Cheyenne left their reservation because they were starving, they were actually eating much better than if they were "still in the wild." It described the Indians as, "fat, sleek and wealthy," and claimed if the Indians were within reach of their reservation, bountiful sup-plies of beef and flour were available.[18] The source of the *Bee*'s information is unclear, but it is certain they were wrong. The testimony of the Indian's own agent refuted the *Bee*'s claim. In a contemporary government report, he had described the Cheyenne as "barely surviving."[19]

A wire story in the *Bee* illustrated the controversy on just who was ultimately responsible for the Cheyenne outbreak. The paper reported that the outbreak had been a topic of discussion at the latest cabinet meeting in Washington. According to the wire story, army officers claimed that the Cheyenne left because they were starving, while the Indian Bureau stated that the Indians were well fed and had no reason to "revolt." The army expected the Sioux to join the Cheyenne in raids on the Black Hills settlements, while the Indian Bureau believed that the only fighting the Sioux would do would be on behalf of the government as scouts against the Cheyenne.[20]

While the Omaha newspapers argued who was to blame for the Cheyenne outbreak, the Indians continued to move north. On October 23, 1878, the Cheyenne under Dull Knife were caught by an early snowstorm just two days away from Camp Robinson. As the Cheyenne halted to reconnoiter, spectral forms emerged from the swirling snow; it was a troop of cavalry under Captain John B. Johnson. The Cheyenne were surrounded and ordered by Captain Johnson to turn over their weapons and horses.[21] A few broken guns were turned over, along with bows and arrows. The Cheyenne's best guns were dismantled and hidden under the women's dresses, and springs, locks, pins and cartridges were attached to hair and clothing as decorations.[22]

The *Republican* reported the capture of the Cheyenne under Dull Knife, but the wire story included some inaccurate details. It claimed that when the Cheyenne learned their destination was Camp Robinson, they refused to go and "scattered over the prairie and commenced digging rifle pits with their hunting knives." The paper added that artillery had been sent for to shell the Indians if they refused to surrender. It concluded, "Considerable excitement prevails here over the anticipated trouble."[23] In fact, there was no trouble. No rifle pits were dug. No artillery was called up. The weary Cheyenne, resigned to their fate, surrendered peacefully.

Little Wolf and his band were huddled near their fires in the Niobrara River valley when scouts reported the news that Dull Knife and his people had been captured and taken to Camp Robinson. Little Wolf now felt it was more important than ever to remain free so as to ensure that the Northern Cheyenne people would survive.[24]

At Camp Robinson, Dull Knife and his people were placed in old barracks. Red Cloud, of the Sioux, came to visit them and lamented that he could not shelter them and no longer had the power to protect them. He was a virtual prisoner on his own reservation.[25] The fate of the Cheyenne was left to the inexperienced hands of Captain Henry W. Wessells, the recently appointed commander of Camp Robinson.

Dull Knife met with Wessells and told him that he and his people wished only to end their days here in the North Country where they were born and where their fathers were buried. They could not live in the south; there was no game and their people sickened and died in that hot climate. He asked Wessells to tell the "Great Father" that if they were allowed to stay, they would promise to hurt no one. Dull Knife added, "if he tries to send us back, we will butcher each other with our own knives."[26]

Wessells promised to relay the message, but on January 3, 1879, he received orders from General Phil Sheridan to send the Cheyenne back to Oklahoma. Both Sheridan and Secretary Schurz felt that to allow the Cheyenne to stay would be to invite other tribes to flee their reservations for their homelands. They feared it would be a shock that could endanger the entire reservation system.[27] The Cheyenne were ordered to return immediately to Oklahoma, despite the winter weather. When he was told of the decision, Dull Knife asked Wessells if the "Great Father" wanted them to die. If so they would die right here. They would not go back.

Wild Hog, a subchief of the Cheyenne, argued with the soldiers, and Wessells ordered him to be put in irons and locked up. Wild Hog was wounded in a struggle during the arrest and he, in turn, stabbed one of the soldiers.[28] Wessells then gave the Cheyenne five days to change their minds. They would be given no food, water, or wood for their stove until they agreed to go back.

For five days the Indians huddled in their frigid barracks. They scraped freshly fallen snow from the windowsills to melt for drinking water. Their only food was the scraps left from previous meals.[29] The *Herald* used a wire service story to report that the Cheyenne had grown sullen and repeatedly expressed a desire to die before they would return south. It added that a guard had been posted on their barracks.[30] Dull Knife realized that his people could not hold on much longer, but he also knew they would never agree to return to Indian Territory.

In the darkened barracks the women began to remove the dismantled guns from where they had hidden them under the barracks floorboards. They removed the firing pins, springs and locks from their clothing and hair and reassembled their few remaining rifles and pistols. On the dark night of January 9, 1879, the Cheyenne burst through the boarded windows of their barracks and started a mad dash for freedom across the frozen parade ground of Camp Robinson.

The *Herald* described the scene vividly:

> the savages jumped through the windows of the prison room and made for the cold prairie, which is thickly coated with frozen snow, firing on the guards with revolvers they had concealed since their capture. . . . The main guard rushed out of the guardhouse on hearing the firing. . . . and opened fire and shot and killed over forty savages. Over one hundred and sixty of the cavalry, mounted and dismounted, are still in pursuit of the fleeing savages. The sharp bang of the carbines in the hands of our men can be heard from the hills three miles distant, where the savages have evidently made for. It is thought not one of them will escape.[31]

The *Bee* reported the same basic story but added some details, such as the Indians using floorboards that they had pried loose as makeshift clubs in their escape attempt, and that "the troops are in pursuit of the retreating savages, killing them without mercy." It also reported that Dull Knife was among the dead, having been shot in the head.[32] The *Omaha Herald* disputed the report of Dull Knife's death and reported instead that he was among the 34 Indians, 15 of whom were warriors, who remained at large. The *Herald* was right. Dull Knife had survived the initial skirmish. In fact, Dull Knife lived for several more years, not dying until 1883. The *Herald* added that 37 Indians, almost all women and children, had been recaptured, and 30 Indians had been killed, including 2 children and 8 women.[33]

The main body of Indians did not get far before they were caught and surrounded. Attempts were made to get them to surrender. The *Republican* reported that they were "stubbornly refusing," so a 12-pound Napoleon gun was brought up to help convince them. In the face of this terrifying weapon, the group surrendered. Now only a few small scattered bands remained free. The Republican stated, "It is now authentically reported the number of Indians killed is forty, fifteen wounded and from forty to fifty recaptured."[34]

A correspondent for the *New York Herald* reported "Volley after volley was poured into the fleeing [Cheyenne] and as earnestly returned by the Indians who sped toward the sawmill which lies south[east] and their bleeding bodies, mangled and torn, bucks, squaws and papooses all together, literally strewed the road they had selected for their much hoped for deliverance."[35]

According to the *New York Herald*'s correspondent, some of the wounded Cheyenne were murdered by the soldiers, "aroused to the highest pitch of exasperation." He described the killings as an aftermath of the flight. "And where the first shot did not dispose of the victim, a coup de grace was readily given by final pistol charge."[36]

Editorials commenting on the Cheyenne's fatal flight quickly followed the news stories on the event. The *Herald* called it, "the end of one of the most barbarous and bloody tragedies to be found in the annals of any country pretending to be Christian and civilized." It added that many people begged Secretary Schurz to allow the Cheyenne to stay in the North. He was told they preferred death to returning South:

> But it was all in vain. The Cheyenne must go back to the graveyard Prepared for them in Indian Territory. . . . It drove them to despair. . . . True to their heroic nature, they acted upon their solemn resolutions to perish rather than submit to the slower tortures of the most monstrous and infamous of the rules by which the strong ever oppressed the weak. The result is before us. Wholesale murder is a mild phrase in which to describe the atrocious tragedy.
>
> "None will escape," say the dispatches. Thank God for that! It is a mercy to kill the last Cheyenne, and let Carl Schurz have all the glory of it. He invited the slaughter, and it has come as a red and burning shame upon our country. Let the Secretary of the Interior contemplate the bloody fruit of the indifference to the demands of humanity and justice as he puts the last touches on his rejoinder to [General Philip] Sheridan, and let the country see by the light of the

long tragedy that ended in the wholesale slaughter at Camp Robinson, what a beautiful thing it is to have an Indian Bureau in this country.[37]

If it had followed the pattern of coverage it had established in earlier stories about the Cheyenne Outbreak, the *Bee* would have been expected to come out in support of the course the army had taken. Instead, it castigated Captain Wessells and the civilian officials who it felt had created the tragedy.

The *Bee* wrote, "Many people in this section think a dead Indian is a good Indian. This class will doubtless suffer no pangs of regret at the wholesale slaughter of the Cheyenne who were endeavoring to escape Camp Robinson."[38] It went on to mock Wessells' decision to refuse food, water, and fuel to the Indians for five days in order to get them to acquiesce, all because he did not want to resort to force.

According to the *Herald,* Captain Wessells should not be held responsible for the "slaughter" of the Cheyenne. It stated that no one wanted to avert bloodshed more than he, but he was forced "to do his duty" no matter how much he might deplore it. It added that the escape took place at night, so it was difficult to ascertain the sex or the age of the fleeing individuals. The *Herald* initially placed all the blame for the incident on the Indian Bureau. "The Indian Bureau is the author and actual perpetrator of this cold-blooded massacre and it cannot escape its terrible responsibility. . . . The eyes of the people of the country are no longer so blinded to the main cause of Indian war and atrocity, and the Camp Robinson tragedy will prove only one more bloody record of the crimes committed by the organized band of robbers who compose the Indian Bureau."[39]

An interview with General Philip Sheridan by the *Chicago Inter-Ocean* was carried in the *Bee.* It asked Sheridan for his comments on newspaper criticism of the soldiers' killing of Cheyenne women. He responded that the women had revolvers hidden on their persons and the soldiers were reluctant to search them thoroughly. In addition, the Indian women were known to be adept at the use of revolvers and were therefore as dangerous as the men. Sheridan, continuing in a cold-blooded manner, added, "Of course the soldiers had to do their duty, and the women were in the way. If any of them were killed, they were killed accidentally—the soldiers could not have done otherwise. They could not help what they did, though everybody regrets the necessity."[40]

The *Herald* called for a thorough investigation of the Cheyenne incident, pointing out that the temperature was 30 degrees below zero during the night the Cheyenne had fled Camp Robinson, and the Indians were wearing only the clothes they had brought with them from Indian Territory months earlier. It claimed that all of this was known to the military authorities, who had not sent new clothes for the Indians even though they were being forced to travel in the dead of winter. It called for the investigation to start with General George Crook, commander of the Department of the Platte, to explain exactly what he knew about the incident. That way the important facts would be forthcoming sooner than any other way.[41]

While the Omaha newspapers were editorializing about the causes and effects of the massacre of the Cheyenne at Camp Robinson, Dull Knife and a handful of survivors were still hurrying through the hills of Northwest Nebraska. The *Herald* warned of the possibility of a general Indian war if the surviving Cheyenne linked up with Red Cloud's Sioux.[42] The *Republican* echoed the warning of the *Herald* and stated that "The prevalent impression here is that we are near the eve of a bloody Indian war."[43] Perhaps this fear of a general uprising was sincere on the part of the two papers. However, it revealed a complete lack of understanding of the status of the Sioux under Red Cloud. Although only two years removed from their triumph at the Little Big Horn, everything was forever changed. They had neither the power nor the inclination to wage all-out war on the whites ever again. Except for the brief, tragic events still to come at Wounded Knee, their armed struggle against the whites was done.

In a wire story headlined "The Subtle Savage," the *Bee* described the pursuit of the fleeing Cheyenne. It related an incident in which the Cheyenne escaped from the encircling troops in a way that was "worthy of a Fenimore Cooper Indian romance." The Indians were trapped in a ravine. Guards were posted at regular intervals all around the ravine and the army waited for the coming dawn to round up the few surviving Indians:

> In the face of all these precautions, the savages vacated the ravine during the night. They could only have done so by working their way in a snake like and sinuous manner, and conducting their exit so noiselessly as not to arouse the vigilance of sentinels posted within at least fifty yards of each other. The manner in which the plucky savages accomplished this almost incredible feat of wood-craft and valor has called forth the warmest admiration of even their pursuers, and many are almost tempted to say that they hope they will effect their final escape.[44]

They did not escape. Dull Knife and five other Cheyenne were recaptured within six miles of Camp Robinson, leaving only one small remnant of 32 Cheyenne still free. Within days, they too were surrounded. When the soldiers approached the Indians' defensive position, they were met with a withering fire, which killed three soldiers and wounded several others. Eventually the Indians ran out of ammunition and, armed only with knives, charged the soldiers. The desperate Cheyenne were met with bullets; when the smoke had cleared, only nine Indians remained alive, and six of them were wounded.[45]

Now all that remained was to determine what to do with the survivors. Their tragic flight from Camp Robinson had earned them the sympathy of many Americans. A front-page article in the *Bee* suggested that the government's plan was to make the Indians hungry with poor rations and then destroy them. It added that the "expiring remnants of the red race" were to be "stuffed with Simon pure civilization." Yet the *Bee* had no sympathy for the Indians who continued to oppose the encroachment of civilization. It stated that the "unruly tribes and lawless plunderers [are] only fit for bullets, sabers and hempen cords."[46]

The *Herald* favored transferring the responsibility for the Indians from the Indian Bureau to the army, but it had some concerns, particularly with Generals Sherman and Sheridan. "The bloody-minded Sherman, and the shoot-em-down Sheridan, who say openly that Indians have no rights, are doing much to defeat the transfer of the red men to the Army. We favored this transfer originally because we thought the Indians would get fair treatment at the hands of the Army, and we favor it now because no change could be for the worse. But we shall not be as much grieved if the whole effort at transfer collapses as we should have before seeing the outgivings of a pair of generals who delight in bloodshed and mock at the slaughter of innocents."[47]

The *Herald* made its opinion clear on the Cheyenne outbreak in a brief editorial in late January of 1879. It stated that posterity would forget neither the Cheyenne nor those who brought about their downfall; it reported that it was probable they would "go down to future generations together—the one immortal from having made a gallant fight for what they believed to be their rights; and the other for having hounded to destruction a heroic remnant whose chief fault was their unwillingness to submit to death by starvation."[48] It added: "So far as the Cheyenne are concerned, they have had the best of it. They have preferred to die as men rather than to be starved or hanged like dogs. When posterity comes to make up its judgment on the entire occurrence, it cannot be doubted that the infamy connected with the slaughter of these people will fall on the nation whose treachery to an inferior race was the original cause of the outbreak, and the responsible agent for its consequences."[49]

It is not certain that all the Cheyenne would have agreed with the *Herald* that they had had "the best of it." In a tragic postscript to the story of Dull Knife's band, Wild Hog, who had been locked up in the guardhouse with leg irons and handcuffs the day before the Cheyenne broke out of Camp Robinson, met his wife when she returned to the fort with other survivors of the massacre. She told him that their son had been killed. Later, while grieving in his prison cell, Wild Hog managed to stab himself in the chest four times, despite his manacles.[50] Still he did not die of his wounds. He died a year later from the effects of a bout with pneumonia.[51]

After many months of delay, because of the outpouring of public sympathy, the few survivors from Dull Knife's band joined Little Wolf's band at a newly created reservation on the Tongue River in Montana Territory.

At long last they were home.

CHAPTER 7

❧

The Standing Bear Trial:
April–May 1879

*I*t was a court case that began with the last request of a dying son and ended with a groundbreaking legal decision. In between, Standing Bear of the Ponca became an unlikely hero. Playing an integral role in this legal case were the frontier newspapers of Omaha, Nebraska.

The Ponca were native to the Niobrara and Missouri River valleys of northeastern Nebraska. Unfortunately for them, the Fort Laramie Treaty of 1868 promised their reservation land to the Lakota Sioux. The Ponca protested to the government again and again, but to no avail. To make matters worse, the young men of the Sioux visited the Ponca and demanded horses as tribute and harassed them in other ways. In the hysteria following the Battle of the Little Big Horn in 1876, the Ponca were selected, along with several other northern tribes, to be exiled to Indian Territory. Even though the Ponca had no involvement in the Battle of the Little Big Horn, they too were suffering the consequences of Custer's defeat.[1] The government found it easier to send a small, peaceful band of Indians south rather than risk further trouble with the aggressive Sioux.

The Ponca first learned of their imminent removal when U.S. Indian Inspector Edward C. Kemble visited them in January 1877. Standing Bear, White Eagle, Big Elk, and some other Ponca chiefs were told that they should visit the Indian Territory and see the land selected for them. Kemble said if they saw land they liked they were to inform the "Great White Father," and if they saw land they did not like, they were to let that be known as well. After visiting Indian Territory, the chiefs rejected the land as being barren, full of rocks, and unsuitable for farming. They asked to see the Great White Father as promised, but Kemble refused. They then asked to be given some money so they could return home. Kemble refused again and the Indians, equipped with one pair of moccasins and one blanket each, walked through the winter-shrouded land over 500 miles back to Nebraska.

When they arrived home, Kemble was waiting and told them that they would have to go to Indian Territory or suffer the consequences of forced removal. He was able to convince 170 members to go south with him, but the majority refused to leave.

On May 21, 1877, soldiers came to the Ponca camp and forced the remaining Indians to begin the journey south. Their farms and tools were taken away and they were left with only what they could carry or transport in a few wagons. The *Omaha Bee* reported that the stories circulating that the Ponca would rather die than leave their homeland were untrue:

> The Major [T. S. Clarkson] says he apprehends that the Poncas will make no forcible resistance to their removal. Their change of location has been decided upon by the government, and they will have to go. To be sure, they don't relish the idea of giving up their old reservation. For more than two hundred years they have lived on the lands they now occupy on the Missouri. They look upon their present reservation as their only home and are exceedingly loath to leave it for a new location, one which they now have no positive assurance that they will like or that will be adapted to their tastes and wants. But the Indian can see . . . it will avail him nothing to declare war rather than be removed, for the result would be punishment visited upon himself and his ultimate removal all the same.[2]

The Indian Territory was being called the "red man's sacred soil" by the *Omaha Republican.*[3] The paper reported that the last of the Ponca had been sent to Oklahoma, "with their consent, from their reservation in northeast Nebraska. The tribe is now reduced to about 700, and are a very peaceable and quiet people who have made considerable advancement in civilization."[4]

The Ponca were not moved with their "consent," and many died en route, including Standing Bear's daughter, Prairie Flower. Within a year of their arrival to the Quapaw reservation in Indian Territory, the Ponca lost almost one-fourth of their tribe to starvation and disease. Historian Joe Starita quotes Standing Bear as saying, "The water was bad, and the ground was bad. Everything was strange. A great many of our people were sick."[5]

In the spring of 1878, the Indians were removed to a better site 150 miles away on the west bank of the Arkansas River, but the government neglected to give them provisions or assign an agent to them, and more sickened and died. By the end of that year, only 430 of the 710 Poncas who had been sent to the Indian Territory were still alive. One of the last to die was Standing Bear's 16-year-old son, Bear Shield. His last request was that his body be taken back to the Niobrara and buried with those of his ancestors. Standing Bear promised, and in January of 1879, he and 29 of his people headed north as a burial party. They traveled by trails that avoided towns and forts and reached the Omaha Indian reservation before soldiers caught up with them.[6]

Secretary of the Interior Carl Schurz telegraphed General George Crook and ordered him to arrest the Ponca and return them to their reservation in Indian Territory. Crook sent a company of soldiers to the Omaha Reservation and brought Standing Bear and the other Ponca back to Fort Omaha to await arrangements for their transfer back to Indian Territory. When he saw the Ponca, Crook was saddened by their pitiable condition and impressed with their stoicism. He contacted Thomas Henry Tibbles, an assistant editor of the *Omaha Herald,* and enlisted his help.[7] Crook believed that Schurz's order was cruel but felt powerless to do anything about it himself. He encouraged Tibbles to use his newspaper to "fight against those who are robbing these helpless people." He added, "The American people, if they knew half the truth, would send every member of the Indian Ring to prison."[8]

Tibbles was an appropriate ally for General Crook. He had joined abolitionist John Brown on a raid into Missouri to free slaves and had lived for a while with a band of Omaha Indians. He used that experience as the basis for a lecture tour that later helped finance his college tuition. He served as a journalist and scout with the Union forces in the Civil War and traveled as a circuit-riding Methodist minister in Missouri and Nebraska. He later joined the *Herald* and by 1879 had risen to assistant editor.[9]

Tibbles walked the four miles from the *Herald* to Fort Omaha and met with the Poncas. He then enlisted the aid of local churches in an appeal to the government to allow the Poncas to stay on the reservation of the Omaha Indians.[10] Tibbles's employer, the *Herald,* fired the opening salvo in a war of words with its three-column story in the April 1, 1879, edition. It quoted Ta-zha-but, a Ponca who had returned to Nebraska with Standing Bear, from a speech he had made at a hastily called Indian council:

> I sometimes think that the white people forget that we are human, that we love our wives and children, that we require food and clothing, that we must take care of our sick, our women and children, prepare not only for the winters as they come, but for old age when we can no longer do as when we are young. But one father made us all. We have hands and feet and hearts all alike. We also are men. Look at me. Am I not a man? I am poor. These clothes are ragged. I have no others. But I am a man! . . . I was living peaceably with all men. I have never committed any crime. I was arrested and brought back as a prisoner. Does your law do that? I have been told since the great war [Civil War] that all men were free men, and that no man can be made prisoner unless he does wrong. I have done no wrong and yet I am here a prisoner. Have you a law for white men, and a different law for these who are not white?
>
> If we go back to the reservation in Kansas [sic], we shall have nothing to do, we must live on the government and will soon all die. There will not be one left of us to tell the tale. It would be better for the government, better for us, to stand us out there in a line, bring the soldiers and tell them to shoot us all. Then

our miseries would be ended and the government would have no more trouble. It would be better that way.[11]

The *Herald* also carried portions of the speech by Standing Bear in which he stated that his people had been sent to the Indian Territory without the means to support themselves; he noted that they were soon starving and sick and were ultimately forced to beg help from some of the surrounding tribes. "It was like a great house with a big fire in it, and everything was poison. We never saw such kind of sickness before. One hundred and fifty of our people have died, and more are dying every day. . . . My boy who died down there, as he was dying, looked up at me and said, I would like you to take my bones back to the Omaha agency and bury them where I was born. I promised him I would. I could not refuse the dying request of my boy."[12]

The *Herald* reported that Judge Elmer S. Dundy had granted an application for writ of habeas corpus. It added: "The Case is regarded by the legal fraternity as one of the most important ever brought in the United States courts, and it will undoubtedly attract the attention of the whole country. The Indian, wronged, oppressed, and robbed, as he has ever been since the whites landed on this continent, is at last to have his case presented in the courts by such able advocates as Hon. A.J. Poppleton and Hon. J.L. Webster, who have volunteered to plead his cause for him. Standing Bear's pathetic appeal for someone to help him has been answered."[13]

Standing Bear's lawyers were using the Fourteenth Amendment, enacted in July 1868, as the basis for their case to keep the Ponca in Nebraska. Tibbles stated that the amendment defined the right of any "person" in the United States to life, liberty, and property unless removed by due process of law.[14] *Habeas corpus* literally means "produce the body." The dictionary defines the writ as "Any of several common-law writs issued to bring a party before a court or a judge."[15] Poppleton and Webster were going to try and prove that Standing Bear and the Ponca were entitled to this protection under law. The government, represented by District Attorney G.M. Lambertson, would try to prove that the Indians had no rights.

Owing to Tibbles's influence, the *Herald* led the fight on behalf of the Ponca. It castigated Edward A. Hayt, Commissioner of Indian Affairs, for planning to have the writ of habeas corpus dismissed and for attempting to deny the Poncas benefit of counsel. It claimed that Hayt believed the Indians "may be accused of a crime, tried, sentenced and executed on an ex parte showing without the right to be defended."[16]

It added: "This Indian ring which has so long robbed, swindled and murdered the defenseless Indians, will find before this thing ends, that the people of this republic have made up their minds that this horrible cruelty must stop, and that the Indian has some rights which even Mr. Hayt must respect. The courts of this country will not give their sanction to the taking of a man from his plow and sending him to a pest-hole where certain death awaits him, who has committed no crime, and only asks to be allowed to dig from the ground a living for himself, his wife and his children. No, not even if his skin is somewhat tawny."[17]

The criticism of Commissioner Hayt and the "Indian ring" continued to be featured in the pages of the *Herald*. Criticism of the "Indian ring" was often a way to criticize alleged corruption by the Republican Party and was common practice of papers like the *Herald*, which favored the political views of the Democratic Party.

It chastised Hayt for declaring the Poncas could not hire lawyers unless he allowed it and advised Judge Dundy and defense lawyers Poppleton and Webster, to "see to it that the Washington upstart is properly rebuked for his insolence." It added, "Mr. Hayt says the Indians are "wards" of the country, and that, therefore they have no personal rights under the writ of *habeas corpus,* when, in fact, it is just such people, those who are weak and defenseless, for which the writ is specially intended and to whom it is always applied."[18]

Secretary of the Interior Schurz was also criticized by the *Herald*. He had stated that the Indians should be kept on reservations and out of the way of "bad white men who would excite or provoke them to acts of violence."[19] The *Herald* found this argument specious and called it "beautiful condescension." The newspaper considered the prevailing Indian policy to have been "a policy of murder and outrage for which civilized history has rarely furnished either precedent or parallel."[20] It felt confident the courts would soon relieve the "Indian ring" of "the trouble of discussing either the wisdom or non-wisdom of the 'policy' of dragging such people as Standing Bear and the Poncas from their homes and property as helpless victims of the hard and hellish power of gunpowder and the bayonet. If we mistake not, it will soon be a question of right and not of policy, that shall, in a judicial decree, unloose the grip of tyranny that clutches these unoffending red man by the throat to make them its very slaves; and the Washington managers and murderers of these red men do well when they begin to hail and hedge on the great question that is raised in the Ponca *habeas corpus* case."[21]

Journalist John M. Coward, in "Creating the Ideal Indian," wrote that to frontier America there were two kinds of Indians, "bad" Indians and "good" Indians. " 'Bad' Indians were traditional natives unwilling or unable to become civilized. 'Good' Indians, on the other hand, were Indians willing and able to give up savagery for civilization."[22] Coward stated that attitudes toward Indians were gradually moderating, and many newspapers, both east and west, were fairer in their coverage of Indians in the 1870s. He added, "Slowly but surely, some newspapers were coming to a more complex view of Indians: they might still be 'savage,' but there seemed to be new evidence that Indians could be civilized. By the late 1870s, the idea of the 'civilized savage' was turning up in the press with increasing frequency. It was an idea that Thomas Tibbles began to exploit on behalf of the Poncas."[23]

Reprinted articles supporting the *Herald*'s view on the Ponca question were frequently featured in the pages of the newspaper. Excerpts from the *New York Herald* favorably compared the Ponca to the "rascals" who were responsible for their incarceration. It stated, "In practice, however, the most degraded Ponca is worth more to the country than the whole breed of parasites alluded to, and the sympathies of the public will be almost entirely with the Indians and against the bureau." The *St. Louis Republican* wrote, "We have been so accustomed to regard and treat the Indians as brutes that an attempt to treat them as human beings astonishes us as much as it probably does them."[24]

Not to be outdone, the *Omaha Bee* also printed excerpts from other newspapers regarding the Ponca case. It quoted the *New York Tribune* in an article titled, "How We Treat the Indians":

> Nothing more glaring, unjust and absurd can be found in our treatment of the Indians than the mismanagement of the Poncas. Under the direction of Protestant Episcopal mission, these people had reached a degree of civilization and steady prosperity far surpassing that of most Western colonies of white men. . . . All that we demand or hope for the Indians was answered in the successful progress of the tribe.
>
> But in one fell swoop, without pretense of a reason; at the mere whim of the Commissioners, they were routed out of their homes and whisked off to a wilderness. The United States government had no more right to disturb these people in the homes they had worked and paid for than it would have to remove the inhabitants of a New England village and set them down in Kansas.[25]

Journalist John M. Coward pointed out that supporting the Ponca was "easy" for the New York and Chicago newspapers: "No Indians threatened their readers and the problems of the frontier were readily 'solved' on paper. Moreover, these sympathetic newspapers, relying on information from Tibbles and other Ponca supporters, treated the Ponca as an exceptional case, a tribe readily distinguished from less civilized natives."[26] However, the fact that Omaha's four newspapers were also sympathetic to the plight of the Ponca is remarkable. Nebraska was still a frontier state and many of its citizens still feared the possibility of an Indian war.

In the days leading up to the trial, the *Herald* continued to plead the case of the Indians. It stated that since the government had entered into treaties with the Indians, recognizing them as owners of the land, certain "rights" were implied. It added:

> In practice we have said, "Indian, you are in our way," but in theoretical phrase, they have made independent concessions to us, and wherever we have found them "In flagrante delicto," breaking the peace or battling with our citizens, we have seldom stopped to ask why; but have met them at the front of the battle and ended the contest by "a new treaty" in which the Indian has conceded some reserved rights, and if words mean anything, "by consent of parties."
>
> Is not the Indian entitled to the pursuit and practice of liberty and happiness, while he have life, if he did not invade our law-girt system of society, or

infringe any of the "rights" we have left him. If there be any doubt of that, let it be solved at once and forever.[27]

A report by the *Republican* revealed some sympathy for the Ponca. It was head-lined "Standing Bear Tells the Story of His Wrongs," and it argued that it was up to the court to disprove the Ponca rights to liberty, not for the Ponca to prove their rights to freedom.[28]

The *Bee* also carried a preliminary report on the Ponca court case, headlined, "The Poor Poncas." It related the story of the Ponca return to Nebraska, their cap-ture at the Omaha reservation, and their stop at Fort Omaha. The *Bee* added that it was while they were at Fort Omaha that "the sympathetic and philanthropic T. H. Tibbles, a *Herald* scribbler, put up a job on the government, and got out a writ of habeas corpus. The writ was issued by Judge Dundy to Gen. Crook, requiring him to show cause and by what authority he detained and deprived the Poncas of their liberty."[29]

The trial lasted only two days, but the *Herald* believed the principles being ad-dressed were of paramount importance:

> The case involves constitutional questions and those rights of personal liberty for the conservation of which the Anglo-Saxon race has shed rivers of blood and which they have secured for themselves only after centuries of bloody con-tests. A report of the testimony will be found on another page, but the great issues which are at stake in this contest are not such as can be settled by oral testimony. They are questions of law. Does the law vest absolute power in the hands of the commissioner of Indian affairs or the Secretary of the Interior, over Indians who are not at war, and who are engaged in the peaceful pursuits of agriculture, so that he can arrest them at whim, move them where he pleases, confine them in prisons, force them to live in pest holes, confiscate the property they have accumulated around them by their own labor, take their lands which have been guaranteed to them by solemn treaties ratified by the Senate of the United States, make them prisoners for life within certain described limits, and all, when they have committed no crime against the person or property of any man. Everyone of these things has Commissioner Hayt done or attempted to do with these Ponca Indians.
>
> Messrs. [Andrew J.] Poppleton and [John L.] Webster are not simply arguing Standing Bear's case. The principles involved are wider than this nation and older than the foundation of the government, and in their defense men have poured out their blood like water on a thousand battle fields. Have the Indians an absolute monarch over them in the person of the commissioner at Washing-ton, who can say to any one of them, come, and he must come; and go, and he must go? And who can say to a man who is plowing in the field, "Take your wife and little children and go to a pest hole of sickness and stay there till you die,"

and if he refuses to go, has he the power to command the army to force him there at the point of the bayonet? If there is an unlimited monarch like that over the Indians, let Mr. Lambertson read the law which created him.[30]

In an article headlined "'The Celebrated Case' Finally Comes to a Hearing," the *Herald* used three columns to report the first day's court testimony. Standing Bear was called as a witness, and G. M. Lambertson, the district attorney, objected. Judge Dundy responded, "Anybody can be sworn. This court recognizes no distinctions on account of race, color or previous condition." Standing Bear recounted his story of going down to Indian Territory and finding the land unsuitable, and also how many of his people had died, including two of his own children. At one point, Standing Bear was asked what his people were doing to become white men. He replied they were farming and sending their children to school and added, "I want to work and become like a white man. I have been trying my best to do so for a long time."[31]

The *Herald* continued to devote extensive coverage to the Ponca court case. There were large, multicolumn stories on May 3 and 4, 1879, that detailed the speeches of Poppleton and Webster and summarized the words of Standing Bear, while using extensive excerpts from his testimony.

Webster commented that much had been said about Indian cruelty, but that it did not compare to the cruelties of whites. The paper added that Webster had stated, "Nothing in all the history of savages equaled the cruelty which has been practiced by the whites." Webster continued by stating that the title to the Ponca land had not been disputed but had been recognized by treaty. How could it now be taken away?

He quoted from the Fourteenth Amendment of the Constitution, which states that all *persons* born or naturalized in the United States are citizens of the United States and cannot be deprived of life, liberty, or property without due process of law and are entitled to equal protection under the law. Webster inferred that the Indians must then be citizens since they were born "on our soil." If not citizens, what are they, he said. "Are they wild animals, deer to be chased by every hound?" He even cited the case of an Oneida Indian [*Jackson vs. Goodell*] who was declared a citizen when he left his tribe.[32] District Attorney Lambertson countered with the claim that the "Indian could not appear in court, was not entitled to the writ of habeas corpus, he was not a citizen, that Indian tribes were independent communities, and based his argument principally upon Judge Tansy's decision in the Dred Scott case."[33]

Standing Bear's other lawyer, Andrew J. Poppleton, began his "argument" by stating he was appearing on "behalf of a feeble remnant of a class of beings who seem, for two or three hundred years to have had no friends and to have never had any rights." He added, "these Indians are honestly desirous of adopting the ways of civilization and becoming civilized men; of pursuing the habits and industries of the present age, there is no power, human or divine, that has the right to interpose a barrier between them and the goal to which they seek to march."[34]

Poppleton criticized District Attorney Lambertson's argument that the Indians had no rights and are not even recognized as having rights to "breathe the pure air of heaven."[35] He stated that in having entered into treaties with this tribe, the U.S. government "guarantees them certain rights, certain lands and certain privileges in connection with these lands, and now to turn back on those guarantees is a most infamous act."[36]

The climax of the second day of the trial came with Standing Bear's testimony. The *Herald* quoted him as saying: "You see me standing here. Where do you think I come from? From the water, the woods or where? God made me and he put me on my land. But, I was ordered to stand up and leave my land. Who the man was, I don't know. He told me to leave and I had to go. I objected to going. I looked around for someone to help me, but I found no one. Now I have found someone to help me and it makes me glad. When I got down there it seemed as if I was in a big fire. One-hundred and fifty-eight of my people were burned up; now I stand before you. I came away to save my wife and children and friends. I never want to go back there again. I want to go back to my old reservation to live there and be buried in the land of my fathers."[37]

According to Tibbles in his book *Buckskin and Blanket Days,* Standing Bear's speech was a little more dramatic. Tibbles claimed Standing Bear held out an upraised arm and said:

> That hand is not the color of yours, but if I pierce it I shall feel pain. If you pierce your hand, you also feel pain. The blood that will flow from mine will be the same color as yours. I am a man. The same God made us both.
>
> I seem to stand on the banks of a river. My wife and little girl are beside me. In front the river is wide and impassable, and behind are perpendicular cliffs. No man of my race ever stood there before. There is no tradition to guide me.[38]

Tibbles stated that Standing Bear then began to talk of a great flood that began to rise around them. Standing Bear led his family up the side of the cliff and saw a break in the rocks where they could find safety: "But a man bars the passage. He is a thousand times more powerful than I. Behind him I see soldiers as numerous as the leaves of the trees. They will obey that man's orders. I too must obey his orders. If he says I cannot pass, I cannot. The long struggle will have been in vain. My wife and child and I must return and sink beneath the flood. We are weak and faint and sick. I cannot fight. [Looking at Judge Dundy he says] You are that man."[39]

The content of the two versions of Standing Bear's speech are similar, but Tibbles's version is much more dramatic than the one quoted by the *Herald.* It seems curious that the more dramatic version, if accurate, was not used by the *Herald.* Tibbles published *Buckskin and Blanket Days* 36 years after the Standing Bear trial. In addition, he had spent several years following the trial in pursuit of justice for the Indians, so he strongly identified with their cause. It is possible that he embellished the speech somewhat when he wrote his book many years later.

While it did not devote quite as much coverage to the Standing Bear trial as the *Herald,* the *Republican* also offered extensive reporting. It described the Indians in the courtroom as not being the stereotypical "stoic" Indian. It described the emotion on their faces during Standing Bear's testimony and stated that Standing Bear's wife, "Suzette," broke down and cried when the chief told of their son's dying wish to be buried in the land of his ancestors. The *Republican* added:

> He did not come from the woods but from God's hand, and he had remained where God had placed him. Then comes the hand of power and takes him away against his will—took him and cast him into the fire of a burning climate, where scores and scores of them died. Escaping from a land of death, of idleness, they seek to return to liberty and to labor.
>
> All he wished was liberty—to be free to go back to the home of his fathers, to bury his dead there, to build and labor and to live and die there. He saw before him the example of the whites; he asked only the poor privilege of being permitted to follow it, and earn a living as honest as the words he spoke for himself and his for the labors of his own hands. He admired, wherever he saw, the works of the civilization of the whites. He liked to watch them at their labor—to see them plow and build—to see their children learn to read and write. And for the truth of his every word he appealed to the God of the white men, before whom, with uplifted hand, he had taken solemn oath.[40]

The *Republican* agreed that the Standing Bear trial had "wider significance than the liberty or restraint of twenty-five Indians. It involves largely the extent of the power of the government over all Indian tribes."[41] The *Republican* praised the work of Poppleton and Webster on behalf of a "wronged, but savage people." Yet, it also wanted its readers to "hear both sides." It summarized Lambertson's arguments against the "citizenship rights" of the Indians, where he declared that the Indians did not really own the land because they did not fully use it. They had rights of occupancy only. Lambertson continued by stating that the Indians "disdain to pay homage to the soil by cultivating it and exhibit a noble scorn of labor. The enduring sentiment and rule of action for all ages, 'In the sweat of thy brow shalt thou earn they bread,' never became a tenant of the Indian brain. The motto of the noble red man is, 'In the sweat of my squaw's brow shall I earn my bread.' The Indian will not toil, will not seek a time and place to submit to the laws of God, will not provide for the future, saying he will take no thought for the morrow for the morrow will take thought for the things of itself. The life of an Indian is so entirely foreign to that of an industrious people that only a mind with a vast imagination could suggest a resemblance."[42]

The first paper to publish the news of Judge Dundy's decision was the *Republican.* It featured the news on its front page one day before its competitor, the

Herald. One can only imagine the satisfaction the *Republican* took in scooping its competitor, especially on a story that the *Herald* had launched and championed for weeks. In a story headlined "The Indian Has Rights which the White Man is Bound to Respect," the *Republican* pointed out that this was the first decision in a U.S. court concerning the rights of the Indian and that the Poncas could now join the Omaha Indians on their reservation and "live something like white men."[43]

The *Republican* prefixed its report on Judge Dundy's decision by noting that it would have "far sweeping effects upon the policy of the Indian Bureau." It stated that the decision not only released the Ponca from the custody of the army but prohibited the government's use of the army to force other Indian tribes to stay on their reservations against their will. This meant that all the tribes now in Indian Territory, including the Ponca, Cheyenne, and Nez Perce, could now begin heading north, and that the "Indian ring" could no longer "force the Army to hold up the hands of the Indians while they are robbed by thieves."[44]

The headline on the *Herald's* story on Dundy's decision trumpeted "Standing Bear's Victory." It also called Dundy's decision far-reaching and stated the "Indian Ring is Shorn of Its Power." Unlike the *Republican,* it did not preface Dundy's decision with an opinion on its effects but began its story with a summary of the case:

> An Indian is a *person* within the meaning of the *habeas corpus* act, and as such is entitled to sue out a writ of *habeas corpus* in the federal courts, when it is shown that the petitioner is deprived of liberty under color of authority of the United States, or is in custody of an officer in violation of the constitution, or of a law of the United States, or in violation of a treaty made in pursuance thereof.
>
> The right of expatriation is a natural, inherent, and inalienable right, and extends to the Indian as well as the more fortunate white race.
>
> In time of peace no authority, civil or military, exists for transporting Indians from one section of the country to another without the consent of the Indians, nor to confine them to any particular reservation against their will, and where officers of the government attempt to do this, and arrest and hold Indians who are at peace with the government, for the purpose of removing them to, and confining them on, a reservation in the Indian Territory, they will be released on *habeas corpus.*[45]

Not all of the Omaha newspapers agreed with the *Herald's* opinion on Indian issues, but they seemed to have sympathy for the Ponca predicament. The *Omaha Evening News* stated it believed that Judge Dundy's decision was "in every way superior." The *Evening News* clarified its position by pointing out that it was not generally sympathetic with Indian issues, but the Standing Bear case was different:

> We have a feeling very different from sympathy for the palaver over the Indian question generally indulged in by the tract societies of the East and the senile

and hare-brained, would-be humanitarians of the west, who, by some strange freak of providence, are sometimes thrown into the editorial chair of some unlucky journal. The romance surrounding the Indian character is in most instances maudlin, conceived in the exercise of the perverted taste that seeks Beedle and Cooper for its sole source of knowledge. We do not believe that, as a general thing, the treaties with the Indians have been first broken by the white man, nor do we believe that most of the wild tribes have enough intellect to understand a compact or enough honor to keep it if they understood it. But there are exceptions, and under this head comes the Poncas, who have been the first to apply to a court for the protection of violated rights."[46]

As an illustration as to just how much attitudes had changed toward the Indians, at least in the case of the Ponca, both the *Herald* and the *Republican* ran editorials supporting a fund of food, supplies, and money, that would help give the Ponca a fresh start. The *Herald* opined, "No other case will ever appeal to the sympathy of an ever generous Omaha public more strongly than this. Send around your contributions to Mr. [L. S.] Reed and let us repair in some slight degree the great wrong which has been done to Standing Bear."[47]

In support of its own editorial stance, the *Republican* reprinted editorials on the Standing Bear case from other newspapers across the country. The *Chicago News* wrote that the district court in Nebraska had "rendered an important decision in the case of a number of Ponca Indians; if sustained by the Supreme Court of the United States it must overturn the entire Indian policy and system of the government." The *Kansas City Mail* stated: "This decision merely recognizes the fact that the Indian is a human being and not a wild beast; that so long as he violates no law he is entitled to the protection of the law, and has some personal rights which both the white man and the white man's government ought to respect; and finally that there is no class of persons under the jurisdiction of our government over whom an administration can rule with despotic sway, without authority of law, denying them even the liberty to live in peace where the law permits them to eke out a miserable existence."[48]

The *Bee* also believed that Judge Dundy's decision in the Standing Bear case was to have far-reaching consequences. Despite its history of demonizing Indians, the *Bee* was sympathetic to correcting the plight of the Ponca. The *Bee* made it clear that it admired Standing Bear's intelligence and "earnestness" in pleading the cause of his people.[49]

The *Bee* hoped that Judge Dundy's decision might open the door for a whole new way of dealing with the "Indian problem." It used an editorial reprinted from the *Chicago Tribune* to help support its position: "It makes no difference what degree of civilization an Indian may possess, he is controlled by the same laws as are those most savage. There can be no question that many Indians, and indeed some entire tribes, are now in a condition to permit of their receiving the rights of citizenship. Many of them are as capable of taking care of themselves and of performing the ordinary civil duties as the average white man. Such Indians have laid aside their savage instincts and customs, and they are now law-abiding, frugal and industrious. These Poncas are of this class."[50]

Now that the dust had settled following Judge Dundy's decision, the possible repercussions of the case were being discussed across the country. Commissioner Hayt of the Indian Bureau was concerned that by letting Standing Bear go, a damaging precedent would be set, and he vowed to fight the decision to the Supreme Court if needed. Hayt instructed District Attorney Lambertson to take the necessary steps to carry the case to a higher court. Hayt believed Dundy's decision would make the Indians "virtual citizens" with the right to go where they pleased and that "if sustained will prove extremely dangerous alike to whites and Indians. If the power of the government to hold Indians upon their reservations and to return them when they escape is denied, the Indians will become a body of tramps moving without restraint wherever they please and exposed to attacks of frontiersmen without redress from the government."[51]

Judge Dundy's ruling was called "The Righteous Decision" by the *Herald,* which claimed that it had gone "thundering through the press" and awakened the people to its importance. The *Herald* did not believe that Commissioner Hayt would be successful in his efforts to overturn Dundy's decision: "It is righteous and just in itself in asserting human rights and personal liberty that we do not see how any court can contravene it. And as to that part of it which determines that the government cannot take these people from their lands, at the point of a bayonet in the absence of any law authorizing such a proceeding, the idea that the government can do such things would be absurd if we had not been so long accustomed to seeing these red men trodden down as so many beasts who had no rights which a corrupt government and a mercenary people were bound to respect."[52]

There was a paternalistic theme that ran through the newspapers' coverage of the Standing Bear case. All three newspapers made repeated references to Standing Bear's professed desire to be just like the white man. The *Republican* quoted him as saying he admired the civilization of the white man and enjoyed watching them at work.[53] The *Herald* stated that Standing Bear wanted to work and "become like a white man." It was as if they were proud parents watching their young child walk down the stairs dressed in "grownup" clothes.

Following the decision in the Standing Bear trial, the agent for the Ponca, William H. Whiteman, tried to discredit Standing Bear and the others by calling them renegades. Big Snake, Standing Bear's brother, petitioned Whiteman for permission to journey north to join his brother, but permission was denied. Determined to test the court case, Big Snake led some 30 of his people to the Cheyenne reservation 100 miles to the west. Agent Whiteman asked the military to arrest Big Snake and detain him at Fort Reno in Indian Territory until the furor over the Standing Bear case had died down. Secretary Carl Schurz agreed to Whiteman's request and asked General William T. Sherman to give the order to arrest Big Snake. Sherman agreed, stating that Judge Dundy's decision was unique to the

Standing Bear case and did not apply anywhere else.[54] In this he was correct. Dundy had written his decision to apply only to the Standing Bear case.

On October 31, 1879, Big Snake was arrested on trumped up charges. When he resisted, he was shot and killed. The Interior Department issued a statement that Big Snake had been shot "resisting arrest." There was a public outcry to investigate the incident, but it was shoved under the rug and nothing was ever done.[55]

The first attempt by Indians to fulfill the high hopes engendered by Judge Dundy's decision had ended in the tragic death of an innocent man. Standing Bear, who had started the entire process by his simple desire to return his dead son to the land of his birth, now had a brother to bury as well. It had only been a few months since newspapers across the country had called for citizenship rights for peaceful Indians, but it was not until 45 years later, in 1924, that those citizenship rights, which had seemed so attainable in the spring of 1879, would finally be given to the first Americans.

The coverage of the Standing Bear case by the Omaha newspapers differed from the typical coverage of Native Americans by frontier newspapers. The Omaha reporters were on the scene and were able to cover the action gavel to gavel. The event they were covering was not an Indian campaign, so they were not subject to the vagaries of weather and distance, and they were not dependent on the military to provide them with information. They were in a court of law, with well-defined rules and regulations. All of this lent the coverage a high degree of *accuracy* and also provided the *selection* or balance that Martin and Nelson describe as two of the four measures used to judge historical coverage by the press.[56]

It is in the other two measures cited by Martin and Nelson—*judgment* and *prediction*—that the Omaha newspapers did not perform as well. The *Republican* predicted that, as a result of Dundy's decision, tribes like the Ponca, Cheyenne, and Nez Perce would soon be heading north.[57] However, when Big Snake of the Ponca traveled to a nearby reservation, he was killed. There was no mass exodus to the north by the tribes. The *Bee* had predicted that Dundy's decision heralded a new way of dealing with the age-old "Indian problem," but nothing had really changed. Violent solutions and imprisonment on reservations were still the most popular answers to the "Indian problem." The *Herald* predicted that the decision in the Standing Bear case would cause the "Indian Ring to be shorn of its power." However, it remained strong for many more years and, some would argue, continues even to this day in the guise of the Bureau of Indian Affairs.

All three newspapers expressed confidence that a new day was coming in the handling of Indian affairs and that the Standing Bear decision would reverberate through the halls of power and affect Indian policy for years to come. It did not, as so starkly illustrated by Big Snake's death a few short months after the decision. It is true that it helped to mobilize public sympathy for the plight of the Indian, but it did not have an immediate effect on the policy of the government. Today it is a little known event that is best remembered for the stoicism of Standing Bear and the poignant illustration that in 1879 it took a U.S. court to finally recognize the Indian as a "person"—a human being with rights under the law.

CHAPTER 8

Ghost Dance and Wounded Knee:
1890–1891

It was the last day of December 1890 and the snow and the cold had frozen the bodies into grotesque poses. Big Foot lay on his side, his arms half raised as if to ward off a blow. Dozens of other bodies lay scattered across the Wounded Knee battlefield. The soldiers gathered them up and dumped them into a mass grave. The survivors had already been taken to the agency at Pine Ridge.

Suzette La Flesche, a member of the Omaha tribe and a reporter for the *Omaha World-Herald,* described the scene at the agency:

> There was a woman sitting on the floor with a wounded baby on her lap and four or five children around her, all her grandchildren. Their father and mother were killed. There was a young woman shot through both thighs and her wrist broken. Mr. Tibbles had to get a pair of pliers to get her rings off. There was a little boy with his throat apparently shot to pieces.
>
> They were all hungry and when we fed this little boy we found he could swallow. We gave him some gruel and he grabbed with both his little hands a dipper of water. When I saw him yesterday afternoon, he looked worse than the day before, and when they feed him now, the food and water come out of the side of his neck.
>
> I have been thus particular in giving horrible details in the hope of rousing such an indignation that another such causeless war shall never again be allowed by the people of the United States. Soldiers and Indians have lost their lives through the fault of somebody who goes scot free from all the consequences or blame. . . . The Sioux firmly believe it has been brought about because their land was wanted. If the white people want their land and must have it, they

can go about getting it some other way than by forcing it from them by starving them or provoking them to war and sacrificing the lives of innocent women and children, and through the suffering of the wives and children of officers and soldiers.[1]

Wounded Knee is considered by most historians to be the death knell of the Indian wars of the Great Plains. It occurred more than a decade after the last battle between the Sioux and the army. It was a final tragedy that had its roots in the policies of the federal government toward the Indians and a longing by the Sioux to return to a way of life that was forever lost.

Twenty-two years had passed since the Treaty of 1868 at Fort Laramie established the Great Sioux Reservation. It was a desperate time for the Sioux. Historian Robert M. Utley describes it in his book *The Lance and the Shield*: "The reservations had destroyed the very foundations of the Indian way of life. . . . The government warred on spiritual beliefs and practices, on the office of chief, and on the tribe itself. . . . By 1890 all the Lakota tribes verged perilously on cultural breakdown."[2]

The Sioux were ripe for the coming of Wovoka, the latest Indian messiah, and his message of a return to the old ways. Wovoka was a Paiute, living in Nevada close to Lake Tahoe. On New Year's Day 1889 there was a solar eclipse in Nevada. The Paiutes called it "the day the sun died." According to historian Rex Allen Smith, on that same day, Wovoka had a vision that he was taken to heaven. He was told the old world was to be destroyed and replaced by a fresh one. The dead would live again and everyone would be young and happy. The buffalo would return and the white man would disappear. All the Indians had to do was to perform the dance of the souls departed—the ghost dance.[3]

Wovoka's vision was peaceful, but as it radiated out to other Indians it was imbued with the flavor of individual tribes. The Sioux added a strain of militarism. "The Sioux read more hostility to the whites into the prophet's words than did the other tribes. When the Sioux thought they had heard Wovoka speaking of knocking the soldiers 'into nothingness,' other tribes heard him to say that he would send soldiers against any tribe that 'misbehaved' . . . others understood that he had come for all of God's children and that 'all whites and Indians are brothers.' "[4]

Adding volatility to the mix was the Sioux leader Sitting Bull, who had returned with his people to the United States from Canada in July 1881. Life on the reservation did not suit him and he longed for the old ways. Among his own people, he became a symbol of resistance and a hindrance to the plans of men such as James McLaughlin, agent at Standing Rock Reservation. Elements of the frontier press alternately feared and despised him.

It is likely that the ghost dance would have spread on the Sioux reservations anyway, but Sitting Bull's support lent a potent symbol to the cause of the new religion. For a people who had seen their way of life unalterably changed, requiring adjustment to strange new customs and rhythms, the lure of a return to the old ways that the ghost dance promised was hard to resist. There are no reliable figures regarding the number of converts to the new religion across the Sioux reservations, but it is thought that perhaps one-third of the Sioux were involved in the dance at some time. The largest group of dancers, perhaps 3,500 people, was located in a section of the Bad Lands northwest of the Pine Ridge Agency that came to be known as "the Stronghold."[5]

The new religion, which drew heavily from Christian tenets and beliefs, resulted in increasing numbers of Indians professing a belief in the Christian God. In addition, Wovoka told the Indians to farm and to send all their children to school. These were all things that should have been desirable to the whites. In fact, one of the primary duties of an Indian agent was to replace native religious beliefs with Christian dogma. It would seem that the new Indian religion was doing just that. However, Standing Rock agent James McLaughlin called it an "absurd craze" and described the dance as "demoralizing, indecent and disgusting." He found no reason to change his opinion when he finally witnessed a dance a month after submitting his original assessment.[6]

Historian Elmo Scott Watson states that although the ghost dance was called variously an "uprising," an "outbreak," and a "war," it was "none of these—except in the columns of the contemporary press." He quotes Dr. Valentine T. McGillicuddy, former Indian agent at Pine Ridge, as telling General L. W. Colby, commander of Nebraska's mobilized state troops, on January 21, 1891, that no citizen of either Nebraska or Dakota has been killed or molested and that no property had been destroyed off the reservation. Watson adds that when it seemed likely that the Sioux would again "take the warpath, the journalistic practices of a quarter of a century earlier were repeated. Unverified rumors were presented as 'reports from reliable sources' or 'eye-witness accounts;' idle gossip became fact; and once more a large number of the nation's newspapers indulged in a field day of exaggeration, distortion and plain faking."[7]

The *Leadville Evening Chronicle* offered a typical example of frontier newspaper coverage of the crisis. Under the headline "Insane Indians," the newspaper claimed that the Indians were "lashing themselves into a frenzy of excitement. They lose all their senses in the dance. They think they are animals, some get down on all fours and bob like buffaloes. When they cannot lose their senses from exhaustion, they butt their heads together, bang them on the ground and do everything to become insensible, so that they may be ushered into the presence of the new Christ."[8] The actual ghost dance was a slow circular shuffle and bears little resemblance to the dance described in the *Chronicle*.

The *Omaha World-Herald* took an early editorial stance on the new Indian religion when it commented on the ghost dance in a story headlined, "Let Them Alone." It declared that

The United States takes this matter very stupidly—it always takes everything connected with the Indians stupidly. Troops have been sent to the agencies most affected by this belief, and all the ministers are preaching fiercely against this new Jesus and endeavoring to break up the "Jesus dance." All this is but a part of the general impression which this government and the people in it have always cherished, that the Indian has no right to any ideas of his own, or indeed to any nationality of his own.

The Indian is not an idolater. He is distinctly religious. His ideas concerning the unknown are far from contemptible, yet they have never been respected and they are not respected now.[9]

Although the first news stories had been concerned mostly with the religious aspects of the ghost dance, mentioning fears of a general Indian uprising, there had been no overt panic among the frontier citizens. All of this began to change by mid-November 1890. According to a wire story in the *World-Herald*, settlers in North Dakota were abandoning their ranches and farms because they felt unprotected and vulnerable to Indian attack. Reports circulated that the Indians were armed with "Custer's rifles, which had never been found," and that local hardware men had sold out all their ammunition to the Indians.[10]

The *Aspen Weekly Times*, fanned these new fears. "The last news from Wounded Knee, which came in last night, was to the effect that the ghost dances were being held nightly, and that all the Indians collected there were excited, threatening and boisterous. The rumor that the troops were coming was repeated there and only elicited threats in response. The Indians declared their Messiah was advising them and encouraging them every day and that the dancers could not be stopped."[11]

Historian Watson wrote that these settlers worked themselves into such a panic that they abandoned their ranches. Sometimes even whole villages were deserted. These people fled into railroad cities with "vivid stories of murder, scalping and desolation that had no foundation whatever in fact." Watson adds that "Apparently the degree of alarm was in reverse ratio to the nearness of the 'theater of war.' Country weeklies took the 'danger' much more calmly than did their daily brethren in the more distant big cities."[12]

The *Aspen Daily Chronicle* headlined a story "Fanatical Redskins" and warned its readers that there were 364 lodges with over 6,000 Indians at Wounded Knee. "He [Plenty Bear, a "friendly" Sioux Indian] said they were forming into a regular war dance and were swearing vengeance upon the whites for conspiring to stop their Ghost Dance. They have taken an oath to resist interference if it costs them the last drop of their heart's blood."[13] The *Chronicle*'s numbers were ridiculously exaggerated, but its mention of an Indian encampment at Wounded Knee was eerily prescient.

Watson described the *Omaha Bee* as "a gossipy tabloid, strewn with stories about sex, violence, crime and intrigue." He considered [Charles H.]Cressey's writing style to be sensationalistic. "He depended on imagination, rumor, and hearsay to keep his stories exciting. Whether by assignment or disposition, Cressey's stories about Pine Ridge seethed with impending violence and conflict. His sensational accounts spread to newspapers around the nation and, amazingly, he became a prime source of information about the Pine Ridge troubles."[14]

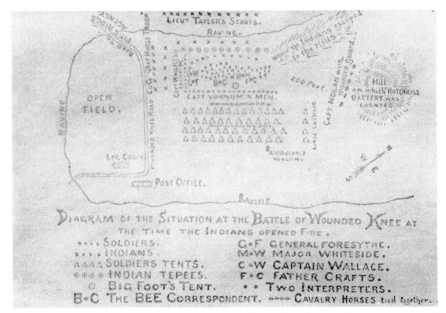

Diagram of the situation at Wounded Knee just before the shooting began. Courtesy of Denver Public Library, Western History Collection.

The *World-Herald*'s Carl Smith developed an early antagonistic relationship with Dr. Daniel F. Royer, the newly appointed agent at the Pine Ridge agency. Smith was unusually blunt in his reporting. He wrote that since the presence of troops was a major boon to the local economy, the locals would invent "cock and bull" stories just to keep them there.[15]

In headlines that screamed, "Fears of an Ambush," and "A Squaw's Warning," the *Bee* continued to report on the trouble that always seemed to be just on the verge of erupting into a full-scale Indian war. One headline even read, "False Rumors of a Real Battle."[16]

Cressey, the *Bee*'s primary correspondent, delighted in painting a graphic picture of the situation in South Dakota. He made the most mundane event seem sinister. For example, he predicted that the Indians would "make a charge and stampede the beef herd" at the next beef rationing. Of course, he did not explain that this had been standard practice for years and was simply a pale reenactment of the traditional buffalo hunt. Instead of admitting that nothing new was happening, he sent back stories headlined, "The Redskins are Dancing—the Much Dreaded Ghost Dance" and "Crazed Red Men Continue to Look for Promised Messiah."[17]

In stark contrast to the excited prose of the *Bee*, the *World-Herald* had a more measured approach to the events in the Dakotas. In an editorial headlined "No Need For War," the paper cautioned its readers not to get too caught up in all the melodrama:

Patriotism has not died in the piping times of peace. On the contrary, if one is to judge by present signs, it has grown. From every town in Nebraska come the courageous cries of young men, pining to die on the altar of their country. They wish to arm themselves and rush upon an Indian reservation, in spite of the fact that treaties signed by the always trusting Indian, specifically agreed that soldiers should not again set foot upon those reservations. But then why should young men concern themselves with matters of moral responsibility when the government does not do so? But what has the government to do with moral responsibility anyway—especially where the Indian is concerned.

They stand with their faces to the setting sun, thinking of all this till oblivion falls upon their overwrought senses. That is, they are afflicted with a contagious hysteria. So were many of the early Christians. So were the British Druids. So were the Crusaders. So were the followers of Mahomet. So has been many a holy monk in his cell. So were the pioneer Methodists, the civilizers of the great central west. And yet, no arms were brought to bear on them. No retributions were prepared in the shape of a Hotchkiss gun or otherwise.[18]

While the *World-Herald* pleaded for understanding, the *Bee*'s headlines during the same few days screamed "Fanatical Ghost Dancers Threaten Anyone Who Interferes" and "Their Orgies Wilder Than Ever."[19] It was hard to believe that the two newspapers were covering the same event.

The *Bee* seemed to relish the idea that it was driving public opinion in the ghost dance business. It took credit for a flood of "Appeals for Aid and Arms," citing an exclusive story it had run in its morning paper. "Since the exclusive publication in the *Bee* this morning, of the proposed plot of the supposed friendly Indians to murder all of General [John Rutter] Brooke's forces, a panic seems to have seized the settlers living near the Pine Ridge agency. All day long telegrams have come pouring into Governor Thayer's office appealing for aid and arms."[20] Of course the plot was nonexistent and the expected massacre never occurred, but that did not seem to matter to the *Bee* or its correspondent.

In the style established by the *Bee*, the *Aspen Daily Chronicle* printed a story from a correspondent in Indian Territory [present-day Oklahoma]: "He states there are 4,000 Indians in different sections west of his place [Guthrie, Indian Territory] trading off their ponies, blankets and ammunition. They are daubed with war paint and dancing and screaming in their half-nude condition. Never before, during the Ghost craze, has the aspect of the Indian Territory looked so serious."[21] It was another example of misleading and inaccurate reporting. There was no ghost dance problem in Indian Territory.

Even as November of 1890 ended, the *World-Herald* continued to downplay the threat of trouble at Pine Ridge. In an editorial, it referred to General Nelson A. Miles's claim that the frontier troubles were more of a "correspondents'" than an Indian scare." The paper replied that Miles was mistaken; that some correspondents, and particularly the correspondent from the *World-Herald*, had claimed almost from the first that the alarm was unjustified. It added that everyone except Agent Royer now admitted that it had all been a "tempest in a teapot."[22]

The feud between Smith and Royer continued through the latter half of November 1890. Royer threatened to expel Smith several times and each time he did, Smith responded with a personal attack in the pages of the *World-Herald*. Smith wrote, "You would not put a man who never saw a cow at the head of a big cattle company. Yet the Indian department goes even further than that and selects men who never saw an Indian to run Indian agencies."[23]

Historian Watson described Smith as a "brash youngster with journalistic shortcomings." According to Watson, in addition to criticizing Royer, Smith also "made himself *persona non grata* with the military."[24] This latest attack proved to be too much for Agent Royer, and the *World-Herald* was forced to recall Smith. The paper replaced him with two familiar names, Thomas H. Tibbles, who also served as a correspondent for the *Chicago Express,* and his wife Suzette La Flesche, also known as Bright Eyes. She was one of the first female war correspondents to be officially employed by any American newspaper and was certainly America's first female Native American war correspondent.

Bright Eye's reporting on the action is a little-known but truly remarkable occurrence. It may not have been an attempt to provide balance and accuracy, but simply a cynical ploy to create reader interest owing to the novelty of an Indian woman reporting on an Indian war. Nevertheless, her reporting did provide a unique perspective missing from the coverage of earlier Indian wars.

Typical of her writings was an article that attempted to explain the "Messiah scare." Headlined, "What Bright Eyes Thinks," her article tried to give the *World-Herald*'s readers a glimpse of the ghost dance from an Indian perspective:

> Picture to yourself the effect were you to have lived your life thus far with all its dissatisfactions, unsatisfied aspirations and weariness, without having heard of the life of Christ, and someone were to come suddenly before you, someone in whom you had perfect faith and trust, and were to tell you for the first time the story of the Bible in all its simplicity, and of a deliverer who would satisfy all your needs and aspirations. Would you not feel tempted to believe because of your need? And if you have lived all your lives in the environment which the highest known to the world has brought around you, a civilization based on the idea of the Messiah, can you not realize what that story would seem when told to a human being for the first time, even though the human being were only an Indian who had lived all his life without the blessings of your civilization.
>
> I have no doubt that the excitement in the belief of the Messiah's coming added to the excitement of the religious dances. Many knowing of no other way by which they could do homage to the coming deliverer, wrought the Sioux up to such a pitch that a newly arrived agent in his alarm would call for help. . . . The best thing for the agent to have done, and what I believe an experienced agent would have done, would have been to have gone among the peace

abiding element of the Indian community and interested the leading men whose opinion had weight with the others to cooperate with him in persuading the Indians to drop the dancing of their own accord for the time being.[25]

In contrast, the *Bee*'s correspondent painted an insulting picture of "cigar sign models" who sat all day in the same spot "absolutely motionless." Cressey added that if one speaks to the Indians, all you receive in return is a "grunt and a foolish look." He described the reservation as a place which must be monotonous in normal circumstances. He stated, "Without the trimmings and spirit given it by reflections from the ghost dance and the military, life on Indian reservations must be dull enough to cause the half-animated, long-haired, blanket-swathed musk bags that make up nine-tenths of the inhabitants, swim their teepee in tears and then go blind."[26]

In response to some of the sensational stories printed in the eastern papers, the *World-Herald*'s Tibbles stated that there was "not a word of truth in them. There has been no fight and no bloodshed. A part of the hostiles have come in."[27] Tibbles added that he thought all of the hostiles except 60 lodges would come in right away and there would be no war. "Everything looks favorable and there cannot possibly be any damage inflicted upon settlers in the Black Hills by roving bands of Indians, as there is now a cordon of troops between the hostiles and the ranchmen. The dispatches are highly colored and sensational in the extreme. If trouble occurs, it will be outside of the hills in the Bad Lands."[28] Tibbles was absolutely correct. There was no possible danger for area settlers. The Indians were completely surrounded by thousands of troops. And the trouble, when it finally did occur, happened in the unpopulated Badlands.

On December 10, 1890, under pressure from agent McLaughlin, General Miles ordered General Thomas Ruger to "secure the person of Sitting Bull using any practical means."[29] Shortly before 6:00 A.M. on December 15, Indian policemen arrived at Sitting Bull's cabin to arrest him. According to historian Robert M. Utley, Sitting Bull initially agreed to go peacefully, but as he was leaving his cabin a crowd began to gather. They jostled the policemen and shouted at them to release Sitting Bull, who began to struggle with his captors. Catch-the-Bear, one of Sitting Bull's followers, shot Bull Head, one of the Indian policemen. As he fell, Bull Head fired a shot into Sitting Bull's chest, and Red Tomahawk, another policeman, fired a shot into the back of the unarmed Sitting Bull's skull, killing him instantly. A fierce, brutal battle then erupted, and when it was all over Sitting Bull, his young son Crow Foot, and six other tribesmen lay dead. In addition, four Indian policemen were dead and three were wounded, two of them mortally.[30]

Both the *Bee* and the *World-Herald* carried the same wire story on the death of Sitting Bull in their December 16, 1890, editions. The article did not include many details except to report that Sitting Bull and several other Indians had been killed when Indian policemen sent to arrest the chief became embroiled in a struggle with his followers.[31] The *Bee* included a brief summary of Sitting Bull's life, stating that he had "probably done as much 'injun devilment' in his time as any savage since Tecumseh."[32] In contrast, in an editorial published just a day after it printed the news of Sitting Bull's death, the *World-Herald* called for someone to accept responsibility for the chief's death:

> Somebody is responsible for the death of Sitting Bull and the other Indians killed at the same time. The killing was only part of the unwarranted severity and oppression that the United States is now inflicting on the Indians. Somebody is responsible. Not those, merely, who did the killing. Nor those merely who ordered the military to the scene of the so-called trouble. Nor those merely who misjudged the danger and called for troops. Nor even those who annually cheat, rob and despoil the miserable red men through Indian rings. Not one of these alone, but altogether, forming as they do, our so called "system" are responsible for the unhappy death of Sitting Bull.
>
> There seems to be no end to the blunders, crimes and atrocities into which the government is led in the treatment of the Indians. It is time for a change.[33]

The *Bee*'s Cressey stated that the news of Sitting Bull's death had "thus far produced no excitement whatever among the Indians here, though none can tell what they are thinking about." He added, "The fact is, however, that Bull was considered during the last years of his life a little better than the average coffee cooler, a term synonymous with a vagabond. At least such is the estimation in which he was held by very many, if not all, the friendlies here."[34]

However, a contradictory story in the *Bee* two days later was headlined, "The Warriors of the Dead Chief Bound to Have Blood."[35] The editors of the *Bee* could not seem to make up their minds as to whether Sitting Bull was to be feared or ridiculed.

L. Frank Baum, who later gained fame as the author of the *Wizard of Oz* books, used Sitting Bull's killing as the spark for proposing genocide. In the Aberdeen, South Dakota, *Saturday Pioneer,* he wrote a venomous editorial a week after Sitting Bull's death. "The proud spirit of the original owners of these vast prairies . . . lingered last in the bosom of Sitting Bull. With his fall, the nobility of the Redskin is extinguished, and what few are left are a pack of whining curs who lick the hand that smites them. The Whites, by law of conquest, by justice of civilization, are masters of the American continent, and the best safety of the frontier settlements will be secured by the total annihilation of the few remaining Indians. Why not annihilation? Their glory has fled, their spirit broken, their manhood effaced; better that they should die than live [as] the miserable wretches that they are."[36]

The *World-Herald* credited Bright Eyes with remaining calm instead of reacting with "rage" at the degradation of her "race." It stated "the racial placidity of Bright Eyes comes to her protection even in this fevered hour. From her height she sweeps a calm eye over all the puerile tumult and wonders what the Great Father thinks of this petty show of church and state, of masquerading civilization and undisguised savagery in which a nation is slowly going down and out."[37] Despite the flowery praise, Tibbles, in his book *Buckskin and Blanket Days,* said the *World-Herald* and the *Chicago Express* were not always satisfied with their reporting: "Our newspapers had grown indignant with us for not turning in anything interesting about this 'great Indian war' all around us. Other dailies had whole columns of thrilling stuff, but our readers, finding no exciting 'news from the front,' flung down their papers in disgust. Because we absolutely refused to manufacture tales about a 'war' which simply did not exist, we soon were sharply ordered home as complete failures. Only a personal appeal to the various powers from General Miles . . . made it possible for us to stay on at Pine Ridge, where we so greatly wanted to stay until we could see the whole problem solved—thinking that we might help somehow to bring about a peaceful solution."[38]

While Tibbles and Bright Eyes were searching for a peaceful solution, the final tragic players had entered the stage. A mixed band of Sioux Indians under Minneconjou Chief Big Foot had fled the Cheyenne River reservation. Big Foot headed for the safety of Pine Ridge, hoping that Red Cloud could protect his people. He feared that the killing of Sitting Bull might be the first action in an all-out war. Suspecting that Big Foot was heading to the Badlands to join the hostiles, Major Samuel Whitside, with four troops of the Seventh Cavalry, was sent to capture him. The *World-Herald* reported that Big Foot had "eluded the troops and joined the hostiles,"[39] and the *Bee* reported that "slippery Big Foot" had deceived the soldiers and slipped away.[40]

Watson relates that the correspondents hanging around Pine Ridge thought that the military would have no trouble rounding up Big Foot, so the majority decided to stay where they were, believing that the expected surrender of Kicking Bear, a leader of the ghost dance, would be a much bigger story. Only William Fitch Kelley of the *Nebraska State Journal,* Charles W. Allen of the *Chadron Democrat,* and Cressey of the *Bee* accompanied Whitside's troops.[41] Undecided on the importance of the story, Tibbles of the *World-Herald* waited two hours before grabbing horse and following.[42]

Near Wounded Knee Creek, Big Foot—with his band of 120 men and 230 women and children—was intercepted by Whitside, commanding Custer's old Seventh Cavalry. It was December 28, 1890. Later that night Colonel James W. Forsyth, Whitside's superior, assumed command and told Whitside that the Indians were to be disarmed and shipped to a military prison in Omaha, Nebraska.[43]

Big Foot had developed pneumonia on the flight through the Badlands and was now so weak he could barely sit up. Despite his illness, a council was called and Forsyth told the assembled warriors they would be asked to give up their guns. Fearful of being unarmed and vulnerable, Big Foot decided to give up his broken and useless guns and keep the good guns handy. The following day, when the Indians turned over their guns, the soldiers collected an assortment of broken and outdated weapons. Forsyth and Whitside knew there were more guns, so they ordered a search of the camp to gather up all the remaining weapons. It was considered a delicate process that could easily lead to a violent reaction. As a precaution, only officers were allowed to enter teepees and search the women.[44]

Despite all these prudent efforts, the tension began to increase palpably. Yellow Bird, a Minneconjou medicine man, started to dance and chant and he threw handfuls of dirt into the air. He called upon the young men to have brave hearts and told them their ghost shirts would protect them from the soldiers' bullets. The soldiers began to search the men for weapons, and one young man leapt to his feet, angrily holding aloft his gun and saying he had paid good money for it and would not give it up. Some Indian witnesses said he was named Black Coyote and others said it was a man named Hosi Yanka, which means "deaf." Two soldiers came behind the young man and tried to seize his weapon. In the scuffle it went off. At that point several young warriors threw off their blankets and fired a brief volley into the soldiers' ranks. Lieutenant James Mann remembered thinking "The pity of it! What can they be thinking of?" Almost simultaneously the soldiers' lines erupted with fire. Big Foot was one of the first to die.[45]

The soldiers had surrounded the camp. As they fired at the Indians, some of their bullets carried through the crowd and hit their fellows on the opposite side of the camps. Many of the Indians who had survived the initial fury slipped away into a nearby ravine, seeking protection from the lethal fighting. That proved to be a deadly mistake. Now that the Indians had separated from the soldiers, the Hotchkiss guns on the ridge began to rake the camp with a withering fire. As more and more Indians sought refuge in the ravine, the deadly artillery turned its attention there and began to rain shells on the crowded mass of Indians. Men, women, and children were slaughtered in its close confines. Only a few survived the murderous barrage. Some survivors were hunted down and killed miles from the camp. The exact number of Indian dead is not known, but it is certain that at least 170 were killed, most of them women and children.[46] There were also casualties among the soldiers, 25 killed and 39 wounded, most by friendly fire.[47]

Thomas H. Tibbles had decided that there would be no trouble and had left the camp in the morning to get his dispatches to the telegraph office at Pine Ridge. He had not gone far when he heard a single shot, quickly followed by several more. By the time he returned, most of the fighting was over and he was witness only to the rounding up of the few survivors. However, he was able to interview participants shortly after the event.[48]

The *Bee*'s Cressey was present when the gunfire erupted. Historian Watson states that "the part Cressey played in the fight is not known. It is probable that he saw at least part of the fighting, but it is doubtful that he had any such valorous role as he later claimed."[49]

The *Bee* was the first to carry a story on the battle at Wounded Knee. It rushed a brief account that made it into the evening edition of the paper the same day the battle occurred. The story—headlined "A Bloody Battle" and "Many Red Devils Bite the Dust"—covered only the basic fact that a battle had occurred and there had been heavy casualties.[50]

The *Bee* carried a report from Cressey in the following day's edition, with headlines that trumpeted "Ghastly Work of Treacherous Reds" and "Capt. [George] Wallace Tomahawked to Death." After briefly describing the soldiers' search of the Indians for weapons, the *Bee* stated:

> About a dozen of the warriors had been searched when, like a flash, all the rest of them jerked guns from under their blankets and began pouring bullets into the ranks of the soldiers who, a few moments before, had moved up within gun length. Those Indians who had no guns rushed on the soldiers with tomahawk in one hand and scalping knife in the other.
>
> Their first volley was almost as one man, so that they must have fired a hundred shots before the soldiers fired one. But how they were slaughtered after their first volley.
>
> The troops were at a great disadvantage fearing the shooting of their own companions. The Indian men, women and children then ran to the south the battery firing on them rapidly. Soon the mounted troops were after them, shooting them down on every side. To the south many took refuge in a ravine, from which it was difficult to dislodge them. It is estimated that the soldiers killed and wounded about fifty. Just now it is impossible to state the exact number of dead Indians.
>
> To say that it was a most daring feat, 120 Indians attacking 500 cavalry, expresses the situation but faintly. It could only have been insanity which prompted such resistance. The members of the Seventh Cavalry have once more shown themselves to be heroes in deeds of daring. Single handed conflicts were seen all over the field. In the first rush of the Indians those of them who had no guns attacked the troopers with knives, clubs and tomahawks.[51]

The *World-Herald* took a different approach in its coverage of the conflict at Wounded Knee. Its first story on the battle was headlined "All Murdered in a Mass," with subheads such as "Big Foot and His Followers Shot Without Regard to Sex" and "Men Women and Children Said to Have Been Shot Wherever Found." The *World-Herald* reported the same basic facts as the *Bee* but treated the event as a massacre and not a battle. It reported:

> Nearly all the bucks were killed off. There are only a handful left. Whether Big Foot survived is not reported, particulars at this hour being meager. The Indians scouts who have come in say that but few of Big Foot's band are left.
>
> It is said that when the Major [James W. Forsyth] took them they were coming into the agency and endeavoring to elude the troops so that their surrender might be made to appear voluntary. They were half starved, the reports of quantities of jerked beef stored in the Bad Lands being a fiction of the half breeds and squaw men.[52]

Gathering up the dead of the battlefield of Wounded Knee, South Dakota. Courtesy of Denver Public Library, Western History Collection.

The *Aspen Daily Chronicle* gave its description of the encounter a day after the *Bee* and the *World-Herald*. It seemed to imply that the Sioux had prepared an ambush and were merely waiting for a signal to begin.

It was thought the order to search had been a signal. . . . The reply was immediate however, and in an instant, it seemed [that] the draw in which the Indian's camped was a sunken Vesuvius. The soldiers, maddened at the sight of their fallen comrades, hardly awaited the command and in a moment the whole front was a sheet of fire, above which the smoke rolled obscuring the central scenes from view. Through this horrible scene, single Indians could be seen flying before the fire. But after the first discharge of the carbines of the troops, there were few of them left. They [the Sioux] fell on all sides like the grain in the course of a scythe.

With the Indians flying, it was easier to reach them. The Gatling and Hotchkiss guns were trained and began a heavy firing that lasted half an hour with frequent heavy volleys of musketry and cannon.

It was a war of extermination now with the troops. It was difficult to restrain them. Tactics were almost abandoned. For several minutes the engagement went on until not a live Indian was in sight.[53]

In an editorial, the *World-Herald* called Wounded Knee a "Crime Against Civilization" and outlined its anger and regret over the causes of the conflict:

The first blood has been shed in this absurd and criminal war upon the Indians. A large number of Indians are dead, a few officers and soldiers—and for what reason? What is the principle for which they are fighting? What sentiment dignifies and raises it from the low estate of murder to that of war?

It is proper now to cast a reflective eye back over the last few weeks. A body of half starved Indians indulged in a religious ecstasy which made them forget for a time the cold in their teepees and their empty cupboard. A foolish and apprehensive agent grew as hysterical as the Indians, and begged for help. The help came in the shape of troops. Meanwhile, the Indians, fearful of being killed, ran away to the Bad Lands, and the settlers, fearful of being killed, ran for the cities. The settlers were not asked to return. They were extended sympathy. But the Indians were immediately termed "hostiles," and the government resolved to bring them back, if need be, at the point of a bayonet. . . . It is not the injustice of slaughtering the Indians alone that the *World-Herald* laments. It is asking the soldiers of this country to die on a field on which there can be no honor except that created by their own bravery—a field unbeautified by a cause for which any man would care to die. It is a crime, this war, and the soldiers and the Indians alike are the victims.[54]

Calling it "A Deadly Triangle," the *Bee* predicted that Wounded Knee was just the first of many battles and that "further desperate fighting will occur there seems no doubt." The paper stated that 156 Indians had "bit the dust," among them 40 "squaws." It claimed the "squaws were not killed with particular intent, notwithstanding that they had been running around with scalping knives trying to stab the soldiers. They were killed principally by reason of being so mixed with squads of bucks that made dashes to the ravines and were mowed down by the battery."[55]

While the *World-Herald* was trying to convince its readers that there should never be another Wounded Knee, the *Bee* was warning its readers that the "greatest battle in Indian history is almost at hand."[56] Never one to shy away from self-congratulation, the *Bee* sought to bolster its opinions by quoting the *Kearney Hub* as stating that of the three war correspondents for Nebraska newspapers present at Pine Ridge, the best reports came from the *Bee,* with the *Lincoln Journal*'s reports second and the "poorest reports of all" coming from the *World-Herald.*[57]

The *Daily Chronicle*'s editorial policy was similar to the *Bee*'s. It wrote that "300 'good Indians' were made at the late fight with the hostiles. Now look for a howl from the New Englanders, whose only knowledge of Indians comes from [James Fenimore] Cooper's novels. . . . But all this romance is knocked higher than a kite by actual contact with the fierce, brutal savages, whom nothing can tame or civilize."[58]

The *Castle Rock Journal* was also determined to milk the trouble at Wounded Knee for more articles, sarcastically mocking the opinion that the crisis in South Dakota was over. It pointed out that there were 2,800 "loving, tenderhearted 'friendlies'" within a mile of the agency with only 500 troops to protect it. It also wrote of a recent alleged attack on an army officer. "When the officer and his two companions turned their backs to ride back to camp, the sneaking, treacherous, dastardly pets of the government shot him down from behind. Yet there is no war here. Come out gentle lover of the Indian and you shall sup on horrors."[59] In fact, there would be no more "battles" and the vast majority of the casualties of this one were women and children.

Once the bodies had been counted and a little time had passed, the nation's newspapers began asking for answers to the question of who was to blame for the Wounded Knee tragedy. The *World-Herald* identified several villains, including Colonel James Forsyth. When General Miles relieved Forsyth of his command, the paper headlined its story "He Will Answer Before a Court Martial for the Big Foot Butchery." The story, however, was not as accusatory as its headline. The *World-Herald* claimed that the army's principal accusation against Forsyth was that he had placed his troops so that, when the battle began, they fired upon each other.[60] Despite General Miles's best efforts, Forsyth was found to have acted reasonably and was eventually restored to command.[61]

Historian Smith states that prior to Wounded Knee most of the nation's press had been "hollering for blood." He adds, "There is substantial evidence indicating that without the newspapers' distortion of the facts and a continual agitation of both whites and Indians, there would not have been a battle of Wounded Knee. . . . But once it had obtained the blood it was 'hollering for,' much of the press had faced about and began working the other side of the street." Smith wrote that the newspapers who had been calling the Indians "treacherous" and "murderous" were now calling them "innocent victims." In addition, soldiers they had been describing as "heroic defenders of the frontier" were now murderers and were guilty of "slaughter without provocation." Smith points out that Democratic newspapers [such as the *World-Herald*], saw a chance, in Wounded Knee, to brand the Republican administration with the guilt of a brutal bloodletting.[62]

The *Bee* did not think the Indians were innocent victims. It was outraged by Forsyth's removal and felt sure he would be exonerated. It still expected a bloody climax to the troubles and featured headlines such as "Omens of Bloodshed" and "Terrified Settlers Desert Their Homes and Swarm into Town."[63] The paper also found time to run a brief story from the *Philadelphia Ledger* that praised Cressey's coverage of the ghost dance troubles and compared him to other "great" war correspondents.[64]

In contrast to its neighbor, the *Aspen Daily Chronicle,* the *Leadville Evening Chronicle* seemed more empathetic to the Indians' side of the story. It printed an interview with Sioux chief Red Cloud where he stated that the Indians had been promised many things but that very few of the promises were kept. "Our food is poor, our clothing bad and very little has been done to help us farm. . . . Year after year our rations have been cut down. . . . We want to learn the ways of the white man, but that cannot be done in a day or a year. We can go hungry, but we must have something to keep the children alive."[65] The Leadville paper wrote that Red

Cloud's viewpoint might be slanted, but it was hard to argue against his claim of broken promises.

The *Aspen Daily Chronicle* took time to lambast some of the coverage of the Wounded Knee affair by eastern newspapers. It minimized the slaughter of women and children and predicted that these writers would change their tune if they were living on the frontier. "The long-haired philanthropists are now bewailing the fact that some squaws and papooses were killed at the Wounded Knee affair as the result of the treachery of the bucks, but they have no tears for Uncle Sam's soldiers and officers who were treacherously murdered in the same affair. What a blessed thing it would be if these eulogists of savage murderers could be drafted into the army and be made to serve on the frontier for about five years. Their love of the 'noble red man' would soon cool."[66]

The *Leadville Evening Chronicle* also did some editorial mocking of eastern newspapers, but it was in direct contrast to the *Aspen Daily Chronicle.* "A New York paper calls the Wounded Knee battle a 'glorious victory' for the United States troops. Well, hardly. The slaughter of sucking babes and fleeing squaws was not glorious. The whole business was a hideous, ghastly mistake."[67]

While the *Bee,* the *Aspen Daily Chronicle,* and the *Castle Rock Journal* were fanning the flames of hysteria, the *World-Herald* was still looking for someone to blame:

> Somebody is to blame that over thirty brave soldiers lie dead and forty more are suffering from their wounds, that over 300 Indians, men, women and children, lie dead under a winter sky with coyotes and dogs preying on their unburied bodies, and over 4,000 destitute people are fleeing from their homes in midwinter, fearing the same fate.
>
> Of course the Indian is always to blame. He neither writes nor owns a newspaper. His opinions are never consulted. He has been starved, robbed and lied to until he has no right to expect anything else and he should at once be put to death or lamely submit to an unending succession of Royers that will be inflicted upon him whether he wants them or not.
>
> Yet we are a Christian people, for murder, starvation and death is still the portion of the heathen as it was in the days of Pizzarro, Cortez and the noble Pilgrims of New England.[68]

The worst fears of the frontier newspapers were never realized. Within two weeks, the "war" was over. On January 13, 1891, the *Bee* declared, "The End Almost in Sight,"[69] and on January 17, 1891, it announced, "The Indian War Is Over."[70] A "war" that had begun with panic over the pathetic attempt of the Indians to dance back the old days, fueled by wild stories from breathless correspondents, had ended with a whimper.

Historian Watson stated that "Despite all their violations of news writing principles—rumor-mongering, exaggeration, distortion and faking—the corps of correspondents who covered the Ghost Dance troubles. . . . are entitled to some recognition in the history of American journalism."[71] Author Oliver Knight was not as kind. He felt that Wounded Knee was not journalism's finest hour. He wrote, "With rumor, exaggeration, distortion and falsifying, despite some accurate reporting, the reporters at Pine Ridge signed an unfitting '30' [end of story] to newspaper coverage of the Western war."[72]

It is not totally clear whether the *Bee* and the Colorado newspapers really understood the significance of Wounded Knee and the events that led up to it. They may have perceived that it was only a feeble attempt by the Indians to forestall the inevitable. However, if only for the sake of selling newspapers, they portrayed the events as a harbinger of a catastrophic assault on the white settlers and their cherished way of life. In contrast, the *World-Herald* and, to a lesser degree, the *Leadville Evening Chronicle* recognized the true significance of the events and lamented the starvation, ignorance, and greed that ultimately led to the suffering and slaughter of so many innocent men, women, and children.

CHAPTER 9

Closing the Circle

During the last third of the 19th century, the Indians of the Great Plains went from being rulers of thousands of square miles of territory to paupers cooped up on parcels of barren land. Much had changed in the newspaper business as well. Improvements in technology and the settling of the frontier meant that a story about the battle of Wounded Knee could appear in the evening edition of an Omaha paper on the same day that the event took place. In contrast, just 14 years earlier, it took 12 days for the news of Custer's death to reach the readers of Omaha's newspapers. However, not everything had changed. For example, Indian stereotypes that were popular in 1862 found renewed popularity in 1890.

In the coverage of the Great Sioux Uprising in Minnesota, the *Mankato Semi-Weekly Record* featured some initial inaccuracy in its reporting, inflating the casualty count and inflaming emotions. Later it tried to calm the public's fears and put things in perspective. The Minnesota papers ran the gamut in terms of their portrayal of the Sioux. The *St. Cloud Democrat*'s editorials promoted genocide and encouraged paying bounties for scalps. In contrast, the *St. Paul Pioneer* covered the mass hanging of 38 Sioux in a sensitive and sympathetic fashion.

In what would become a theme repeated in the coverage of several Indian wars, the description of the Sand Creek Massacre was colored by the politics of the newspapers that covered it. The *Rocky Mountain News* championed Colorado Governor John Evans and Colonel John Chivington, praising them as heroes. It featured editorials that would be judged blatantly racist by today's standards.

In contrast the *Daily Mining Journal* of Black Hawk, Colorado, initially praised Chivington's actions but eventually severely criticized both him and Governor Evans. Its attitude toward the Indians was at best paternalistic, but at least it recoiled in horror at some of the atrocities committed by Chivington and his men.

Its change of attitude may have been due to new details of the massacre, but it was certainly also seen as an opportunity to disparage its political rivals.

During the late 1860s, the *Omaha Republican* and the *Omaha Herald* both did a fairly accurate job of covering the Fort Laramie Treaty of 1868. The *Herald* did a much more thorough job of covering the event than did the *Republican*. However, the *Republican*'s cynical prediction that the peace treaty would not last proved to be more prescient than the *Herald*'s cautious hope for a lasting peace. Both papers occasionally used the term *savages* to describe the Indians, but the overall tone of the stories was far less derogatory than later coverage would be.

There was little balance in the two newspapers' coverage of the treaty. The story was told almost exclusively from the whites' point of view. Oliver Knight, in his book *Following The Indian Wars,* writes that the "Western war correspondent reported the story in detail, but did not and could not have had the Indian side of the story. Often, however, the reporter did reveal the Indian side when he sought to explain the cause of the conflict, not in terms of Indian interpretations, but in terms of criminal mismanagement of Indian affairs by civilians. In that connection, the reporter generally reflected the feelings, attitudes and thoughts of the military."[1] This remained relatively true throughout the coverage of the Indian wars by the Omaha papers with the striking exception of Bright Eyes' stories about the ghost dance and Wounded Knee for the *Omaha World-Herald.*

In examining the history of the western Indian wars, the Battle of the Little Big Horn created more myths than any other single event. This myth making also affected the coverage of the event by the frontier newspapers. Journalist Barbara Cloud writes, "In considering the frontier press, one must deal with the legends and mythology that have developed, both about the region and about the press itself. Western literature, both fiction and nonfiction, has created people and places larger than even the wide-open spaces of the West can accommodate with honesty, and journalism history has added its own mystique."[2]

The frontier newspapers were shocked by the death of Lieutenant Colonel George Armstrong Custer. To them, he had been an indestructible hero who had weathered the Civil War. It was unthinkable that he had met his end at the hands of "ignorant savages." While the Omaha newspapers demonized the Indians somewhat, this attitude was not as intense as in their coverage of other events. The newspapers, especially the *Bee* and the *Republican,* concentrated their efforts on glorifying Custer. If Custer were to be painted in the most heroic of colors, he had to have been defeated by worthy opponents. This attitude led to stories portraying Sitting Bull as a military genius who had studied the campaigns of Napoleon, or the even wilder tale that as a taciturn cadet known as "Bison," he had graduated from West Point. There were many stories about the overwhelming number of Indians that Custer faced, and that the Indians were better armed than the soldiers. There is no doubt that Custer was heavily outnumbered, but that was simply one factor in his defeat. Of the three Omaha newspapers, only the *Herald* gave credit to the Sioux and their allies for their military prowess.

The search for scapegoats became a focus of many newspapers in the aftermath of Custer's defeat. Major Marcus Reno, Custer's second in command, was blamed by many, including Custer's widow, Libby Custer. He was exonerated following a court martial. Others blamed the government and some even blamed Custer himself. The *Herald* saw the Custer debacle as political ammunition it could use against President Ulysses S. Grant and the Republican Party. It was a theme that the *Herald* was to use throughout its coverage of Little Big Horn.

When stereotypes were used, the "murdering redskin" stereotype dominated, but there were a few instances in which the "degraded Indian" was also used. There were many exaggerations in terms of Indian casualties and reports of the overall number of Indians present at Little Big Horn. Even more disturbing were false reports of the total annihilation of troops under the command of General Alfred Terry and Major Marcus Reno. In the weeks following the battle, the frontier newspapers competed with each other to provide details of the battle, ensuring very comprehensive coverage of this epochal event for their readers. Despite the in-depth coverage, few stories were written from the viewpoint of the Indians. While the *Bee* and the *Republican* warned of an even greater gathering of the tribes, the *Herald* correctly predicted that the large camp could not hold together and would soon break up, influenced more by the movements of buffalo herds than by the those of the soldiers.

The Nez Perce campaign presented an interesting opportunity for frontier newspapers. For the first time, Chief Joseph represented an Indian leader who fit the "noble savage" stereotype quite well. Unlike Sitting Bull, Chief Joseph had no history of militancy against the whites; in fact he had a reputation for peaceful relations with his white neighbors. Joseph was different. Not only was he given credit not only for a string of surprising victories over his white opponents but also for having a just cause—trying to get his people to safety while fighting overwhelming odds.

In the early reporting on the Nez Perce campaign, the newspapers used negative stereotypes to describe the actions of the Indians, particularly the murder of the civilians who precipitated the outbreak. However, as the campaign continued and the Nez Perce successfully defended themselves, the coverage began to turn sympathetic, especially in the *Herald*. In addition, most of the inaccuracies occurred in the early stages of the coverage. Once the campaign was in full swing, the reporting was fairly accurate.

A notable exception was the story that appeared in both the *Omaha Bee* and the *Colorado Miner* about the slaughter of Chinese miners by the Nez Perce. It was a massacre that was vividly described despite the fact that it had never taken place.

The *Bee* and the *Republican* showed poor judgment when they called for an extensive use of volunteer militia to corral the Nez Perce. In both instances where militia had been present during a battle, their performance had been at best inept and at worst disastrous. The regular army received both criticism and praise. The *Colorado Transcript* criticized the military prowess of General Oliver O. Howard, and the *Boulder News* praised General Nelson Miles.

Several papers predicted—inaccurately—that the flight of the Nez Perce would lead to a general uprising of the Indians of the Northwest. The *Pueblo Chieftain* thought that Joseph's success would inspire hundreds of young Indian men from other tribes to join him. The *Herald* went so far as to claim an alliance, in support of the Nez Perce, between the Crow and their traditional enemies the Sioux. In spite of these relatively few inaccuracies, it was the most balanced reporting to date, with several stories written from the Indian perspective.

The theme of the "noble savage" continued in the *Herald's* coverage of the Cheyenne outbreak. It called the Cheyenne men of gentle nature who were forced to choose between starvation and warfare. In contrast, other papers, especially the *Bee,* preferred to use the "murdering redskin" stereotype. As in the coverage of the Nez Perce campaign, most of the inaccuracies in reporting appeared in the early coverage of the campaign. The *Bee* was guilty of perhaps the most grievous errors when it reported the death of Dull Knife in the first encounter of the campaign and when it stated that the Cheyenne were fat, sleek, and wealthy and had no reason for discontent. The *Herald* also made its share of mistakes. At one point it claimed that Spotted Tail had taken his band of Sioux on the warpath to aid the Cheyenne. In fact, some Sioux acted as scouts for the army.

The initial predictions by all the newspapers of the army's imminent capture of the fleeing Cheyenne were overly optimistic. In addition, all the papers warned of danger to the civilians in the path of the Cheyenne. In fact, with the notable exception of the settlers in the Sappa Valley in western Kansas, the Indians tried to avoid conflict with white settlers. While the *Wichita Daily Beacon* romanticized an early encounter between the Cheyenne and the Cavalry, the *Dodge City Times* tried to downplay the danger of the flight of the Cheyenne. They seemed to fear that settlers would panic, flee the region, and never come back.

As the campaign progressed, the *Herald* became more and more sympathetic to the plight of the Cheyenne. Following the last bloody flight of Dull Knife's band from Camp Robinson, even the *Bee* and the *Republican* evinced sympathy for the surviving Cheyenne. The significance of the Cheyenne outbreak—whether the military or the civilian Indian Bureau should have jurisdiction over the Indians—was recognized by all three Omaha newspapers.

The Standing Bear trial also featured wrangling over who had jurisdiction over the Indians. Unlike the newspaper coverage of previous events, the Standing Bear trial was not subject to the vagaries of time, distance, or geography. Most of the action took place within the confines of a courtroom and the reporters had easy access to the court records. This resulted in unmatched levels of balance and accuracy in the reporting of the event by the Omaha newspapers. Despite opposite predictions by the *Bee* and the *Herald,* both turned out to be incorrect. The *Bee's* prediction that Judge Elmer Dundy's decision would lead to a mass exodus of disgruntled tribesmen proved to be no more correct than the *Herald's* assertion that the outcome of the trial would have a lasting impact on relations between the Indians and the whites.

Stereotyping played a smaller role in the coverage of the Standing Bear trial. Almost no negative stereotypes were used. A rare exception was the *Republican's* reference to a "wronged, but savage people." The *Herald's* coverage did feature some use of the "noble savage" stereotype, especially in its descriptions of Standing Bear. If any stereotype dominated, it was the stereotype of the "degraded Indian." There were references to a "feeble class of beings," and "poor and ragged Indians" by the *Herald* and a paternalistic tone was evident throughout the newspaper's coverage of the trial.

In August 1890, the *Republican* folded and left the *Bee* and the *World-Herald* to battle it out in their editorials. As a result, the *Republican* missed the last great Indian story of the 19th century—the ghost dance and the battle at Wounded Knee. The *World-Herald* had been formed in 1889 when Gilbert M. Hitchcock, owner and publisher of the *World,* had purchased the *Herald* and merged the two papers.

It had been a few years since the Omaha newspapers had been given a story of this magnitude right in their own backyard. The first brief stories appeared in the October editions of the papers, and by November, conflict with the Indians dominated the front pages of both the *Bee* and the *World-Herald.* The *Bee* was much more inclined to sensationalize the story and use stereotypes with abandon. It described the Indians as "red devils," "fanatical ghost dancers," "crazed red men" and the "savage foes of civilization." The paper left little doubt as to how it felt about the Indians.

Most of the Colorado papers followed the pattern set by the *Bee.* In fact, many of them reprinted stories written by the *Bee's* correspondents. The *Aspen Weekly Times, Aspen Chronicle,* and *Leadville Daily, and Evening Chronicle* offered sensationalized coverage of the events unfolding in South Dakota. The newspapers regularly inflated the numbers of the Indians involved in the events and romanticized the ghost dance, making it seem mysterious and ominous. It portrayed the Indians as "maniacs, crazed Indians" and "fanatical Redskins."

In contrast, the *World-Herald* was more sympathetic in its coverage. It was more likely to refer to the Sioux simply as Indians, although following the battle of Wounded Knee, it did warn that the Indians were "out for blood." Both papers occasionally employed the "degraded Indian" stereotype in their coverage. The *Bee* called the Sioux "cigar store models" and described them as "half-animated, long-haired, blanket-swathed musk bags." The *World-Herald* referred to the Indians as "miserable" and "destitute" as well as "helpless and ignorant."

While neither paper was entirely accurate in its coverage of the events, the *World-Herald* generally refrained from making bold claims and tended to downplay the reports of bloodshed and imminent disaster that were featured almost daily in the *Bee* and the Colorado newspapers. In contrast, the *Bee* gleefully reported on battles that had never taken place and once even went so far as to report specific casualties for a nonexistent battle. The *Bee* and the Aspen and Leadville newspapers also made frequent predictions of disaster and warned almost daily of a massive uprising that would engulf the west in a wave of blood and fire. It often assured its readers that within 24 or 48 hours a catastrophe was certain to occur.

When disaster did not occur, the *Bee* blithely ignored its earlier predictions and crowed that it was widely viewed as having the most accurate grasp of the "facts."

Its sensationalized style of reporting the ghost dance did seem to be copied by the Aspen and Leadville papers. The *World-Herald* took a more measured approach to covering the events and was reluctant to make rash predictions. For the most part, it accurately predicted the scope and duration of the violence that was to occur.

It is in the area of balance that the papers differ most. The *Bee* and the Colorado newspapers saw menace in every move of the Indians. At one point, a reporter from the *Bee* even attached evil intent and fears of an ambush to the glances of Indians traveling on the train with him to South Dakota. The paper made it clear that the Indians were solely to blame for any trouble that might occur. The sole exception to that theme was an admission that hunger on the part of the Indians might have had a role to play in their unrest. The *World-Herald,* on the other hand, went out of its way to provide balance to its coverage of the events. It actively sought out the Indian side of the story and presented a measured tone throughout its coverage. It even took the unprecedented step of employing an Omaha Indian as one of its correspondents in hopes that she would provide a valuable insight into Sioux beliefs and practices.

There was a basic consistency in the coverage of all the frontier newspapers throughout all the events of this period. With the notable exception of the *Herald* and later the *World-Herald,* the frontier papers mostly maintained a single philosophy regarding the "Indian problem." While the coverage varied somewhat depending on the event, it did not vary greatly. Many of the newspapers tended to treat the Indian as subhuman, little better than wild animals to be tamed or eliminated. The extent of their vitriol was at times astounding.

However, the newspapers did show some signs of balance in their coverage of the Great Sioux Uprising, the Sand Creek Massacre, the Nez Perce war, and the Cheyenne outbreak. While they were far from sympathetic, they did at least sometimes strike a conciliatory note. The exception to the rule for the Omaha papers was their sympathetic coverage of the Standing Bear trial. Of course, the fact that the Ponca posed no threat may have had something to do with that. The *Bee* returned to its traditional approach during coverage of the ghost dance and Wounded Knee episodes. The coverage of the ghost dance by the Aspen and Leadville papers was also almost universally sensationalistic and often inaccurate.

In marked contrast, the *Herald* and later the *World-Herald* remained sympathetic to the plight of the Indian throughout all the events. This is truly surprising considering that Omaha was a frontier town and that generally public opinion toward the Indian was anything but favorable. The *Herald* and *World-Herald's* editorial opinions flew in the face of this traditional frontier attitude. The *Republican,* and especially the *Bee,* were not slow to criticize the *Herald,* and later the *World-Herald,* for their unpopular stands. The *Herald* and its successor returned the favor in their editorial columns. The *Rocky Mountain News* and the *Daily Mining Journal* also used their columns to snipe at their political and business rivals. All of the newspapers used their discussion of the "Indian problem" to further their own political philosophy and especially to criticize the philosophy of their competitors.

While all of the newspapers made inaccurate claims and utilized racial stereo-types in their reporting, there is little doubt that the *Herald* and especially the *World-Herald* outperformed their rivals in terms of accuracy, prediction, balance, and judgment. Never is the contrast as apparent as in a comparison of the coverage of the events of Wounded Knee by the *World-Herald* and the other newspapers. While the *Bee* and the Colorado newspapers succumbed to exaggeration, omission of pertinent facts, and sometimes outright fabrication, the *World-Herald* presented an accurate, balanced, and calm portrayal of the events to its readers. It also took the unprecedented and almost revolutionary step of employing an Indian reporter to give its readers better insight to the Indian side of the story.

When it came to coverage of the "Indian problem," it is safe to say that the frontier newspapers performed as well as, and in some cases better than, many newspapers in large metropolitan areas. The *Herald* and the *World-Herald* can be especially singled out for the quality of their reporting. These two papers earned prominent mention in the history of the frontier press.

Notes

INTRODUCTION

1. David Dary, *Red Blood and Black Ink* (New York: Alfred A. Knopf, 1998), p. 22.

2. John Myers Myers, *Print in a Wild Land* (Garden City, NY: Doubleday, 1967), p. 60.

3. Ibid., p. 61.

4. Ibid., p. 108.

5. Benjamin Pfeiffer, "The Role of Joseph E. Johnson and His Pioneer Newspapers and the Development of Territorial Nebraska," *Nebraska History* 40 (June 1959), p. 129.

6. Richard H. Dillon, *North American Indian Wars* (New York: Facts on File, 1983), p. 110.

7. Pfeiffer, "The Role of Joseph E. Johnson and His Pioneer Newspapers and the Development of Territorial Nebraska," p. 128.

8. Ibid., p. 126.

9. Ibid., p. 124.

10. Alfred Sorenson, *The Story of Omaha From the Pioneer Days to the Present,* 3rd ed. rev. (Omaha, NE: National Printing Co., 1923), p. 431.

11. Ibid., p. 430.

12. James Savage and John T. Bell, *A Brief History of the City of Omaha, Nebraska* (New York, 1894), p. 141.

13. James W. Savage, "George L. Miller," *Magazine of Western History,* 9 (March 1889), reprinted (Omaha, NE: Gibson, Miller and Richardson, 1889), p. 616.

14. Ibid., p. 623.

15. Ibid., p. 623.

16. Sorenson, *The Story of Omaha,* pp. 430–433.

17. Victor Rosewater, "How I Came to Go Into Newspaper Work," *Nebraska History,* 17 (July–September, 1936), pp. 181–188.

18. Walter Christensen, "Gilbert M. Hitchcock; The Newspaperman," *Nebraska History,* 17 (July–September, 1936), p. 191.

19. Ibid., p. 189.

20. *Omaha Republican,* April 13, 1873, p. 2.

21. Elmo Scott Watson, "The Indian Wars and the Press, 1866–1867," *Journalism Quarterly,* 17 (1940), p. 302.

22. Barbara Cloud, *The Business of Newspapers on the Western Frontier* (Reno: University of Nevada Press, 1992), p. 150.

23. Ibid., p. 74.

24. Ibid., p. 111.

25. Pfeiffer, "The Role of Joseph E. Johnson and His Pioneer Newspapers and the Development of Territorial Nebraska," p. 121.

26. Myers, *Print in a Wild Land,* p. 60.

27. Ibid., p. 30.

28. Ibid., p. 30.

29. Robert F. Berkhofer, *The White Man's Indian* (New York: Alfred A. Knopf, 1978), p. 28.

30. Ibid., p. 28.

31. Ibid., p. 30.

32. *Omaha Daily Herald,* May 7, 1873, p. 2.

33. John L. Martin and Harold L. Nelson, "The Historical Standard in Press Analysis," *Journalism Quarterly,* 33 (1956), p. 457.

34. Ibid., p. 458.

35. Ibid., p. 463.

36. Berkhofer, *The White Man's Indian,* p. 3.

37. Ibid., p. 91.

38. Josiah Nott and George R. Glidden, *Types of Mankind: Or, Ethnological Researches Based Upon the Ancient Monuments, Painting, Sculptures and Crania of Races,* 6th ed. (Philadelphia: Lippincott, Grambo & Co., 1854), p. 461.

39. Cloud, *The Business of Newspapers on the Western Frontier,* p. xiii.

40. Ibid., p. xiv.

41. Oliver Knight, *Following the Indian Wars* (Norman: University of Oklahoma Press, 1960), pp. 5, 6.

42. Robert M. Utley, *Cavalier in Buckskin: George Armstrong Custer and the Western Military Frontier* (Norman: University of Oklahoma Press, 1988), p. 55.

43. Watson, "The Indian Wars and the Press, 1866–1867," p. 302.

44. Office Memoranda, Adjutant General's Office, *Chronological Lists of Actions &c., with Indians, From January 1, 1866 to January 1891,* pp. 2–56.

45. Knight, *Following the Indian Wars,* p. 6.

46. Ibid., p. 29.

47. John Finerty, *Warpath & Bivouac* (Chicago: M. A. Donoghue & Co., 1890), p. 120.

48. Knight, *Following the Indian Wars,* p. 326.

49. Watson, "The Indian Wars and the Press, 1866–1867," pp. 302, 303.

50. Ibid., p. 310.

51. Knight, *Following the Indian Wars,* p. 326.

CHAPTER 1: GREAT SIOUX UPRISING

The epigraph for this chapter comes from Paul Mazakootemane, "Narrative of Paul Mazakootemane." Minnesota Historical Society Collections, 1869, Vol. 3, 1870–1880.

1. Kellian Clink, "Historiography of the Dakota War," paper given at the Northern Plains History Conference, October 2001, p. 3.

2. Ibid., p. 4.

3. William Folwell, *A History of Minnesota,* Vol. 2. (St. Paul: Minnesota Historical Society Collections, 1924), p. 214.

4. Carol Chomsky, "The United States-Dakota War Trials: A Study in Military Injustice," *Stanford Law Review* 43, no. 1 (1990), p. 17.

5. Jerome Big Eagle, "A Sioux Story of the War," *Minnesota Historical Society Records* 6 (1894), p. 389.

6. Chomsky, "The United States-Dakota War Trials," p. 18.

7. Big Eagle, "A Sioux Story of the War," p. 389.

8. Chomsky, "The United States-Dakota War Trials," p. 18.

9. *Mankato Semi-Weekly Record* 4, no. 16 (August 23, 1962), p. 1.

10. Chomsky, "The United States-Dakota War Trials," p. 19.

11. *Mankato Semi-Weekly Record,* p. 2.

12. Ibid.

13. *Mankato Semi Weekly Record* 4, no. 18 (August 30, 1862), p. 1.

14. Ibid., p. 2.

15. Ibid.

16. Ibid.

17. Ibid., p. 3.

18. Ibid.

19. Ibid.

20. *St. Cloud Democrat,* "Scalps," September 11, 1862, p. 2.

21. *Mankato Semi-Weekly Record,* 4, no. 20 (September 6, 1862), p. 2.

22. Ibid.

23. Ibid, p. 3.

24. *Mankato Semi-Weekly Record* 4, no. 22 (September 12, 1862), p. 1.

25. Ibid.

26. *Mankato Semi-Weekly Record* 4, no. 22 (September 20, 1862), p. 1.

27. *Mankato Semi-Weekly Record* 4, no. 28 (October 10, 1862), p. 1.

28. Ibid.

29. *Mankato Semi-Weekly Record* 4, no. 30 (October 11, 1862), p. 1.

30. *Mankato Semi-Weekly Record* 4, no. 32 (October 18, 1862), p. 1.

31. Ibid.

32. *Mankato Semi-Weekly record* 4, no. 34 (October 25, 1862), p. 1

33. Chomsky, "The United States-Dakota War Trials," p. 21.

34. *Mankato Semi-Weekly record* 4, no. 34 (October 25, 1862), p. 2.

35. *Mankato Semi-Weekly Record* 4, no. 36 (November 11, 1862), p. 2.

36. *Mankato Semi-Weekly Record* 4, no. 26 (September 27, 1862), p. 1.

37. *The St. Paul Pioneer,* "Letter from Northern Minnesota," no. 237 (October 5, 1862), p. 1.

38. Chomsky, "The United States-Dakota War Trials," p. 20.

39. *Mankato Semi-Weekly Record* 4, no. 28 (October 4, 1862), p. 1.

40. Letter from Maj. Gen. John Pope to Col. Henry Sibley, September 28, 1862.

41. *Mankato Semi-Weekly Record* 4, no. 40 (November 15, 1862), p. 1.

42. *St. Paul Pioneer,* "The Indian Trials," no. 292 (December 11, 1862), p. 1.

43. Chomsky, "The United States-Dakota War Trials," p. 15.

44. Ibid., p. 28.

45. *Mankato Semi-Weekly Record* 4, no. 41 (November 11, 1862), p. 1.

46. Chomsky, "The United States-Dakota War Trials," p. 30.

47. *Mankato Semi-Weekly Record* 4, no. 20 (November 15, 1862), p. 1.

48. *Mankato Semi-Weekly Record* 4, no. 47 (December 13, 1862), p. 1.

49. Ibid., p. 2.

50. Ibid.

51. Ibid.

52. *The Mankato Semi-Weekly Record* 4, no. 49 (December 20, 1862), p. 1.

53. Ibid.

54. *St. Paul Pioneer,* "Execution of Sioux Murderers," no. 309 (December 28, 1862), p. 4.

55. Ibid.

56. Ibid., p. 1.

57. Ibid.

58. Ibid.

59. Angela Wilson Waziyatawin, "Little Crow," in *The Encyclopedia of American Indian History,* Vol. 3, ed. Bruce E. Johansen and Barry M. Pritzker (Santa Barbara, CA: ABC-CLIO, 2008), p. 771.

CHAPTER 2: SAND CREEK MASSACRE

1. Alvin M. Josephy Jr., *The Civil War in the American West* (New York: Alfred A. Knopf, 1991), p. 299.

2. Ibid., p. 300.

3. *Daily Mining Journal* 1, no. 152 (May 27, 1864), p. 3.

4. Alan C. Downs, "Sand Creek Massacre," in *The Encyclopedia of American Indian History,* Vol. 1, ed. Bruce E. Johansen and Barry M. Pritzker (Santa Barbara, CA: ABC-CLIO, 2008), p. 262.

5. Josephy, *The Civil War in the American West,* p. 306.

6. Ibid., p. 305.

7. Ibid.

8. Ibid.

9. *Rocky Mountain News Weekly* 6, no. 15 (July 27, 1864), p. 1.

10. Ibid.

11. *Rocky Mountain News Weekly* 6, no. 24 (September 28, 1864), p. 1.

12. Ibid.

13. "Massacre of Cheyenne Indians," in *Report of the Joint Committee of the Conduct of the War,* Vol. 3. U.S. Senate Report 142, 38th Congress, 2nd Session, Washington, D.C., 1865, p. 18.

14. George Bird Grinell, *The Fighting Cheyenne* (Norman: University of Oklahoma Press, 1915), p. 167.

15. Josephy, *The Civil War in the American West,* p. 308.

16. Testimony of 2nd Lt. Joseph A. Cramer in "Report of the Secretary of War," Senate Executive Document 26, 39th Congress, 2nd Session, Washington, D.C., 1867.

17. Josephy, *The Civil War in the American West,* p. 310.

18. Ibid., p. 311.

19. Ibid.

20. *Rocky Mountain News* 5, no. 92 (December 7, 1864), p. 2.

21. *Daily Mining Journal* 11, no. 7 (December 8, 1864), p. 2.

22. *Rocky Mountain News* 5, no. 96 (December 12, 1864), p. 2.

23. Ibid.
24. *Rocky Mountain News* 1, no. 35 (December 14, 1864), p. 2
25. Ibid.
26. *Daily Mining Journal* 2, no. 12 (December 14, 1864), p. 2.
27. *Rocky Mountain News* 1, no. 36 (December 21, 1864), p. 2.
28. *Rocky Mountain News Weekly* 1, no. 37 (December 28, 1864), p. 2.
29. Josephy, *The Civil War in the American West,* pp. 311, 312.
30. *Daily Mining Journal* 2, no. 26 (December 30, 1864), p. 3.
31. *Rocky Mountain News* 5, no, 111 (December 30, 1864), p. 2.
32. Ibid.
33. *Rocky Mountain News* 1, no. 38 (January 4, 1865), p. 4.
34. Ibid., p. 2.
35. Ibid., p. 3.
36. *Daily Mining Journal* 2, no. 30 (January 5, 1865), p. 2.
37. Ibid.
38. Ibid.
39. *Rocky Mountain News* 6, no. 39 (January 11, 1865), p. 2.
40. *Daily Mining Journal* 2, no. 78 (March 2, 1865), p. 2
41. Josephy, *The Civil War in the American West,* p. 312.
42. *Rocky Mountain News* 6, no. 39 (January 14, 1865), p. 2.
43. *Rocky Mountain News* 1, no. 141 (February 4, 1865), p. 4
44. *Rocky Mountain News* 1, no. 43 (February 8, 1865), p. 1.
45. Ibid.
46. *Rocky Mountain News* 2, no. 103 (March 31, 1865), p. 2.
47. *Rocky Mountain News* 5 no. 164 (March 3, 1865), p. 3.
48. *Daily Mining Journal* 2, no. 122 (April 25, 1865), p. 2.
49. *Rocky Mountain News* 1, no. 47 (March 8, 1865), p. 1.
50. *Daily Mining Journal* 2, no. 177 (June 29, 1865), p. 3.
51. Ibid.
52. "Massacre of the Cheyenne Indians," *Report of the Joint Committee on the Conduct of the War.*
53. Ibid.
54. Ibid.

CHAPTER 3: FORT LARAMIE TREATY

1. Loring Benson Priest, *Uncle Sam's Stepchildren: The Reformation of United States Indian Policy, 1865–1887* (Lincoln: University of Nebraska Press, 1875), p. 6.
2. LeRoy R. Hafen and Francis Marion Young, *Fort Laramie and the Pageant of the West, 1834–1890* (Glendale, CA: Arthur H. Clark Co., 1938), p. 358.
3. Report to the President by the Indian Peace Commission, January 7, 1868, in *Annual Report of the Commissioner of Indian Affairs for the Year 1868,* p. 31.
4. *Omaha Weekly Herald,* February 2, 1868, p. 1.
5. *Omaha Weekly Herald,* March 11, 1868, p. 1.
6. *Omaha Weekly Herald,* March 15, 1868, p. 1.
7. *Rocky Mountain News Weekly* 10, no. 3 (May 6, 1868), p. 1.
8. *Omaha Weekly Herald,* May 6, 1868, p. 1.
9. *Rocky Mountain News* 10, no. 4 (May 13, 1868), p. 1.

10. *Omaha Weekly Herald,* May 20, 1868, p. 1.

11. *Omaha Republican,* May 20, 1868, p. 1.

12. *Omaha Republican,* May 26, 1868, p. 1.

13. *Rocky Mountain News Weekly* 10, no. 5 (May 20, 1868), p. 2.

14. Ibid.

15. *Omaha Republican,* May 26, 1868, p. 1.

16. *Omaha Weekly Herald,* March 15, 1868, p. 1.

17. *Omaha Weekly Herald,* February 2, 1868, p.1.

18. *Omaha Weekly Herald,* May 20, 1868, p.1.

19. Dee Brown, *Bury My Heart at Wounded Knee* (New York: Bantam Books, 1970), p. 265.

CHAPTER 4: THE LITTLE BIG HORN CAMPAIGN

1. Richard H. Dillon, *North American Indian Wars* (New York: Facts On File, 1983), p. 57.

2. Robert M. Utley, *Cavalier in Buckskin: George Armstrong Custer and the Western Military Frontier* (Norman: University of Oklahoma Press, 1988), p. 4.

3. *Omaha Daily Herald,* July 7, 1876, p. 1.

4. *Omaha Bee,* July 6, 1876, p. 2.

5. *Omaha Republican,* July 8, 1876, p. 2.

6. Rex C. Myers, "Montana Editors and the Custer Battle," *Montana, The Magazine of Western History* 26 (April 1976), p. 21.

7. Brian W. Dippie, "The Southern Response to Custer's Last Stand," *Montana, The Magazine of Western History* 21 (April 1971), p. 24.

8. Myers, "Montana Editors and the Custer Battle," p. 24.

9. Ibid., p. 24.

10. Marie L. Schulte, "Catholic Press Reaction to the Custer Disaster," *Mid-America* 37 (October 1995), p. 206.

11. Dippie, "The Southern Response to Custer's Last Stand," p. 21.

12. Ibid., p. 22.

13. Ibid., p. 25.

14. Ibid., p. 28.

15. Ibid., p. 29.

16. *New York Herald,* July 7, 1876.

17. Myers, "Montana Editors and the Custer Battle," p. 31.

18. Evan S. Connell, *Son of the Morning Star: Custer and the Little Big Horn* (New York: Harper & Row, 1984), pp. 223–225.

19. Knight, *Following the Indian Wars.*

20. Lewis O. Saum, "Colonel Custer's Copperhead: The Mysterious Mark Kellogg," *Montana, The Magazine of Western History* 28 (Autumn 1978), p. 16.

21. Ibid., p. 20.

22. Ibid., p. 21.

23. Utley, *Cavalier in Buckskin,* p. 165.

24. Saum, "Colonel Custer's Copperhead," p. 21.

25. Utley, *Cavalier in Buckskin,* p. 192.

26. *Omaha Daily Herald,* July 8, 1876, p. 1.

27. James Donovan, *A Terrible Glory: Custer and the Little Bighorn* (New York: Little Brown, 2008), p. 318.

28. Knight, *Following the Indian Wars,* p. 216.

29. Donovan, *A Terrible Glory,* p. 318.

30. Saum, "Colonel Custer's Copperhead," p. 23.

31. *Omaha Daily Herald,* July 8, 1876, p. 2.

32. *Omaha Republican,* January 15, 1876, p. 2.

33. *Omaha Republican,* January 22, 1876, p. 1.

34. *Omaha Republican,* January 22, 1876, p. 2.

35. *Omaha Republican,* February 5, 1876, p. 1.

36. Robert M. Utley, *The Lance and the Shield: The Life and Times of Sitting Bull* (New York: Henry Holt & Company, 1993), p. 128.

37. *Omaha Republican,* February 5, 1876, p. 1.

38. Utley, *The Lance and the Shield,* p. 128.

39. Ibid., p. 129.

40. *Omaha Republican,* February 26, 1876, p. 2.

41. *Omaha Republican,* March 4, 1876, p. 2.

42. *Omaha Republican,* March 18, 1876, p. 2.

43. *Omaha Bee,* March 23, 1876, p. 2.

44. *Omaha Republican,* March 25, 1876, p. 2.

45. *Omaha Bee,* March 27, 1876, p. 1.

46. Utley, *The Lance and the Shield,* p. 130.

47. *Omaha Republican,* March 29, 1876, p. 3.

48. Utley, *The Lance and the Shield,* p. 130.

49. *Omaha Republican,* March 26, 1876, p. 2.

50. *Omaha Republican,* April 8, 1876, p. 1.

51. *Omaha Republican,* April 29, 1876, p. 3.

52. *Omaha Bee,* May 30, 1876, p. 2.

53. *Omaha Daily Herald,* June 24, 1876, p. 2.

54. *Omaha Bee,* June 28, 1876, p. 2.

55. *Omaha Daily Herald,* June 28, 1876, p. 1.

56. Ibid.

57. Ibid.

58. Utley, *The Lance and the Shield,* pp. 141, 142.

59. Ibid., p. 142.

60. *Omaha Daily Herald,* July 6, 1876, p. 2.

61. *Omaha Daily Herald,* July 9, 1876, p. 2.

62. Utley, *Cavalier in Buckskin,* p. 179.

63. *Omaha Daily Herald,* July 6, 1876, p. 1.

64. Utley, *Cavalier in Buckskin,* p. 179.

65. *Omaha Bee,* July 6, 1876, p. 1.

66. Ibid., p. 2.

67. Ibid.

68. Ibid.

69. *Omaha Republican,* July 8, 1876, p. 1.

70. Ibid.

71. Utley, *Cavalier in Buckskin,* p. 188.

72. Ibid., p. 192.

73. *Omaha Daily Herald,* July 7, 1876, p. 2.

74. *Omaha Bee,* July 7, 1876, p. 1.

75. Ibid.

76. *Omaha Daily Herald,* July 7, 1876, p. 2.
77. Ibid.
78. Ibid., p. 1.
79. Connell, *Son of the Morning Star,* p. 47.
80. *Omaha Daily Herald,* July 8, 1876, p. 2.
81. Connell, *Son of the Morning Star,* pp. 10, 11.
82. *Helena Herald,* July 15, 1876, p. 1.
83. Connell, *Son of the Morning Star,* p. 316.
84. *Omaha Bee,* July 8, 1876, p. 1.
85. *Omaha Daily Herald,* July 9, 1876, p. 2.
86. *Omaha Bee,* July 11, 1876, p. 2.
87. Ibid., July 13, 1876, p. 1.
88. *Omaha Daily Herald,* July 12, 1876, p. 2.
89. Ibid.
90. Ibid.
91. Ibid.
92. *Omaha Daily Herald,* July 13, 1876, p. 1.
93. Connell, *Son of the Morning Star,* pp. 374, 375.
94. Ibid., p. 410.
95. Ibid.
96. *Omaha Bee,* July 14, 1876, p. 1.
97. Connell, *Son of the Morning Star,* p. 420.
98. Utley, *The Lance and the Shield,* pp. 160, 161.
99. *Omaha Daily Herald,* July 13, 1876, p. 2.
100. Ibid.
101. *Omaha Republican,* July 15, 1876, p. 1.
102. Utley, *Cavalier in Buckskin,* p. 189.
103. *Omaha Republican,* July 15, 1876, p. 3.
104. Ibid., p. 2.
105. *Omaha Daily Herald,* July 15, 1876, p. 2.
106. *Omaha Daily Herald,* July 16, 1876, p. 2.
107. *Omaha Republican,* July 22, 1876, p. 1.
108. Connell, *Son of the Morning Star,* p. 383.
109. Ibid., p. 308.
110. *Omaha Daily Herald,* July 16, 1876, p. 2.
111. *Omaha Daily Herald,* July 22, 1876, p. 2.
112. *Omaha Daily Herald,* July 23, 1876, p. 2.
113. Ibid.
114. Ibid.
115. *Omaha Daily Herald,* July 29, 1876, p. 1.
116. Utley, *The Lance and the Shield,* p. 166.
117. Ibid., p. 165.
118. *Omaha Bee,* July 24, 1876, p. 2.
119. Ibid.
120. *Omaha Bee,* August 1, 1876, p. 1.
121. Utley, *Cavalier in Buckskin,* p. 200.
122. *Omaha Daily Herald,* July 11, 1877, p. 2.

123. Neil Asher Silverman, "Custer's Ghostherders," *Military History Quarterly* 2, no. 2 (Winter 1990), p. 88.

CHAPTER 5: THE FLIGHT OF THE NEZ PERCE

1. Richard H. Dillon, *North American Indian Wars* (New York: Facts on File, 1983), p. 224.
2. Ibid., p. 224.
3. David Lavender, *Let Me Be Free: The Nez Perce Tragedy* (New York: HarperCollins, 1992), pp. 189–192.
4. Dillon, *Indian Wars,* p. 224.
5. Lavender, *Let Me Be Free,* p. 234.
6. Ibid., p. 238.
7. *Omaha Republican,* June 19,1877, p. 1.
8. Ibid.
9. *Omaha Republican,* June 20, 1877, p. 1.
10. *Omaha Daily Herald,* June 20, 1877, p. 1.
11. Dillon, *Indian Wars,* pp. 224–225.
12. *Omaha Bee,* June 22, 1877, p. 1.
13. *Omaha Republican,* June 19, 1877, p. 1.
14. Lavender, *Let Me Be Free,* p. 248.
15. *Omaha Daily Herald,* June 21, 1877, p. 1.
16. *Omaha Republican,* June 21, 1877, p. 1.
17. *Omaha Bee,* June 23, 1877, p. 1.
18. Ibid., p. 2.
19. Ibid.
20. *Omaha Republican,* June 23,1877, p. 1.
21. *Omaha Daily Herald,* June 26, 1877, p. 1.
22. Ibid., p. 2.
23. *Omaha Bee,* June 26, 1877, p. 2.
24. *Omaha Republican,* June 25, 1877, p. 1.
25. *Omaha Daily Herald,* June 27, 1877, p. 1.
26. Ibid.
27. *Omaha Bee,* June 27, 1877, p. 1.
28. *Omaha Republican,* June 29, 1877, p. 1.
29. Ibid.
30. *Omaha Bee,* June 27, 1877, p. 1.
31. *Omaha Daily Herald,* June 29, 1877, p. 2.
32. *Omaha Daily Herald,* June 30, 1877, p. 2.
33. Dillon, *Indian Wars,* p. 112.
34. *Omaha Republican,* June 30, 1877, p. 1.
35. *Omaha Bee,* June 30, 1877, p. 1.
36. *Omaha Bee,* July 6, 1877, p. 2.
37. Lavender, *Let Me Be Free,* p. 347.
38. *Omaha Republican,* July 6, 1877, p. 1.
39. Ibid.
40. Lavender, *Let Me Be Free,* p. 254.

41. *Omaha Republican,* July 6, 1877, p. 1.
42. Lavender, *Let Me Be Free,* p. 261.
43. Ibid.
44. *Omaha Republican,* July 10, 1877, p. 1.
45. *Omaha Bee,* July 18, 1877, p. 2.
46. *Omaha Bee,* July 14, 1877, p. 1.
47. *Colorado Miner* 11, no. 11 (July 21, 1877), p. 2.
48. *Omaha Daily Herald,* July 22, 1877, p. 1.
49. Dillon, *Indian Wars,* p. 225.
50. *Omaha Republican,* July 15, 1877, p. 1.
51. Ibid.
52. Ibid.
53. Dillon, *Indian Wars,* p. 225.
54. *Omaha Republican,* July 20, 1877, p. 1.
55. Ibid.
56. Lavender, *Let Me Be Free,* p. 268.
57. *Denver Daily Times,* July 21, 1877, p. 1.
58. *Omaha Daily Herald,* July 22, 1877, p. 1.
59. Ibid.
60. *Omaha Bee,* July 26, 1877, p. 2.
61. *Omaha Republican,* July 31, 1877, p. 1.
62. Dillon, *Indian Wars,* p. 226.
63. *Omaha Republican,* August 12, 1877, p. 1.
64. *Omaha Daily Herald,* August 17, 1877, p. 1.
65. *Omaha Bee,* August 13, 1877, p. 1.
66. Dillon, *Indian Wars,* p. 226.
67. *Omaha Daily Herald,* August 14, 1877, p. 2.
68. *Omaha Republican,* August 14, 1877, p. 2.
69. *Omaha Bee,* August 13, 1877, p. 2.
70. Ibid.
71. Lavender, *Let Me Be Free,* p. 286.
72. *Omaha Bee,* August 14, 1877, p. 2.
73. *Omaha Bee,* September 20, 1877, p. 1.
74. *Omaha Republican,* August 22, 1877, p. 1.
75. Ibid.
76. *Omaha Republican,* August 24, 1877, p. 1.
77. Ibid.
78. *Omaha Daily Herald,* August 28, 1877, p. 1.
79. *Omaha Bee,* August 30, 1877, p. 1.
80. *Omaha Republican,* August 25, 1877, p. 1.
81. *Pueblo Chieftain* 11, no. 483 (August 23, 1877), p. 2.
82. *Pueblo Chieftain* 11, no. 483 (August 26, 1877), p. 1.
83. *Colorado Transcript* 11, no. 37 (August 15, 1877), p. 2.
84. *Colorado Transcript* 11, no. 37 (August 28, 1877), p. 1.
85. Lavender, *Let Me Be Free,* p. 297.
86. Ibid., p. 298.
87. *Omaha Daily Herald,* October 10, 1877, p. 2.
88. *Omaha Daily Herald,* August 30, 1877, p. 2.

89. Dillon, *Indian Wars*, p. 227.

90. Lavender, *Let Me Be Free*, p. 307.

91. *Omaha Republican*, September 19, 1877, p. 1.

92. Lavender, *Let Me Be Free*, p. 309.

93. Ibid., pp. 309–310.

94. Ibid., p. 311.

95. *Omaha Bee*, September 29, 1877, p. 1.

96. *Omaha Bee*, October 2, 1877, p. 1.

97. Lavender, *Let Me Be Free*, pp. 314–317.

98. *Omaha Bee*, October 8, 1877, p. 1.

99. Lavender, *Let Me Be Free*, p. 317.

100. *Omaha Republican*, October 10, 1877, p. 1.

101. Dillon, *Indian Wars*, p. 228.

102. *Omaha Bee*, October 10, 1877, p. 1.

103. *Boulder News* 8, no. 48 (October 12, 1877), p. 2.

104. Ibid., p. 2.

105. *Omaha Daily Herald*, October 11, 1877, p. 2.

106. *Colorado Miner* 11, no. 25 (October 27, 1877), p. 2.

107. Dillon, *Indian Wars*, p. 229.

108. Lavender, *Let Me Be Free*, pp. 325–326.

109. Lavender, *Let Me Be Free*, pp. 252–253.

110. *Omaha Bee*, July 26, 1877, p. 2.

111. *Omaha Daily Herald*, August 28, 1877, p. 1.

112. *Omaha Bee*, August 14, 1877, p. 2.

113. *Omaha Republican*, August 28, 1877, p. 1.

114. *Omaha Republican*, October 11, 1877, p. 2.

115. Robert R. McCoy, *The Encyclopedia of American Indian History*, Vol. 3, ed. Bruce E. Johansen and Barry M. Pritzker (Santa Barbara, CA: ABC-CLIO, 2008), p. 763.

CHAPTER 6: THE CHEYENNE OUTBREAK

1. George Bird Grinnell, *The Fighting Cheyennes* (Norman: University of Oklahoma Press, 1955), p. 398.

2. John H. Monnett, *Tell Them We Are Going Home* (Norman, University of Oklahoma Press, 2001), p. 31.

3. *Omaha Herald*, September 17, 1878, p. 1.

4. *Wichita Daily Beacon*, September 25, 1878.

5. *Omaha Herald*, September 19, 1878, p. 1.

6. *Omaha Herald*, September 25, 1878, p. 2.

7. *Dodge City Times*, September 14, 1878.

8. *Omaha Bee*, October 4, 1878. p. 1.

9. *Omaha Bee*, October 5, 1878, p. 1.

10. *Omaha Bee*, October 4, 1878, p. 2.

11. Monnett, *Tell Them We Are Going Home*, pp. 79, 80.

12. Mari Sandoz, *Cheyenne Autumn* (New York: Hastings House Publishers, 1953), pp. 129–136.

13. *Omaha Herald*, October 5, 1878, p. 1.

14. *Omaha Herald*, October 6, 1878, p. 1.

15. *Omaha Republican,* October 6, 1878, p. 1.
16. Grinnell, *The Fighting Cheyennes,* p. 409.
17. *Omaha Bee,* October 9, 1878, p. 2.
18. Ibid.
19. Grinnell, *The Fighting Cheyennes,* p. 398.
20. *Omaha Bee,* October 10, 1878, p. 1.
21. Sandoz, *Cheyenne Autumn,* pp. 163–164.
22. Ibid., pp. 176–177.
23. *Omaha Republican,* October 25, 1878, p. 1.
24. Sandoz, *Cheyenne Autumn,* p. 195.
25. Brown, *Bury My Heart at Wounded Knee,* p. 325.
26. Ibid., p. 327.
27. Ibid., p. 328.
28. Monnett, *Tell Them We Are Going Home,* p. 123.
29. Grinnell, *The Fighting Cheyennes,* p. 419.
30. *Omaha Herald,* January 11, 1979, p. 1.
31. Ibid.
32. *Omaha Bee,* January 10, 1879, p. 1.
33. *Omaha Herald,* January 11, 1879, p. 1.
34. *Omaha Republican,* January 12, 1879, p. 1.
35. Monnett, *Tell Them We Are Going Home,* pp. 131, 132.
36. Ibid., p. 132.
37. *Omaha Herald,* January 11, 1879, p. 4.
38. *Omaha Bee,* January 11, 1879, p. 2.
39. *Omaha Herald,* January 12, 1879, p. 4.
40. *Omaha Bee,* January 14, 1879, p. 1.
41. *Omaha Herald,* January 17, 1879, p. 4.
42. Ibid., p. 1.
43. *Omaha Republican,* January 17, 1879, p. 1.
44. *Omaha Bee,* January 16, 1879, p. 1.
45. *Omaha Bee,* January 24, 1879, p. 1.
46. *Omaha Bee,* January 31, 1879, p. 1.
47. *Omaha Herald,* January 29, 1879, p. 4.
48. *Omaha Herald,* January 26, 1879, p. 4.
49. Ibid.
50. *Omaha Republican,* February 1, 1879, p. 1.
51. Sandoz, *Cheyenne Autumn,* p. 306.

CHAPTER 7: THE STANDING BEAR TRIAL

1. Brown, *Bury My Heart at Wounded Knee,* pp. 334–335.
2. *Omaha Bee,* June 20, 1877, p. 1.
3. *Omaha Republican,* April 27, 1879, p. 1.
4. Omaha *Republican,* June 2, 1877, p. 1.
5. Joe Starita, *I Am a Man* (St. Martin's Press, New York, 2008), p. 88.
6. Brown, *Bury My Heart at Wounded Knee,* pp. 340–341.
7. Ibid., pp. 341–342.

8. John M. Coward, "Creating the Ideal Indian: The Case of the Poncas," *Journalism History* 21 (Autumn 1995), p. 112.

9. Ibid., pp. 114–115.

10. Thomas Henry Tibbles, *Buckskin and Blanket Days: Memoirs of a Friend of the Indians* (New York: Doubleday and Company, 1957), p. 196.

11. *Omaha Herald,* April 1, 1879, p. 4.

12. *Omaha Herald,* April 9, 1879, p. 4.

13. Ibid.

14. Tibbles, *Buckskin and Blanket Days,* p. 199.

15. *Funk and Wagnall's Standard Desk Dictionary,* Vol. 1 (New York: Funk and Wagnall's, 1979), p. 288.

16. *Omaha Herald,* April 10, 1879, p. 4.

17. Ibid.

18. *Omaha Herald,* April 11, 1879, p. 4

19. *Omaha Herald,* April 12, 1879, p. 5.

20. *Omaha Herald,* April 13, 1879, p. 4.

21. Ibid.

22. Coward, "Creating the Indian Ideal," p. 113.

23. Ibid., p. 114.

24. *Omaha Herald,* April 16, 1879, p. 4.

25. *Omaha Bee,* April 30, 1879, p. 2.

26. Coward, "Creating the Ideal Indian," p. 116.

27. *Omaha Herald,* April 24, 1879, p. 2.

28. *Omaha Republican,* May 2, 1879, pp. 1–2.

29. *Omaha Bee,* May 1, 1879, p. 4.

30. *Omaha Herald,* May 2, 1879, p. 4.

31. Ibid., p. 8.

32. *Omaha Herald,* May 3, 1879, p. 8.

33. Ibid.

34. *Omaha Herald,* May 4, 1879, p. 2.

35. Ibid.

36. Ibid.

37. *Omaha Herald,* May 3, 1879, p. 8.

38. Tibbles, *Buckskin and Blanket Days,* p. 201.

39. Ibid.

40. *Omaha Republican,* May 4, 1879, p. 2.

41. *Omaha Republican,* May 9, 1879, p. 1.

42. Ibid.

43. *Omaha Republican,* May 12, 1979, p. 1.

44. Ibid.

45. *Omaha Herald,* May 13, 1879, p. 2.

46. *Omaha Evening News,* May 13, 1879, p. 2.

47. *Omaha Herald,* May 15, 1879, p. 5.

48. *Omaha Republican,* May 18, 1879, p. 2.

49. *Omaha Bee,* May 1, 1879, p. 4.

50. *Omaha Bee,* May 21, 1879, p. 2.

51. *Omaha Herald,* May 15, 1879, p. 5.

52. *Omaha Herald,* May 22, 1879, p. 4.
53. *Omaha Republican,* May 4, 1879, p. 2.
54. Brown, *Bury My Heart at Wounded Knee,* pp. 345–346.
55. Starita, *I Am a Man,* p. 181.
56. John L. Martin and Harold L. Nelson, "Historical Standard in Press Analysis," *Journalism Quarterly* 33 (1956), p. 457.
57. *Omaha Republican,* May 12, 1879, p. 1.

CHAPTER 8: GHOST DANCE AND WOUNDED KNEE

1. *Omaha World-Herald,* January 2, 1891, p. 1.
2. Robert M. Utley, *The Lance and the Shield: The Life and Times of Sitting Bull* (New York: Henry Holt & Company, 1993), p. 281.
3. Rex Alan Smith, *Moon of the Popping Trees: The Tragedy of Wounded Knee and the End of the Indian Wars* (Lincoln: University of Nebraska Press, 1981), pp. 67–68.
4. Smith, *Moon of the Popping Trees,* p. 74.
5. Richard E. Jensen, R. Eli Paul, and John E. Carter, *Eyewitness at Wounded Knee* (Lincoln: University of Nebraska Press, 1991), p. 12.
6. Jensen, Paul, and Carter, *Eyewitness at Wounded Knee,* p. 6.
7. Elmo Scott Watson, "The Last Indian War, 1890–1891: A Study of Newspaper Jingoism," *Journalism Quarterly* 20 (September 1943), p. 205.
8. *Leadville Evening Chronicle,* November 20, 1890, p. 1.
9. *Omaha World-Herald,* November 8, 1890, p. 2.
10. *Omaha World-Herald,* November 17, 1890, p. 1.
11. *Aspen Weekly Times,* November 22, 1890, p. 1.
12. Watson, "The Last Indian War, 1890–1891," p. 206.
13. *Aspen Daily Chronicle,* November 29, 1890, p. 1.
14. Watson, "The Last Indian War, 1890–1891," p. 44.
15. Ibid., p. 47.
16. *Omaha Bee,* November 20, 1890, p. 1.
17. *Omaha Bee,* November 22, 1890, p. 1.
18. *Omaha World-Herald,* November 28, 1890, p. 2.
19. *Omaha Bee,* November 22, 1890, p. 1.
20. *Omaha Bee,* November 24, 1890, p. 7.
21. *Aspen Daily Chronicle,* December 9, 1890, p. 1.
22. *Omaha World-Herald,* November 28, 1890, p. 1.
23. *Omaha World-Herald,* December 1, 1890, p. 1.
24. Watson, "The Last Indian War, 1890–1891," p. 211.
25. *Omaha World-Herald,* December 7, 1890, p. 1.
26. *Omaha Bee,* December 8, 1890, p. 3.
27. *Omaha World-Herald,* December 12, 1890, p. 1.
28. *Omaha World-Herald,* December 13, 1890, p. 1.
29. Utley, *The Lance and the Shield,* p. 293.
30. Ibid., pp. 300–303.
31. *Omaha World-Herald,* December 16, 1890, p. 3.
32. *Omaha Bee,* December 16, 1890, p. 1.
33. *Omaha World-Herald,* December 17, 1890, p. 2.
34. *Omaha Bee,* December 17, 1890, p. 1.

35. *Omaha Bee,* December 19, 1890, p. 1.
36. *Aberdeen Saturday Pioneer,* December 20, 1890.
37. *Omaha World-Herald,* December 17, 1890, p. 2.
38. Tibbles, *Buckskin and Blanket Days,* p. 305.
39. *Omaha World-Herald,* December 26, 1890, p. 1.
40. *Omaha Bee,* December 27, 1890, p. 5.
41. Watson, "The Last Indian War, 1890–1891," p. 213.
42. Tibbles, *Buckskin and Blanket Days,* p. 309
43. Brown, *Bury My Heart at Wounded Knee,* pp. 414–415.
44. Smith, *Moon of the Popping Trees,* pp. 184–186.
45. Ibid., pp. 188–190.
46. Ibid., pp. 193–197.
47. Brown, *Bury My Heart at Wounded Knee,* p. 418.
48. Tibbles, *Buckskin and Blanket Days,* pp. 311 312.
49. Watson, "The Last Indian War, 1890–1891," p. 214.
50. *Omaha Bee,* December 29, 1890, p. 1.
51. *Omaha Bee,* December 30, 1890, p. 1.
52. *Omaha World-Herald,* December 30, 1890, p. 1.
53. *Aspen Daily Chronicle,* December 31, 1890, p. 1.
54. *Omaha World Herald,* December 30, 1890, p. 2.
55. *Omaha Bee,* December 31, 1890, p. 1.
56. *Omaha Bee,* January 5, 1891, p. 1.
57. Ibid.
58. *Aspen Daily Chronicle,* December 31, 1890, p. 2.
59. *Castle Rock Journal,* January 14, 1891, p. 1.
60. *Omaha World Herald,* January 5, 1891, p. 1.
61. Smith, *Moon of Popping Trees,* pp. 202–203.
62. Ibid., p. 203.
63. *Omaha Bee,* January 6, 1891, p. 1.
64. *Omaha Bee,* January 7, 1891, p. 1.
65. *Leadville Evening Chronicle,* January 16, 1891, p. 2.
66. *Aspen Daily Chronicle,* January 15, 1891, p. 2.
67. *Leadville Evening Chronicle,* January 6, 1891, p. 2.
68. *Omaha World-Herald,* January 4, 1891, p. 2.
69. *Omaha Bee,* January 13, 1891, p. 5.
70. *Omaha Bee,* January 17, 1891, p. 1.
71. Watson, "The Last Indian War, 1890–1891," p. 219.
72. Oliver Knight, *Following the Indian Wars* (Norman: University of Oklahoma Press, 1960), p. 315.

CHAPTER 9: CLOSING THE CIRCLE

1. Knight, *Following the Indian Wars,* p. 327.
2. Barbara Cloud, *The Business of Newspapers on the Western Frontier* (Reno: University of Nevada Press, 1992), p. xiv.

Bibliography

Aberdeen Saturday Pioneer. December 20, 1890.

Ambrose, Stephen. *Crazy Horse and Custer: The Parallel Lives of Two American Warriors.* New York: Doubleday, 1975.

Andrist, Ralph K. *The Long Death.* New York: Macmillan, 1964.

Aspen Daily Chronicle. November 29, 1890, to January 15, 1891.

Aspen Weekly Times. November 22, 1890.

Babcock, Willoughby. "Minnesota's Indian War." *Minnesota History* 38 (September 1962): 93–98.

Barnard, Sandy. *I Go With Custer: The Life and Death of Reporter Mark Kellogg.* Bismarck, ND: Bismarck Tribune, 1996.

Berkhofer, Robert F. *The White Man's Indian.* New York: Alfred A. Knopf, 1978.

Big Eagle, Jerome. "A Sioux Story of the War." Minnesota Historical Society Records, Vol. 6, 1894.

Boulder News. October 12, 1877.

Bourke, John G. *On the Border With Crook.* New York: Charles Scribner's Sons, 1981.

Boye, Alan. *Holding Stone Hands: On the Trail of the Cheyenne Exodus.* Lincoln: University of Nebraska Press, 1999.

Brady, Cyrus Townsend. *Indian Fights and Fighters.* New York: McClure, Phillips, 1904.

Brown, Dee. *Bury My Heart at Wounded Knee: An Indian History of the American West.* New York: Bantam Books, 1970.

Carley, Kenneth. *The Sioux Uprising of 1862.* St. Paul: Minnesota Historical Society, 1961.

Carley, Kenneth, ed. "As Red Men Viewed It: Three Indian Accounts of the Uprising." *Minnesota History* 38, no. 3 (September 1962): 126–149.

Castle Rock Journal. January 14, 1891.

Chomsky, Carol. "The United States–Dakota War Trials: A Study in Military Injustice." *Stanford Law Review* 43, no. 1 (November 1990).

Christensen, Walter. "Gilbert M. Hitchcock; The Newspaperman." *Nebraska History* 17 (July–September 1936): 188–197.

Clink, Kellian. "Historiography of the Dakota War," Paper given at the Northern Plains History Conference, October 2001.

Cloud, Barbara. *The Business of Newspapers on the Western Frontier.* Reno: University of Nevada Press, 1992.

Colorado Miner. July 21, 1877.

Colorado Transcript. August 15, 1877.

Connell, Evan S. *Son of the Morning Star: Custer and the Little Big Horn.* New York: Harper & Row, 1989.

Coward, John M. "Creating the Ideal Indian: The Case of the Poncas." *Journalism History* 21 (Autumn 1995): 112–121.

Custer, George Armstrong. *My Life on the Plains.* Reprint. Norman: University of Oklahoma Press, 1962.

Daily Mining Journal. May 27 1864, to June 29, 1865.

Dando-Collins, Stephen. *Standing Bear Is a Person: The True Story of a Native American's Quest for Justice.* Cambridge, MA: Da Capo Press, 2004.

Dary, David. *Red Blood and Black Ink: Journalism in the Old West.* New York: Alfred A. Knopf, 1998.

Denver Daily Times. July 21, 1877.

Dillon, Richard H. *North American Indian Wars.* New York: Facts on File, 1983.

Dippie, Brian W. "The Southern Response to Custer's Last Stand." *Montana, The Magazine of Western History* 21 (April 1971): 18–31.

Dodge City Times. September 14, 1878.

Donovan, James. *A Terrible Glory: Custer and the Little Bighorn.* New York: Little Brown and Company, 2008.

Finerty, John. *Warpath & Bivouac.* Chicago: M. A. Donoghue & Co., 1890.

Folwell, William. *A History of Minnesota,* Vol. 2. St. Paul: Minnesota Historical Society, 1924.

Fowler, Gene. *Timber Line: A Story of Bonfils and Tammen.* New York: Covici Friede Publishers, 1933.

Goodrich, Thomas. *Scalp Dance: Indian Warfare on the High Plains 1865–1879.* Mechanicsburg, PA: Stackpole Press, 2002.

Graham, Col. William T. *The Custer Myth: A Sourcebook of Custeriana.* Harrisburg, PA: Stackpole, 1953.

Greene, Jerome A. *Nez Perce Summer 1877: U.S. Army and the Nee-Me-Poo Crisis.* Helena: Montana Historical Society Press, 2000.

Grinnell, George Bird. *The Cheyenne Indians: Their History and Ways of Life.* 2 Vols. New Haven, CT: Yale University Press, 1923.

Grinnell, George Bird. *The Fighting Cheyennes.* Norman: University of Oklahoma Press, 1955.

Hafen, Leroy R., and Francis Marion Young. *Fort Laramie and the Pageant of the West, 1834–1890.* Glendale, CA: Arthur H. Clark Co., 1938.

Helena Herald. July 15, 1876.

Howard, James H. *The Ponca Tribe.* Lincoln: University of Nebraska Press, 1995.

Jensen, Richard, Eli Paul, and John E. Carter. *Eyewitness to Wounded Knee.* Lincoln: University of Nebraska Press, 1991.

Johansen, Bruce E., ed. *Enduring Legacies: Native American Treaties and Contemporary Controversies.* Westport, CT: Praeger, 2004.

Johansen, Bruce E., and Barry M. Pritzker, eds. *Encyclopedia of American Indian History,* 4 Vols. Santa Barbara, CA: ABC-CLIO, 2008.

Josephy, Alvin M. Jr. *The Civil War in the American West.* New York: Alfred A. Knopf, 1991.

Klein, Christina. "Everything of Interest in the Late Pine Ridge War Are Held for Sale: Popular Culture and Wounded Knee." *The Western Historical Quarterly,* 25 (Spring 1994): 45–63.

Knight, Oliver. *Following the Indian Wars.* Norman: University of Oklahoma Press, 1960.

Lane, Harrison. "Custer's Massacre: How the News First Reached the Outer World." *Montana, The Magazine of Western History* 3 (Summer 1953): 46–53.

Lavender, David. *Let Me Be Free: The Nez Perce Tragedy.* New York: HarperCollins, 1992.

Leadville Evening Chronicle, November 20, 1890, to January 16, 1891.

Letter from Maj. General John Pope to Col. Henry Sibley, September 28, 1862.

Mankato Semi-Weekly Record. August 23, 1862, to December 20, 1862.

Marshall, S.L.A. *Crimsoned Prairie.* New York: Charles Scribner's Sons, 1972.

Martin, John L., and Harold L. Nelson. "The Historical Standard in Press Analysis." *Journalism Quarterly* 33 (1956): 456–466.

"Massacre of the Cheyenne Indians." Report of the Joint Committee on the Conduct of the War. U.S. Senate Report 142, 38th Congress, 2nd Session. Washington, D.C., 1865.

Mazakootemane, Paul. "Narrative of Paul Mazakootemane." Minnesota Historical Society Collections, 1869, Vol. 3, 1870–1880.

Miller, David Humphreys. *Custer's Fall: The Indian Side of the Story.* New York: Duell, Sloan and Pearce, 1957.

Monnett, John H. *Tell Them We Are Going Home: The Odyssey of the Northern Cheyennes.* Norman: University of Oklahoma Press, 2001.

Meyers, John Meyers. *Print in a Wild Land.* Garden City, NY: Doubleday and Co., 1967.

Myers, Rex. "Montana Editors and the Custer Battle." *Montana, The Magazine of Western History* 26 (April 1976): 18–31.

Neidhardt, John G. *Black Elk Speaks.* Reprint, Lincoln: University of Nebraska Press, 2000.

New York Herald, July 7, 1876.

Nott, Josiah, and George R. Gliddon. *Types of Mankind: Or, Ethnological Researches Based Upon the Ancient Monuments, Painting, Sculptures and Crania of Races,* 6th ed. Philadelphia: Lippincott, Grambo & Co., 1854.

Office Memoranda, Adjutant General's Office. *Chronological Lists of Action &c., with Indians.* January 1, 1866, to January 1891, 2–56.

Omaha Bee. March 15, 1873, to January 1, 1891.

Omaha Daily Herald. February 2, 1868, to May 20, 1879.

Omaha Evening News. May 13, 1879.

Omaha Republican. May 20, 1868, to May 12, 1879.

Omaha World-Herald. October 16, 1890, to January 2, 1891.

Paul, R. Eli, ed. *The Nebraska Indian Wars Reader, 1865–1877.* Lincoln: University of Nebraska Press, 1998.

Pfeiffer, Benjamin. "The Role of Joseph E. Johnson and His Pioneer Newspapers and the Development of Territorial Nebraska." *Nebraska History* 40 (June 1959): 119–136.

Priest, Loring Benson. *Uncle Sam's Stepchildren: The Reformation of United States Indian Policy, 1865–1887.* Lincoln: University of Nebraska Press, 1975.

Prucha, Francis Paul. *American Indian Treaties: Documents of U.S. Indian Policy.* Berkeley: University of California Press, 1994.

Prucha, Francis Paul. "The Settler and the Army in Frontier Minnesota." *Minnesota History* 29, no. 3 (September 1948): 231–246.

Pueblo Chieftain. August 23, 1877.

Reilly, Hugh. "The First Civil Rights Victory." *Home & Away* (July–August 2004): 19a.

Report to the President by the Indian Peace Commission, January 7, 1868, in *Annual Report of the Commissioner of Indian Affairs for the Year 1868.*

Rocky Mountain News. December 7, 1864, to March 8, 1865.

Rocky Mountain News Weekly. July 27, 1864 to May 20, 1868.

Roddis, Louis H. *The Indian Wars of Minnesota.* Cedar Rapids, IA: Torch Press, 1956.

Rosewater, Victor. "How I Came to Go Into Newspaper Work." *Nebraska History* 17 (July–September 1936): 181–188.

Sandoz, Mari. *Cheyenne Autumn.* New York: Hastings House Publishers, 1953.

Sandoz, Mari. *Crazy Horse: The Strange Man of the Oglalas.* Lincoln: University of Nebraska Press, 1942.

Saum, Lewis O. "Colonel Custer's Copperhead: The Mysterious Mark Kellogg." *Montana, The Magazine of Western History* 28 (Autumn 1978): 12–25.

Savage, James W. "George L. Miller." *Magazine of Western History,* 9 (March 1889). Reprinted, Omaha: Gibson, Miller and Richardson, 1889: 615–625.

Savage James W., and John T. Bell. *A Brief History of the City of Omaha, Nebraska.* New York: no publisher, 1894.

Schulte, Marie L. "Catholic Press Reaction to the Custer Disaster." *Mid-America* 37 (October 1995): 204–214.

Sievers, Michael A. "The Historiography of the Bloody Field. . . . That Kept the Secret of the Everlasting Word: Wounded Knee." *South Dakota History* 6 (1975): 33–54.

Silverman, Neil Asher. "Custer's Ghostherders." *Military History Quarterly* 2 (Winter 1990): 84–93.

Smith, Rex Alan. *Moon of the Popping Trees: The Tragedy at Wounded Knee and the End of the Indian Wars.* Lincoln: University of Nebraska Press, 1981.

Sorenson, Alfred. *The Story of Omaha from the Pioneer Days to the Present,* 3rd ed. rev., Omaha, NE: National Printing, 1923.

Starita, Joe. *The Dull Knifes of Pine Ridge: A Lakota Odyssey.* New York: G. P. Putnam's Sons, 1995.

Starita, Joe. *I Am a Man: Chief Standing Bear's Journey for Justice.* New York: St. Martin's Press, 2009.

St. Cloud Democrat. September 11, 1862.

St. Paul Pioneer. October 5, 1862, to December 28, 1862.

Straight, Michael. *A Very Small Remnant.* New York: Alfred A. Knopf, 1963.

Tate, Michael L. *The Frontier Army in the Settlement of the West.* Norman: University of Oklahoma Press, 1999.

Tate, Michael L. *Indians and Immigrants: Encounters on the Overland Trails.* Norman: University of Oklahoma Press, 2006.

Testimony of 2nd Lieutenant Joseph A. Cramer. "Report of the Secretary of War." Senate Executive Document 26, 39th Congress, 2d Session, Washington, D.C., 1867 p. 47.

Tibbles, Thomas Henry. *Buckskin and Blanket Days: Memoirs of a Friend of the Indians.* New York: Doubleday and Company, 1957.

Tibbles, Thomas Henry. *The Ponca Chiefs: An Account of the Trial of Standing Bear.* Lincoln: University of Nebraska Press, 1972.

Trenerry, Walter N. "The Shooting of Little Crow: Heroism or Murder?" *Minnesota History* 38 (September 1962): 150–153.

Utley, Robert M. *Cavalier in Buckskin: George Armstrong Custer and the Western Military Frontier.* Norman: University of Oklahoma Press, 1988.

Utley, Robert M. *Frontier Regulars: The United States Calvary and the Indians, 1866–1890.* New York: Macmillan, 1973.

Utley, Robert M. *The Lance and the Shield: The Life and Times of Sitting Bull.* New York: Henry Holt and Company, 1993.

Vestal, Stanley. *The Missouri.* Lincoln: University of Nebraska Press, 1945.

Vestal, Stanley. *Sitting Bull: Champion of the Sioux.* Norman: University of Oklahoma Press, 1957.

Watson, Elmo Scott. "The Indian Wars and the Press, 1866–1867." *Journalism Quarterly* 17 (1940): 301–312.

Watson, Elmo Scott. "The Last Indian War 1890–91: A Study of Newspaper Jingoism." *Journalism Quarterly* 20 (September 1943): 205–219.

Webster's Ninth New Collegiate Dictionary. Springfield, MA: Merriam Webster, 1983.

Wichita Daily Beacon. September 25, 1878.

Index

About the Author

HUGH J. REILLY is married and the father of four children. He is an Associate Professor at the University of Nebraska/Omaha's School of Communication and is also a member of UNO's Native American Studies Faculty. He is a past employee of the *Omaha World-Herald* and the *Greeley (CO) Tribune* and is the author or co-author of six books, including *Historical Omaha: An Illustrated History of Omaha and Douglas County* and *Father Flanagan of Boys Town*.